AF194634

WRITINGS FROM THE SUNDARBANS

Studies in Comparative Literature
Jadavpur University

Studies in Comparative Literature, Jadavpur University, is founded on the view that the study of literatures and the arts in multilingual and culturally diverse contexts such as India demands a comparative approach. It is informed by an interdisciplinary and intercultural focus on bhasha literatures, translation, orality and performance as well as other arts and digital humanities, in the context of local, national and international literary and cultural transactions. The series is meant for students, scholars, and teachers of comparative literature as well as of single literature and other humanities departments. It brings together the work of faculty members and scholars at the Department of Comparative Literature, Jadavpur University, as well as of national and international visiting scholars who have enriched its research and debates.

Sub-series I: Texts, Contexts, Methods
  Ia. Histories and Paradigms
  Ib. Approaching New Challenges, Recasting Paradigms

Sub-series II: Indian and Asian Contexts

Sub-series III: Literature and Other Knowledge Systems
  IIIa. Literary Studies and Performance
  IIIb. Literature and Indigenous Knowledge Systems

Sub-series IV: Lecture Series
Contributions based on talks by Visiting Scholars

Series Editors

Kavita Panjabi, Professor, Department of Comparative Literature, Jadavpur University, Kolkata

Samantak Das, Professor, Department of Comparative Literature, Jadavpur University, Kolkata

Sucheta Bhattacharya, Professor, Department of Comparative Literature, Jadavpur University, Kolkata

STUDIES IN COMPARATIVE LITERATURE
JADAVPUR UNIVERSITY

SUB-SERIES II: INDIAN AND ASIAN CONTEXTS

WRITINGS FROM THE SUNDARBANS

Edited by

Indranil Acharya
Sayantan Dasgupta

Orient BlackSwan

All rights reserved. No part of this book may be modified, reproduced or utilised in any form, or by any means, electronic or mechanical, including photocopying, recording or by information storage and retrieval system, in any form of binding or cover other than in which it is published, without permission in writing from the publisher.

WRITINGS FROM THE SUNDARBANS

ORIENT BLACKSWAN PRIVATE LIMITED

Registered Office
3-6-752 Himayatnagar, Hyderabad 500 029, Telangana, India
e-mail: centraloffice@orientblackswan.com

Other Offices
Bengaluru, Chennai, Guwahati, Hyderabad, Kolkata,
Mumbai, New Delhi, Noida, Patna

© Orient Blackswan Private Limited 2023
First published by Orient Blackswan Private Limited 2023

ISBN 978-93-5442-271-3

040896

Typeset in Adobe Jenson Pro 10/12.6 *by*
Shine Graphics, Delhi 110 094

Printed at
Avantika Printers Private Limited, New Delhi 110 020

Published by
Orient Blackswan Private Limited
3-6-752, Himayatnagar, Hyderabad 500 029, Telangana, India
e-mail: info@orientblackswan.com

Contents

Acknowledgements

This volume has benefited from inputs and assistance from a number of people to whom we must acknowledge our debt. We thank Professor Kavita Panjabi and Professor Sucheta Bhattacharya, who, as Series Editors, played an important role steering this project towards publication. No words are enough to express our debt to Professor Samantak Das, whom we miss very much today, and who, as the third Series Editor, was a pillar of support. We are grateful to all the writers and translators who made this anthology a reality. We thank, in particular, Shyamal Kumar Pramanik, who helped in so many different ways to coordinate various aspects of the project. We thank the UGC CAS programme (Phase 3), and the UGC RUSA Phase 2 programme of Jadavpur University, with the support of which this anthology was actuated. We thank the CENTIL project fellows, Ishani Dutta and Tias Basu, for assistance at various points of time on this project.

Last but not the least, the editors are profoundly indebted to the editorial team of Orient BlackSwan—particularly Padmaja Anant, Aditi Jha and other key figures in the production process.

INDRANIL ACHARYA
SAYANTAN DASGUPTA

General Introduction

The first full-fledged department of Comparative Literature in India, and the second in Asia, was established in Calcutta at Jadavpur University in 1956. The reputed Bangla poet, writer and scholar Buddhadeva Bose was its founder and the first Head of the Department. The *Jadavpur Journal of Comparative Literature*, launched here in 1961, is one of the oldest journals in Asia that has continued, regularly, to publish significant research in comparative literature by national and international scholars. In the late 1980s the UGC earmarked the department for promotion of teaching and research under its Special Assistance Programme. In the early nineties the department widened its areas of interest to first introduce courses in the literatures and cultures of Bangladesh, Africa, Canada and Latin America; then it set up centres in the latter three, subsequently a Centre for Translation of Indian Literatures, and, most recently, a Centre for Studies of Islamicate Asia. During the Tenth Plan the department was also selected by the UGC to participate in its ASIHSS (Assistance for Strengthening of Infrastructure for Humanities and Social Sciences) programme. In addition to these UGC programmes and these centres, the UPE—University with Potential for Excellence—programme of the UGC also enabled the establishment of research projects in the department. These included translation and intercultural studies under Project Anuvad; documentation and research relating to performers of traditional dramatic forms in different districts of West Bengal under Project Palagaan; and a unique new venture involving an exploration of Kolkata through narratives of sound under the project Soundscapes. The first and so far only UGC Centre of Advanced Study in Comparative Literature in India was also established in this department in 2005, and it continued promoting research into its third phase. This series, Studies in Comparative Literature, Jadavpur University, is rooted in this academic history of over six decades.

When other departments of Comparative Literature finally began to be established in India in the 1990s, a sharing of our research and pedagogic experience became imperative. As the practice of comparative literature proliferated in centres and newly established departments as well as in single literature departments right across India, we began to face persistent requests for enhanced access to our research from academics, researchers and students alike. Our research, while considerable, had largely been published by local presses and the university, and did not have the national outreach now demanded of it. It was in response to this need that the idea of initiating a series with a reputed mainstream national publisher came about, and we are especially happy about this partnership with Orient BlackSwan, given the important role it has played in the dissemination of scholarship on Indian literatures and cultures.

We hold that the study of literatures and the arts in multilingual and culturally diverse countries such as ours demands a comparative approach; hence, Studies in Comparative Literature, Jadavpur University, is a series for students, scholars and teachers of comparative literature as well as of single literature, arts and other humanities departments. It explores a range of histories, theoretical reflections, as well as innovative approaches and concerns relevant to the field of comparative literature. In keeping with the basic imperatives of comparative literature, it is both intercultural and interdisciplinary in that it engages with the trajectories of literatures across cultures as well as with the relations between literatures and other fields of creative expression. It is thus informed by an interdisciplinary and intercultural focus on *bhasha* literatures, translation, orality and performance as well as other arts and digital humanities, in the context of local, national and international literary and cultural transactions, and also those of the borderlands.

This series brings together the work of faculty and scholars at the department of Comparative Literature, Jadavpur University, and of national and international visiting scholars. It comprises both edited volumes and authored books, as well as monographs by visiting scholars. The series launches the research carried out under the third phase of the UGC Centre of Advanced Study in Comparative Literature, and the publication of these volumes, we hope, will mark the beginnings of a renewed mapping of comparative literary studies in India.

The current studies build on the foundations of creative intellectual vision, innovative pedagogy and several decades of original scholarship that went into the shaping of what was a new field of study, in fact a new mode of inquiry, in the Indian university. Many generations have enriched comparative literary studies in India, and it is impossible to chart all the contributions of even just those at the Department of Comparative Literature at Jadavpur University in the space of a short introduction such as this. What follows however is a brief account of the directions of research, and of the kinds of publications that emerged from this research, as well as in response to pedagogic needs at this department; it is being presented here as an academic contextualisation for the present series that may be useful to other scholars, centres and departments of not just comparative literature but also literary studies in general.

Before mapping the broad areas of research across the decades however, it may be relevant to reflect for a moment on the intellectual and creative range of teachers and scholars who contributed to its making. Buddhadeva Bose and Sudhindranath Dutta were towering modern Bangla poets and writers, and amongst the foremost intellectuals of their time. Joining them in the early years were Fr. Robert Antoine, a Belgian Jesuit priest who was a Sanskritist and a scholar of Greek and Latin, who translated Kalidasa's *Raghuvamsa* from the Sanskrit into English, and also collaborated on a translation of Virgil's *Aeneid* from the Latin into Bangla; Fr. Pierre Fallon, who was also a Belgian Jesuit priest, a professor of French literature, a licenciate in philosophy and theology and an expert in Bangla philology; and David J. McCutchion who had trained in French and German at Jesus College Cambridge, and later became an authority on both the terracotta temples as well as the *patuas* (scroll painters) of Bengal. The next two generations of teacher-scholars, five of whom also trained in M.A. or Ph.D. programmes of North American departments of Comparative Literature and others in France or Germany, included Naresh Guha, Amiya Dev, Deepak Mazumdar, Subir Roychowdhury, Swapan Mazumdar, Bijoya Das, Subha Chakraborty Dasgupta, Ipsita Chanda, Suman Ghosh, Alokeranjan Dasgupta, Pranabendu Dasgupta, Manabendra Bandyopadhyay, Nabaneeta Dev Sen, Sibaji Bandyopadhyay and Debiprasad Bhattacharya. All of them earned international repute as scholars, and while the last was a polyglot and a renowned Sanskritist, the penultimate five were also major creative writers in Bangla.

It is perhaps the wide range of exposure and training, which was as rigorous as it may seem eclectic, that cautioned scholars of this department about strait-jacketing comparative literary studies into any definitive 'school' or methodology, or of limiting Indian literary studies within the political borders of the Indian nation state. So, even in their pioneering role, they refrained from formulating a Jadavpur 'school' of Comparative Literature, or privileging any comparative methodology over others. They also desisted from confining literary studies to inter-Indian literary relations only, and conscientiously trained their lenses on the wider South-Asian and Asian,

Perso-Arabic and Anglo-European fields too; and eventually they reached out to Latin America, Africa and Australia, especially in relation to transactions with Indian literatures and cultures, but also otherwise. Such catholicity, in both approach and range, would naturally give rise to questions of delimitation and focus—and what emerges clearly as a connecting thread across the decades is that, in terms of both literary-cultural focus and methodological approach, scholars here responded to the ground realities and the needs of their times.

It was in the early 1990s that the consolidated programme of publishing started, supported by the Special Assistance Programme of the UGC; the focus in this decade was clearly on creating resources for research. Bibliographies of reception—of World Literature in Bangla periodicals, and of Bangla literature in South Indian languages—formed one thrust area. Translation became a focal point from the beginning: translation of material such as literary manifestoes in Indian languages, and discussions regarding the aesthetics as well as comparative literature methodologies of translation featured in this phase. Literary historiography in India featured as an important concern as did East–West literary interactions of the colonial period. The fourth area of concern was in relation to third-world contexts—to cultures of silence as well as the challenge of envisioning their futures—and this included reflection on African and Latin American literatures and cultures.

The focus on generating resources for comparative research continued through the next five years with translations across several genres (poetry, short stories, plays and excerpts of autobiographies) and several languages (that is, from Bangla into other languages such as Asamiya and English, and from Odia, Gujarati, Marathi and other Indian languages into English as well as Bangla). Also, the first phase had documented debates on comparative literary approaches to historiography; this one brought into focus issues of genology from a comparative perspective, with a volume tracing the *charit* as a genre. A third area of engagement was that of linguistic and cultural formations of self-identity across the literatures of Bengal and Bangladesh, thus bringing the literature of Bangladesh into the purview of our research. This phase was also marked by the publication of three volumes under the rubric of Literary Studies in India: on Literary Historiography, Thematology and Genology; it brought together reflections of comparative literature academics as well as scholars from other literature and humanities departments, on approaches to literary studies in India at the beginning of the twenty-first century.

In the first phase of the Centre of Advanced Study (2005–2010), we continued, on the one hand with the task of generating resources for research, such as the annotated bibliography of Bangla and Asamiya histories of literature; on the other hand we extended the work on historiography to specific areas of study such as Indian English literature. Two new sets of concerns came into focus in this period. One set related to the need to document and study the fast-disappearing body of folk performances—the outcomes included the recordings and studies of *Manasamangal pala* and *Banabibir pala*. The other set of concerns was underlined by the realisation that most of our international focus had been on literary relations with the Anglo-European world, while those with other Asian cultures had not received the attention they deserved; thus the imperative to retrieve and explore these resulted in a focus on travel literature from Asia with focus on the collection of literary material along sea and trade routes, and the publication of a bibliography of travelogues to Asian countries in Bangla as well as an anthology of Bangla and Odia writings on colonial Burma. During this phase the additional support from the Assistance for Strengthening of Infrastructure for Humanities and Social Sciences (ASIHSS) programme of the UGC enabled research in South Asian contexts and resulted in the publication of a South Asian nationalisms reader, as well as a volume on the poetics and politics of Sufism and Bhakti in South Asia.

The following years, in the second phase of the CAS, were marked by more extensive and deeperresearch in the fields already marked out. At least three areas that had clearly emerged as thrust areas were:

- Comparative Literature: Explorations in Discipline and Methodology
- Roots and Routes: Intra-Indian and Intra-Asian Linguistic, Literary and Cultural Relations
- Literature and Other Knowledge Systems

Resources generated for research during this period included a handbook on terms and concepts in comparative literature, a volume on comparative literature in Germany, and textbooks on Indian Nepali literature in English and Bangla. The publications on comparative explorations in genre included a study of the *namah*. Research on folk cultures as knowledge systems resulted in publications on *charak* and *gajan* in Bengal, another on Karbi oral traditions in the Northeast, as well as a volume on literatures and oratures as knowledge systems, based on texts from Northeast India. A comparative study on the *ghumantoo* roadies, or wanderers, of India and Canada added to this set.

In the context of Asian studies, research was published on tales of medieval China. The research on South Asia extended itself to comparative studies of the literatures and cultures of borders in South Asia and the Americas; this last volume marked entry into a new area of research—Comparative Border Studies.

The present series has been envisioned as follows:

Studies in Comparative Literature, Jadavpur University

Sub-series I: Texts, Contexts, Methods

1a. Histories and Paradigms
1b. Approaching New Challenges, Recasting Paradigms

Sub-series II: Indian and Asian Contexts

Sub-series III: Literature and Other Knowledge Systems

IIIa. Literary Studies and Performance
IIIb. Literature and Indigenous Knowledge Systems

Sub-series IV: Lecture Series

Contributions based on talks by Visiting Scholars

In many ways it marks a deepening and consolidation of perspectives across the earlier decades of research; in other ways it also charts new directions in comparative literary studies. The sub-series **Texts, Contexts, Methods** includes two histories in the section *Histories and Paradigms*—one of the emergence and establishment of Indian Comparative Literature, the other a disciplinary and institutional history of comparative literature in India, based on documents preserved at Jadavpur as well as gathered from across the country. Planned along with these are anthologies on texts, contexts and concepts, and on comparative literary studies in India, with contributions from scholars across the country. The section *Approaching New Challenges, Recasting Paradigms* will introduce research in new directions that responds to contemporary challenges. Comparative Literature as a discipline has historically crossed borders in terms of time and space. One of these volumes is a response to the now pervasive trans-national histories of migrants and refugees and, focussing on the Indo-Bangladesh border, it marks a shift from the prism of the 'national' to the prism of borders and frontiers, to the epistemological perspectives of 'borderlanders'; another volume charts the transformations in comparative literary studies in light of the mutual interactions between digital humanities and literary mapping in South Asia.

The sub-series **Indian and Asian Contexts** includes both intra-Indian literary translations and a mapping of linguistic, literary and cultural relations grouped under the rubric of *Roots and Routes*, as well as translations from Bangla and Urdu of fictional and discursive writings of Muslim literati in Bengal from the early twentieth century onward. Included in this sub-series are comparative studies of 'progressive' literatures, South Asian studies of transnational writers such as Ismat Chughtai, and studies of intra-Asian engagements such as Bengal's encounters with Japan in the twentieth century.

The third sub-series, **Literature and Other Knowledge Systems**, includes a volume on reflections on methodology in the translation of performance texts in the sub-section *Literary Studies and Performance*; the sub-section on *Literature and Indigenous Knowledge Systems* carries a comparative study of Karbi and Chakma narrative traditions of Northeast India, as well as another of creation songs from India, Canada, Australia and Southeast Asia.

Finally, the **Lecture Series** comprises volumes based on talks delivered by national and international visiting scholars who have enriched the research and debates of our department, and often taken us in new directions too. We are truly grateful to Alessandro Portelli, Professor Emeritus, University of Rome La Sapienza, and Tridip Suhrud, Professor and Provost, CEPT University, Ahmedabad, for their contributions on oral history and Gandhi's languages respectively, and for their generosity in permitting us to include earlier landmark essays in their volumes. We also extend our gratitude to Robert P Goldman, Professor, University of California at Berkeley, and Daniel Rycroft, Associate Professor at the University of East Anglia for having agreed to write for us on the Valmiki *Ramayana* and the humanities in India, respectively. We thank other scholars, who have collaborated in the research on some of our publications; they include Jatin Nayak, former Professor of Utkal University, Indranil Acharya, Professor at Vidyasagar University, Subha Chakraborty Dasgupta former Professor in our own department, Shraddhanjali Tamang, also a faculty member at Jadavpur University, and writer Manoranjan Byapari.

This series is the collaborative effort of all the faculty members of the Comparative Literature department: Suchorita Chattopadhyay, Kunal Chattopadhyay, Aveek Majumder, Sayantan Dasgupta, Sujit Kumar Mandal, Parthasarathi Bhaumik, Epsita Halder, Debashree Dattaray and Sumit Kumar Barua. They have been working concertedly towards its publication over the last several years; and while the individual volumes will carry their respective names as authors, editors and co-authors, it needs to be put on record that this series is finally seeing the light of day through one of the most devastating pandemics in history only because of their determined collective commitment and mutual intellectual inspiration. We are also grateful to our research fellows—who will be acknowledged individually in the respective volumes—for their selfless and cheerful support. Last but not least we extend our deep gratitude to Padmaja Anant of Orient BlackSwan for her wisdom and infinite patience—it has indeed been a pleasure working with her.

KAVITA PANJABI
SAMANTAK DAS
SUCHETA BHATTACHARYA
Series Editors

The first volumes of this series are being sent to the press with a heavy heart, for Samantak Das is with us no more. May the infallible spirit with which he contributed to the making of this series continue to enrich it in the years to come.

Editor's Introduction

I

Ecological Anthropology is a sub-domain of Anthropology relevant to the understanding of indigenous responses to ecological systems. It is defined as the 'study of cultural adaptations to environments' (Kottak 579). In fact, a scrutiny of the cultural trajectory of some of the governing myths of the Sundarbans' folkloric tradition would surely point at the long process of adaptations of some overseas cultural icons like Bonbibi in the riverine environment. This minor domain is also described as 'the study of relationships between a population of humans and their biophysical environment' (Townsend 104). The focus of this research is on the dynamics of human adaptation to the hostile environments through cultural beliefs and practices. Most importantly, this research attempts to measure how people mobilised cultural materials to maintain their ecosystems.

In the Sundarbans the reciprocity of human and non-human dialogue through a sustained cultural belief system largely determines the equilibrium in the ecosystem. Ecological Anthropology developed from the approach of cultural ecology. Both approaches are quite useful in providing a conceptual framework for understanding the cultural cartography of the Sundarbans. According to Emilio F. Moran (31–32), these approaches offer a better understanding of the wide spectrum of indigenous responses to the challenges of an adverse geo-climatic system. Since 1999, the emergence of a new school of Ecological Anthropology has been more effective in the understanding of a more complex intersection of global, national, regional and local systems. A close reading of the local narratives on the Sundarbans in English translation would definitely reveal the complex intersection of various systems functional in the demographic diversity of this delta region.

The Sundarbans is a mangrove region in the Ganga-Brahmaputra-Meghna delta shared between India and Bangladesh. A land that exists in relative isolation and where metropolitan facilities are often out of bounds, the area is connected by a network of tidal waterways which gives it a unique physiognomy. The name 'Sundarbans' is generally thought to have originated from the Sundari plants which are found in abundance here. The Sundarbans are of immense ecological significance; this has become more and more evident in the context of recent global warming. Loss of the mangrove cover has the potential to render cyclones—extremely common in this part of the world—more devastating in the future.

The Sundarbans has featured prominently in literature with many writers having set their works in the tide country. One of the most influential of these seems to be Amitav Ghosh's very powerful novel, *The Hungry Tide* (2004), which was based largely in the Sundarbans as it traced marine biologist Piyali Roy's sojourn there. The sojourn gives Ghosh an opportunity to not only explore the geography of the Sundarbans, but also revive a forgotten history of displacement, repression and subjugation of human rights. Side by side with this kind of writing exists a long, sustained and powerful tradition of writing in Bangla on and from the Sundarbans, which is what this anthology seeks to foreground. Not much of this writing has been translated into English so far, and so this corpus of writing has remained largely ignored and invisible internationally. We are hopeful that this anthology may make this tradition more widely visible than before.

Writings from the Sundarbans attempts to bring to the limelight the uphill task an author undertakes when they choose to write on the experience from the margins. It tries to break the long-established silence over issues of socio-cultural suppression stemming from the society's neatly charted out mode of upholding the social hierarchy by bringing into play casteism, gender stereotyping, class consciousness and the economic and intellectual divide.

Though ideas of 'purity', 'authenticity' and 'ownership' have long been contested in the superiority/inferiority discourse on language and its use, we have not yet been able to recognise and accept wholeheartedly the 'in-between' space in society. Postcolonial discourses have opened up new vistas for exploration of the 'postcolonial' space and experience of people, just as discourses on power-control-authority and gender inequality have lauded endeavours of 'speaking up'. Subaltern studies made a concerted attempt to free the intellectual space of Puritanism. But translations force us to think of the extent to which these theoretical assumptions and discourses have actually been applied to improve or add value to the everyday struggle for existence of these marginal people—the fishermen, crab-catchers, honey-collectors or the boatmen of this vast delta region of the Sundarbans. To what extent are we, living our sheltered urban life in the midst of modern scientific amenities, aware of the trials and tribulations of lives outside our known orbit? Have we really been able to 'decolonise' our minds? This book makes us hear and see the intricacy, complexity, helplessness and simple beauty of a life lived close to nature both pristine and predatory.

It is important right at the beginning to realise that the Sundarbans are not just about sighting tigers and crocodiles. In the words of one researcher, 'But the Sundarbans are not just forest or *jangol*, they are also an inhabited region or *abad*. I feel that we need to address the urge for omitting people from images and islands of the Sundarbans...' (Jalais 336). This is again underscored in the following comment as well— 'The forest region of the Sundarbans which is famous for the Royal Bengal Tiger is also the home of countless people who eke out an existence from the land and the forest which now yield too little to sustain and feed too many mouths' (Chaudhuri 1914).

It is the people of the Sundarbans and their lives that the stories in this anthology focus upon—something that has often remained outside the purview of the popular image of the Sundarbans— 'Present-day studies on the Sundarbans follow a similar lopsided dichotomy: fascination, on the one hand, for the natural aspects of the Sundarbans, but on the other, an unsettling silence on the social and human facet of the region' (Jalais 337).

The writers of these stories never lose the thread of warm intimacy that they shared with the fishermen, the honey-gatherers, the soothsayers and the crab-hunters of the area. This helpless, downtrodden, exploited population, the intricately woven network of rivers, canals, tributaries and the evergreen mangrove forests of *geoa*, *garan* and *garjan* trees stretched to the far end of the horizon were an unfailing inspiration when they took up writing.

Before we probe further into the crises of the downtrodden people of Sundarbans area it is quite incumbent upon us to attempt to explain the basis to the dangerous livelihoods practised by the poverty-stricken populace in the delta region. The people of the Sundarbans generally eke out their living from one of three categories of occupation: forest workers, prawn seed collectors and landowners. The geographical locations of these three categories directly relate to the geographical-social hierarchy of the Sundarbans islands, with forest workers at the bottom, landowners at the top, and prawn seed collectors finding middle ground between the two. The primary way that these categories are created and divided revolves around how those who work within each occupation regards the forest and its inhabitants, particularly the Bengal tiger. The riverine ecosystem of the Sundarbans region is to be properly understood to realise the nature and extent of human compulsions. Forest workers can be divided into two sub-categories of occupation: there are the forest fishers and there are those who 'do the forest' (honey collectors, wood collectors and poachers). Forest fishers see their work as intrinsically intertwined with the forest, the rivers and all the creatures that inhabit these places. These men leave their homes in groups of three to five for nearly twenty days per month to travel the rivers of the delta region and catch crab and fish. The forest fishers believe that they work under the protection of Bonbibi, Mother of the Forest, whom they pray to before entering the forest. They also firmly adhere to the belief that they may not take more than they need from the forest—neither to deplete its resources nor disturb its inhabitants and their way of life. Because Bonbibi is considered a motherly figure by the forest fishers and to all the beings that live in the forest, they feel as though these beings, especially the royal Bengal tigers, are their 'brothers' or 'friends'. To harm or disturb their brothers is seen as extremely detrimental to the relationship between humans and the forest. Forest fishers think of those who 'do the forest' as disturbing the peace within the forest and depleting it of its resources for their own personal gain. They consider this the utmost kind of greed and arrogance.

As mentioned earlier, honey collectors, wood collectors and poachers are referred to as those who 'do the forest'. This is arguably the riskiest work that one could do in the Sundarbans, as these workers are the most vulnerable to attacks by tigers, snakes, crocodiles and other forest predators. An estimated 150 of such workers are killed in tiger or crocodile attacks annually. Their work is conducted directly within the forest, whereas forest fishers generally remain on the rivers where they are marginally safer. The work is 'high-risk, high-gain', as these workers run the risk of either being relatively successful or being killed in the forest. Honey and wood collection, as well as poaching, are lucrative opportunities because few are willing to take on such risks. In contrast to forest fishers, those who 'do the forest' do not enter the forest peacefully, but rather on high alert and in pursuit of personal gain. They often meet with tragic ends as depicted in some of the narratives of this anthology. For the prawn seed collectors, spirituality is not as necessary in their daily routines as it is for those forest workers who pray to Bonbibi for protection. Neither do they pray to Kali, like those who 'do the forest', as their work does not fall under what Kali represents. This does not mean that they do not need to be protected, however, as women who pull prawn seed nets along the river banks are at huge risk of attack by sharks, crocodiles and even tigers. This anthology is a poignant record of many such unfortunate incidents that devastate the little lives of these ill-starred women.

But frequent devastating cyclonic storms like Aila, Bulbul and very recently Amphan continue to ravage the river embankments and cause severe damage to the farmland. Poverty has driven a lot of people from these islands to migrate and seek jobs elsewhere. They have also been forced to retrace their steps with much difficulty during the lockdown. In a way, the following line sums up the context: 'The inhabited part of the Sunderbans is forbidding, hostile with enormous practical hurdles in the way of the men who have settled there' (Ghosh 352).

Being natives of the Sundarbans, the writers featured in this anthology grew up witnessing the local people worshipping at the sacred seats—at *thaan*s and *darga*s—of the folk deities Bonbibi, Dakshin Rai, Alimadar, Barkhan Gaji, Shahjanguli and Manik Pir. The locals regularly pray and make offerings at these places of worship. Many of the writers featured in this anthology grew up with stories of gods and goddesses appearing in the dreams of the soothsayers and the honey-collectors to instruct them. From the astrologers, soothsayers and witch doctors of the region, they learnt about a plethora of charms and mantras to ward off the wild beasts of land and water. The Sundarbans has a large corpus of rituals that the wives of the fishermen and the honey-collectors perform before their husbands sail off to the forests. The stories featured here highlight these fisher-people, honey-collectors, crab-hunters, their lives and livelihoods, rituals and customs and their magic charms.

Out of the 102 islands of the Sundarbans, 54 were made habitable during the colonial rule in the eighteenth century by clearing the wilderness. 'Lower-caste' people, especially of the sub-castes of Paundra, Namashudra, Bagdi, Kaibarta from places like Khulna, Satkhhira (now in Bangladesh) flocked to the 19 blocks of this arable area, lured by the low cost of land here. Migrant labourers of the Santhal, Munda and Oraon tribes were brought from Ranchi and Chhotonagpur plateau to these islands for forest clearing; a number of homeless people from the flood-hit regions of Medinipur also took shelter here. Naturally, they spoke different languages which differed distinctly from the register of Bangla spoken at the islands of Patharpratima, Kakdwip, Namkhana or Mathurapur. Therefore, the language of the Sundarbans is basically an amalgam of a wide variety of languages and registers of different origin. Even the colloquial language differs from place to place.

But a very different register that the fishermen and the honey-collectors use when they enter the jungles has been called the 'jongla bhasa' (the tongue of the wilderness) by the historian-researcher of the Sundarbans, Satish

Chandra Mitra. In his book titled *Jashor Khulnar Itihas* (vol.1, 1914), Mitra conducted a very comprehensive survey of the dialects and regional variations of the speech communities in several parts of undivided Bengal and the Sundarbans delta. Some such words that have made their way into their writings are—*aksar, al, aur, ari, ala, kwi, kulopak, homeshastra* and *achchamite*. Searching for these words the Dalit author Niranjan Mondal came across an interesting word *daowa* in the sense of 'paddy harvesting'. He was astonished to trace that same word to an eleventh century treatise called *Shunya Purana* by Raman Pandit. Based on the local variations in speech, the articulation patterns of the local language may be sub-categorised into four segments— addition of speech sounds, elision of speech sounds, assimilation of speech sounds and complete phonemic transmutation of words/phrases. However, a cultural insider proficient in the source language of these narratives will be able to appreciate this phonetic salience in the true sense of the term.

II

Let us now take a quick look at the translated stories of this anthology to better ascertain the diversity of themes and concerns manifested in the narratives of various representative authors in this land of hungry tide. The stories translated for this volume not only highlight the realities of the space of the Sundarbans, they also throw into relief a study in contrasts as they focus on the relationship between margin and centre in the context of development. A reading of the stories in the original would also benefit the serious reader to engage in comparative study with regard to the politics of translation.

All the six stories of Shyamal Kumar Pramanik are wonderfully evocative of the weal and woe of the people of the Sundarbans. The first story, "Crocodile", manifests an intense conflict between Kailash Mondal, the human trafficker, and Rashid Ali, the protesting figure. "Kshantoburi's Family" is an emotional narrative of an illiterate and poor widow, Kshantoburi, who lives with her son younger son and daughter-in-law. While the story seeks to highlight the struggles of the people of the Sundarbans ('The people there survive, jousting with tigers and crocodiles every day.'), local customs and myths such as *jhaar phnuk* and *jol pora* are discussed when being used to try and ward off the *brahmadotti* who, it is believed, has assailed her daughter-in-law. As in many of the stories in this anthology, the Matla features prominently here, too, not just as a backdrop within which the narrative is situated, but almost assuming the dimensions of a character itself. The entire narrative is soaked in the grim realities of a fisherman's family.

"The Chronicle of Hariya Dom", set in Sonagaon, a quiet village in the Sundarbans, records a spirited protest of a farmer against land sharks. The caste system figures prominently in this story as we see the struggles faced by the protagonist as he fights to hold on to his piece of land.

"Suleiman Fakir" delineates the character of an extraordinary fakir who searches for the essential harmony between Hindus and Muslims in the annals of the previous generations. It is again a telling political fable apart from being a fascinating narrative.

"Birds of the Forest" is another story by Shyamal Kumar Pramanik that is featured in this volume. This is a wonderful love story that focuses on the relationship between husband and wife who try to support each other in their journey after losing their only son, Gopal, to snakebite. The depiction of the fury of nature and the desperate longing of the grief-stricken couple for solitude, a solitude they can survive only because of the solidarity that binds them together, make this a poignant read.

The single-minded devotion of a village teacher in the story "Pathshala" to teach the low-caste children of the village reminds one of the Ambedkarite slogans of 'Educate, Agitate, Organise'. The story ends with an interesting and significant twist as it presents what he sees when the narrator visits the village many years later.

Niranjan Mondal's story, "The Shrimp-catchers of the Mangrove Forest" is a heart-rending story of a shrimp-catcher somewhere deep in the Sundarbans. Not only does the story throw into sharp relief the lives and lifestyles and struggles of people like Rakhal and his family, it also documents the socio-economic changes and how they affect the lives of these people who depend on catching shrimplets to survive, only for their risky and exhausting labour to provide the opportunity for the rich folk to make themselves richer. This story is a rich treasure trove of customs relating to fishing in the area. It incorporates charms and spells and songs meant to exercise control over the natural world and to make the exercise of fishing safe and more comfortable for the fishing folk.

Utpalendu Mondal, another chronicler of the Sundarbans, depicts the miserable plight of the flood-hit people in this disaster-prone region. The narrative of "Ghost Tiger" is almost fantastical, where fiction and life overlap. In "Tulsi's Chronicle", Mondal draws a pen-picture of Tulsi, an alien in her homeland. Much in this story is indicated rather than stated clearly, and that is what buttresses Mondal's credentials as a powerful short story writer. Through various references throughout the story, the author re-establishes how Dalit women as domestic help in urban colonies suffer perpetually.

"Bhushon and His Family" is a tragic tale of boatman Bhushon who has had to struggle all his life, even forced to sell his boat due to sheer poverty. The narrative is a poignant account of the lives of people like Bhushon and others from his village who very rarely are offered the chance to escape their circumstances and look forward to a better future.

Bimalendu Halder, a veteran Dalit writer, transmutes his personal experiences of this riverine delta into a poignant story titled "Neader". The story is about the eternal quest of the poor, landless people for a place to settle in, the land that keeps slipping away from under their feet, and the sacrifices one has to make to ensure the survival of their near and dear ones.

Prasad Kumar Mandal's story "The Father and the Mother" brilliantly captures the worries and anxieties of the people of the tide country regarding the proposed government plan to construct a ring dam that would take away fertile land from the poor villagers. This story is a fascinating narrative of the uneasy relationship between what passes as development and the traditional way of life.

Pranab Sarkar's story "Silt" is a poignant story of a boatman, Mohor, disillusioned with the political rhetoric of the party leaders. The story shows how the divisive force of mainstream politics aggravates the schism within the fraternity of the boatmen. This is again a story that fuses two major strands—the personal narrative of the poor characters and their relationships, and the larger political narrative that relates to development, capitalism and exploitation.

"The Second Death" by Jaykrishna Kayal is a gripping narrative of the protagonist's encounter with a tiger and all that follows the fateful meeting. The story lays bare the high-risk occupation of the poor islanders venturing out into the heart of the Sundarbans in search of quality wood. The folkloric evocation of Mother Bonbibi and the associated magical spell of chanting reflect the cultural belief system of these islanders. The cult of Bonbibi itself points towards a syncretic religious belief system prevalent in the Sundarbans—several have pointed to a 'religious life that is Islamic in orientation just as it is Hindu in orientation' (Uddin 290).

Four stories of Panchanan Das—"The She-Jackal of Bawaali", "Dokhno", "Shaplas" and "The Museum" weave four very different contexts with great thematic variations. "Dokhno" highlights the centre-margin binary. The misconceived notion of metropolitan folk about the rural people of the Sundarbans as illiterate, uncultured, unsocial and backward is challenged through the portrayal of an illiterate secretary of a school at Pathar Pratima—a humanist par excellence. "Shaplas" focuses on the humble plant that grows beside the canal, and with the use of the child's figure in the narrative, brings in a note of innocence. But beyond that note of innocence lies the hard reality of hunger and labour, which soon becomes the focus of the story. "The She-jackal of Bawaali" is another story by Das that highlights the essential bond between human and beast in a way that is sure to move the reader.

Bikas Kanti Middya's "The Maneater, or Merely an Account of My Travel" and Pabitra Mandal's "The Immersion March" centre around the harrowing experiences of encountering the great predator in the mangrove forests. "Nostalgia or Stories of Roots and Soil" by Aparesh Mondal is a touching tale of leaving one's motherland despite encountering hundreds of perils every day. Archana Mondal's "My Childhood" is an autobiographical account recounting the hardships of a female survivor—the only female voice in the entire oeuvre of narratives.

Biswajit Halder is the youngest of the writers featured in this anthology. His story, "The Will to Live" is set in Saatjelia Colony, on the banks of the river Gomor. It focuses on the girls whose lives depend on the river. The story is a rich catalogue of local customs, beliefs and rituals. Halder's story, much like many others in this anthology, throws up pertinent questions related to development and economics.

"Kanu", the other story by Halder is an essentially humane story which makes skillful use of the child figure. It shows the economic exploitation which forces Kanu's father to take some drastic measures, but the focus lies on the ten-year-old Kanu and his innocence, depicted with rare skill and poignancy.

Over the years, various cultural practices and dialectal conventions have fallen into disuse in this vast tidal community. Large-scale migrations of indigenous people to urban centres have also changed the demographic profile of the delta region. Successive natural calamities have further devastated the subaltern population residing in the riverine villages. Hence, the last vestiges of this folk cultural heritage need to be preserved urgently. This volume seeks to present in English translation a string of stories related to these traditions and lifestyles. The attempt made by the editors is to make readers aware of the knowledge system of communities who inhabit the region. Such attempts will ultimately be instrumental in the manual and digital archiving of literary databases for posterity.

Works Cited

Chaudhuri, Kalyan. "Poverty and Exploitation in Sundarbans." *Economic and Political Weekly*, vol. 11, no. 50, 1976, pp. 1914–15.

Ghosh, Arun. "West Bengal Landscape I: The Sunderbans." *Economic and Political Weekly*, 1988, pp. 352–356.

Jalais, Annu. "The Sundarbans: Whose World Heritage Site?" *Conservation and Society*, vol. 5, no. 3, 2007, pp. 335–42.

Kottak, Conrad Phillip. *Anthropology: Appreciating Human Diversity*. McGraw Hill, 2010, pp. 579–584.

Mitra, Satish Chandra. *Jashor-Khulnar Itihas*, vol.1. Dey's Publishing, 1914, pp. 22–40.

Moran, Emilio F. *People and Nature: An Introduction to Human Ecological Relations*. Blackwell Publishing, 2006, pp. 31–32.

Townsend, Patricia K. *Environmental Anthropology: From Pigs to Policies*. Waveland Press, 2009, pp. 104–105.

Uddin, Sufia M. "Religion, Nature and Life in the Sundarbans." *Asian Ethnology*, vol. 78, no. 2. Nanzan University Anthropological University, 2019, pp. 289–309.

1

Neader

BIMALENDU HALDER

Quite a big mound it was!
Full of *jhati, hatishur* and drooping weeds! A few thorny plants here and there. A dead palm tree and a crooked fan palm tree stood one beside the other at the far end. The endless expanse of paddy fields skirted the mound in the horizon, and on the other side that stretched northwards was an expanse of paved government road for buses to ply.

The mound was occupied by a few houses of people of the Keora, Bagdi and Muchi castes; flood-affected people from the Sundarbans had also settled here. Twigs and branches of trees woven together to prepare fences were plastered with mud to erect the walls of their homes. The ceiling was made of bamboo. Fan palm leaves, dried *kash* leaves and palm leaves had been spread for roofing. The foundation was made of clay and the floors were of mud—most of the time earthworms rose to the surface and grass infested the area. A severe storm could, within seconds, blow away all of this and torrential rain or flood could bring everything down and leave these people homeless again.

These homeless people of the Sundarbans were no vagabonds or gypsies. They were not pig herders, turtle catchers, snake charmers or crow hunters. They had families. They pursued their traditional trades or did menial labour to sustain themselves. But cruel nature, through storms, wind and flood had thrown them out of their land and homes and turned them into landless, poor vagabonds. Almost every other year, homeless and destitute, they made their homes beside roads provided by the government or on any abandoned high grassy plot of land so that no one could raise any objection. After the rains, in the Bengali months of Kartik and Agrahayan or in the winter, they returned to their own ancestral plot skirting the river. Some did not return. In the *haat* or on the roadside on dirty land or beside the rail tracks they raised their own shanties and put themselves up there.

Manti has taken a liking to the mound beside the government road. The earth is hard here. On the far side, long leafy grass spread their heads. No amount of rain would wash away the earth over and above it, and the pucca road nearby would enable them to avoid mud and slush. Just get to the road and off you can go anywhere—the town bazaar, the railway station, the hospital and all over the place, even further ahead.

It is convenient to travel here. There are endless paddy fields on the other side. At the end of a field is a small river and a canal. One can fish there; there was no one to object. Even after the month of Poush had ended, the field was full of dried paddy stems. These stems would be very good fuel. The *aalbheri* of the fields, if rummaged, would yield a profusion of snails to eat. Snail meat curry is heavenly!

Manti throws her hands around Palan's shoulders, embraces him and says with a tone of indulgence, 'This time I shall not leave this place for the Sundarbans.'

'What? What will you eat here?'

'Why? What everyone eats—rice, curry, fish.'

'Stop! How will you get it?'

'Why? You'll earn.'

'Is it so easy? We don't have any acquaintances here, how will you manage?'

'Why? Aren't you a man? Don't you know how to make acquaintances? You know farming—head off to the nearby villages and ask people how to work in their farms.'

'And if that doesn't work out?'

'Then catch fishes, prawns in the river and the canals and sell them in the market. You can collect leaves from fan palm trees around and make hand fans, brooms and mats and sell them in the market. Collect bamboo twigs from the village and make fishing equipment. I shall dig into this *bheri* and collect snails. Have snail meat and sell the shells in the bangle factory nearby. Just a family of two, won't it be enough?'

'Yes, that might be enough, but ...'

'Yes, but what?'

'How many days would it last?'

'Oh! Did you earn more than this in your own village? It was the same work of farming, menial labour, or fishing in the rivers and canals. Of course, sometimes, you went hunting for honey in the forests, stealing wood and catching crabs.'

'*Arey!* I did not say anything about the income.'

'Then what is it?'

'I am saying how long will we be able to stay here like upstarts? Instead, let us go to the village *pradhan*.'

'Why the pradhan again? One pradhan does not do, two pradhans now to give us heartburn. What did your village pradhan do? Not a bit of government aid, nor any help! Instead, you have had to contribute to the party fund every month, and then take leave from work to go to party meetings and processions. There are so many flood victims—has the pradhan come to oversee the situation? Any aid is far-fetched.'

'You are right there, Manti.'

'Listen to me, no more pradhan and all that rubbish! They're the same everywhere. No one will do anything for us. We stay here on this government piece of land as long as we can, then if they drive us out, we shall settle down somewhere else.'

Palan is shocked. What is Manti saying? Lead a causeless life like vagabonds? They are homely householders. Is this good for them? But what could be done?

Nowadays, it is difficult to stay in the Sundarbans. With constant floods and calamities, no one can farm properly. Everyone's condition is poor. Menial work is not available. Moreover, there is constant political pressure. If you catch fish in the rivers and canals, you have to pay your share. Contributions have to be paid every month. A hundred-odd pressures and cruelties and no peace in the heart. It is better to live like this then—roam about from place to place like vagabonds.

Palan takes a deep breath as sorrow overpowers his heart. Vignettes of his village rise before his eyes. Beside the Matla is their home below the *gangbheri*. Where the road passing by Shikri Para reaches the end of the village near the embankment of the river—there lies their two-storeyed mud and thatched house. In front is the small courtyard. Flanking one side is the *pui* thatch, and a chilli plant or two. On one side is a small plot of land growing spinach. Towards the east, flanking the bheri, two-hands-measure below stands an old *banigachh*. Palan has put up a sort of bench with small wooden planks. At times, in the afternoon, he sits on it. Reddish clouds float on the expanse of the sky and waves ripple on the Matla water. The setting sun's rays glitter on the river water. Often, whenever he wakes up from his sleep at night, he goes out and sits on the bench. The white moonlight floods the river, the fields and the heads of the forest afar. He enjoys the beauty of the moon.

Tears drip from his eyes. The familiar village ancestral house, the river, the fields, the forest banigachh! How could he live without these?

Slowly, the rains flit by, and so does autumn. Then the late autumn passes and winter sets in. It is quite cold in Poush. Manti, Palan and the others have not returned to the Sundarbans this time. It is their choice, they have settled well on the mound. Their shack is on the rear, near the mouth of the low-lying land. Behind it stretches the pucca road. If you go down the low-lying land, you will get to the villagers' paddy fields. Some distance away stretches the narrow river. Further ahead lies the village, the market, the mud tracks, the village school, the *baroyaritala* and much much more. Manti has seen it all, she has gone around it all. She has also seen the panchayat office. Palan smiles and ruminates. Manti is very homely and organised. She has managed to get some papaya plants from god knows where and planted them around the shack. These have flowered beautifully and look attractive.

Farming has not begun yet this winter. They sometimes get some work of threshing rice plants and stacking paddy. On days they do not get any work, Palan catches fish in the canal and Manti hawks them around in the village. Many a time, she collects cheap fishes at wholesale price and sells them around. Palan also makes palm leaf mats, brooms and mats woven of *khalbalanga*, and goes around vending them from market to market. For marriages or rice ceremony of children, he catches fishes from ponds for a price. But Manti does not collect snails from the canal with her scythe. It is not needed. They put their heads together and the household is managed quite well.

Some Bauris, Bagdis and Muchis have settled down as well; they are engaged in some odd jobs. They stick to Manti and Palan and agree on one point—if they face any danger, they have to save each other and come together to brave it. They have all agreed and have elected Manti their 'neader'.

Manti is very happy too. She decks herself up quite a bit nowadays. She puts on a *bindi*, applies kohl on her eyes and lipstick to her lips, wears a blouse matching her saree and does not go around hawking to the market or the village locales. Her face is a perfect betel leaf shape and looks cherubic. The full high breasts, the big full eyes brimming with the shade of dark rain clouds, a nice head of hair floating down to the hip; she does not at all look like the wife of a Keora Bagdi—a low-born.

Palan is impressed. 'Do you want to work in films and abandon selling fishes?' Manti smiles. She rolls her eyes and says, 'Yes, why not?'

'Yes, you certainly can. You have the looks. Just a bit of training and you'll be a real heroine.'

'And who'd be my hero? You have advanced in years. You won't do!'

'Arey, getting a hero won't be a problem. So many handsome blokes around. One mention and they'll pick you up and set off for Bombay.'

'Then, then what will happen to you?'

'Me? I shall drive my teeth into this ground and stay on for life here.'

'No, I don't need any young bloke. Whether you are old or anything else, what I have is enough. My priceless Palan.'

Saying so, Manti suddenly breaks into laughter. Then she throws herself at Palan, hugs him and nuzzles his chest. Palan is taken a bit aback but then he shouts with a chortle, 'Hey, what's going on? People around might see us. What's this?'

'Let them see. I am not hugging a stranger; I am loving my husband. What do they have to do with it?'

A half-moon hangs in the sky overhead. A shimmering moonlight pervades all that is around while a cold wind blows across the open field. Manti shuts the door, dims the wall-lamp in the room, embraces Palan closely and then rolls about on the straw spread in the room.

Some days later, this happens. It is early Falgun. The winter has stayed back a bit even though Magh has passed. They could feel the cold in the early morning and evening every day. It was only in the afternoon that it felt somewhat hot and balmy. Palan was at home that day as he was not feeling well. They were just having a siesta after lunch when suddenly a group of people with some documents arrived. The others on the mound had shown them their shack. Manti was the leader, after all. The men were from the panchayat. It was all regarding the voter list and the census.

The men were flabbergasted when Palan listed the names of the inhabitants on the mound. It is illegal to settle here on the mound like this, this cannot go on! They would have to leave this mound as soon as possible. Or else, the people from the panchayat would break everything and turn it all to ruin.

It is evening now. Men and women, old and young, had collected in front of their shack. What do they do now? Where do they go? Wherever they went, it would be government land or land belonging to someone else, and the pradhan would certainly trouble them. What could they do now?

If they left this mound and settled down next to some other road or abandoned high grassland, the panchayat could drive them away. If they put up their shack near the railway tracks, the police could come and destroy it all. If it was near a haat, the haatbabu's local goons could come and beat them up and ransack it all. So, where could they go now? When they had erected this shack on this ground, Manti had said that if they were driven out of here, they would make their home somewhere else. The same Manti was wordless now. She was nervous and dejected. It is not easy to set up home anywhere and everywhere like vagabonds. They are householders now and cannot put up with such inconveniences. They had painstakingly collected bamboos, twigs, leaves and straws and made their homes with a lot of effort. They had had to work hard to find out means of earning money here. They had just settled down, and now they had to leave?

Suddenly Manti stands up and shouts out, 'We won't go. We won't leave. Let's see what they do. We shall fight.'

The people rise up and start to murmur. Palan holds Manti's hand and forces her to sit down.

'Have you gone mad? You want to fight with the crocodile when you live in the water?' He begins reminding her about the floods washing away their village in the Sundarbans, the suffering they had had to go through—he says everything—but to no avail. The pradhan stays unmoved; they would have to leave. They had seven days to do so. Palan and Manti must go to the panchayat office twice or thrice more.

Finally, they decided that they would leave. But Manti was not happy at all. This was a defeat for them. The residents of the mound had appointed her 'neader', and she couldn't do anything at all? This was shameful for her.

How about going to the local police station and letting the OC know all about it? They were citizens of this country. During the elections, the politicians came to beg for votes, but they were nowhere to be seen when the voters were in trouble. What sort of an arrangement was this? Does the rule of law not apply here?

Palan explained to her that the law of the land was not meant for the poor and indigent—it was to beat them and rule over them. The government did not erect dams on the rivers successfully; their house in the village was engulfed by the floods—and no one cared a whiff. Now that they had built a house on vacant, fallow and useless land, now, the panchayat had come running—it was all really, really unjust.

Tomorrow, at daybreak, all the residents of the mound would leave their homes and set off. They do not yet know where they would go but they had to leave, and no one could change that. Manti appeared lost and listless since the afternoon and Palan could not understand what was happening.

It is another night on the mound. There is no moon in the vast expanse of the sky. The only thing that one can feel is the wind blowing across the field—and it is mixed with the sound of someone crying.

There is a sudden pandemonium. Manti is missing since the evening. Palan is frantically looking for her. The others on the mound are also looking around for her. How strange! Has she escaped in fear? Or has she left Palan and run away with someone else? She decks herself up quite a bit nowadays, everyone suspects she has escaped. They are all ashamed they appointed her the 'neader'.

The morning has dawned. A bright, full sun shines on the trees, the fields and everywhere else. The inhabitants of the mound will now be leaving. Everyone has tied up and readied their belongings. Suddenly, they see someone running up the field towards them. A woman it is—dishevelled, hair unkempt with the end of her saree unravelled.

When she draws near, they recognise her as none other than Manti. But why does she look like this? Her blouse is torn in two or three places, the ends of her eyes darkened. There are bloodstains on her saree below the waist.

But she is laughter all over. As she draws near, she laughs out louder and shouts, 'We have won. We have won the battle. We won't have to leave our mound. Everyone can stay on—as many days they want to. Everyone will have their names on the voter's list. Everyone will have a ration card.'

Palan was standing in front of the low-lying land. Manti comes and throws her hands around him. Then she breaks into heart-rending tears.

Translated from Bangla by Keshab Hira
Originally published as "Neader" in *Nona Boner Pnachali*, 2018

2

The She-jackal of Bawaali

PANCHANAN DAS

My friend Parameshwar was a travel enthusiast. His destinations were strange as were the objects of his scrutiny—lanes and by-lanes, ditches and ravines, nooks and crannies, dilapidated houses, ruined temples, mosques, sculptures, coins and all such diverse things. A journey became boring without a companion—a lone man was a fool! But why he preferred to drag along a homebody like me, I never cared to ask.

These last few years I was quite content giving him the slip. Rarely did we meet, and on top of it, there was no dearth of excuses—'Forgot', 'no time', 'lots of work to do', 'not well' and a variety of other explanations. But now with the telephone, all my stratagems have come to an end. Communication or botheration!

I had gone to bed after dinner one winter's night. The phone began to dance in the next room—tring, tring ... tring, tring. Under the shared quilt, my wife kept nudging—'Can't you hear, it's for you!' Getting up before the next instalment of prodding began, I placed the receiver at the appropriate place and released my first word of customary greeting—'Hello...o...o'. From the other end came floating—'Parameshwar here'.

'I can hear your voice, can do without your name. What makes you call so late in the night?'

'Let's suppose there's a ceremony.'

'But...'

'I called once in the morning and heard from your wife that you are perfectly well, loafing about like a lazy oaf. We will be setting off at eight tomorrow morning, will tell you the details later, this is a wonderful wonderfully amusing tale, absolutely fantastic!'

'But where to?'

'Oh, how far can we go? Let's just say it will be within the bounds of South 24-Parganas, and in the night we may...'

'But…'

'No excuse will do, Dhumketu. You have aged now, let your wife have the quilt to herself for a night, I'm hanging up.'

It was a holiday. We sat side by side in the empty train. I did not even have to broach the topic, he did—'I had said we would be going to South 24-Parganas, yet we are heading towards Kolkata; don't you want to know why?'

'What is the point of knowing?'

'I see you lack humour; even a child has curiosity.'

'Is this new to you?'

This way, after a number of blunt questions and callous replies between us for an hour, we alighted and took the Budge Budge-bound train. Somewhat put off, I got down at the station, walking first, then taking a bus, then a van, and then, a final trudge. I was in a bad mood as it was, having sort of clammed up on account of the hurly-burly. Parameshwar understood, but he was not the least bit perturbed; he was a devotee of the league of easy-goers. He could pick up a topic of conversation much like the random scattered rains of autumn—'I have dragged you out of home; so, dear poet, what do you think?'

'Look, I am not a fortune-teller. What is there to understand? Are you asking me to presume my questions and answer them myself?'

'Oh, come on, I just wanted to know what you think of the beauty of rural Bengal since you are a poet.'

'Where do you think you would end up, on the banks of the Hooghly, or on your friend's back?'

'Why so impatient? Listen then. A distant pishima of my distantly related mashima. I had met her at the house of a distant maternal uncle…'

'I understand! That is why you have dragged along a distant friend. I understand everything.'

'But I haven't said anything yet!'

We were walking a meandering path. It was a village fully green. Between the leaves, the blue sky above looked like a crooked trodden track. We walked and walked. One by one, we took off our shawls and other woollens. As soon as it was twelve, my belly and feet gave up. I was hissing in anger, striking blow after blow. In his hunger, my friend digested whatever came his way. In an hour, we had reached the destined place according to directions given. There were three or four stray huts. All around, on the mud walls, grew bottle-gourd and beans, and on each side of the doorway grew *aparajita* creepers. We did not have to knock or call—an elderly woman came as soon as we were at the door and stood before us with a fishing-rod in hand. My friend asked, a little embarrassed—'Grandma, do you recognise me?' Closing her eyes she scratched her head, then smiled broadly and said—'I am old now, is it possible to remember former days in a trice. You had a very beautiful name, some deity...'

'Parameshwar, of Mandir bazar...'

'Yes yes, Parameshwar!' Then shutting her eyes, she touched her forehead with her folded palms and turned her face to the sky and muttered for a while, then laughed heartily. 'You asked me to come, grandma'—Parameshwar said in a low voice.

'Is that why you came? So, who is the dadu with you?'

'My friend, Dhumketu. Dhumketu Das. A distant relative, so to say.'

'Would he have come such a distance if he weren't distantly related? What sort of sense do you have, son? You had said you'd come earlier, but it's taken you this long. If two more years had passed, it would count as an era. Your friend's name ... change it, okay...'

We stood smiling. Then, she said, 'Your faces look worn, your bellies won't listen, sons. Can you cast a net?'

'We can.'

Twin mud ovens, wood and leaves as fuel. She fed us with care; we ate with contentment. Then she said, 'I don't speak of tonight, hope you will stay tomorrow?' Grandma's words sounded as sweet as the mellow receding sunlight. We smiled without replying. She said again, 'You will come again, will you not; how many times will you visit before I die?'

'I will come with my friend', Parameshwar replied.

'Good! So what was it going to be, a tale of a jackal, is it not? Then let me fish out a story from my invisible bag of tales about the deep kinship of the wild, primitive and fierce strangers. This is from a long time ago. It was winter, the day of Saraswati Puja. It rained heavily even before the crack of dawn. Then morning came and I went down to the ghat. I found a puppy curled up in the rain and cold, inside the gap between the wooden steps. At first I thought it was dead. But oh dear, it was alive to the touch! I brought it home, gave it warmth, fed it rice stock. I saw it opening its eyes in the afternoon. It grew with the passing of days and I felt happy in its company. Do you like the story so far?'

'Not much.'

'You will. The instrument that plays the wrong tune jars the ear. Similarly, I too started to feel a little uneasy. After a couple of months, the instrument seemed to completely change its tune. I wouldn't say that the change was complete but whatever was incongruous finally rectified itself. She was no longer a dog's pup, but a jackal's.'

'How did it happen, grandma?'

'I recollect a distant grandpa of yours saying that you study archaeological finds of animal bones. With this sort of intelligence?'

'I simply asked because I was surprised!'

'Wait, I am not done yet. She was really a jackal's offspring. In that stormy night, her mother had come to catch crabs or something but gave birth unexpectedly. She was forced to flee on hearing the barking of the neighbourhood dogs but probably could not carry away her young which had fallen into the gap of the steps. Whatever I say now is what I could guess, and I believe I'm right. After this, she began to grow up. Come. Come with me. You see that hole in the wall behind? I use it in the night to throw things outside, for I live alone. It was a narrow hole; I have made it wider, come and take a look.'

I stood outside and looked. Parameshwar took off the cover from the gaping hole and said—'Quite large! Why did you make it this big? There are the woods behind, snakes...!'

'That is so! But I don't have to explain, you will understand on your own. This hole is never closed at night.'

'Goodness! Why?'

'I keep it closed during the day. Can you see a clay urn on that side of the room?'

'Yes, it is overturned.'

Grandma now rolled over the heavy clay lid to one side and said, 'Come, come and stand by this window. Watch where the sun is receding—Don't look away from the spot, I'm right behind you.'

The sun was setting in the western sky. Its eyes and face glowing crimson with the long day's journey, shreds of its body dangling between the chinks of foliage. How long could it carry on with a sore body! In the twinkling of an eye, it dropped before our eyes, who knew where and when. Grandma placed her hands on each of our shoulders and said—'Are you watching?'

'Yes we are, you told us to,' Parameshwar said.

'A single word, "yes" would have been enough—you have lost the habit of speaking plainly. Keep watching that bush next to the bamboo grove by that narrow path.'

Only Parameshwar knew what went on inside his head. I did not have much of a head for a headache, though never in my life, in the company of two people in a room at evening, had I felt such a thumping in my chest—as though paddy were being pounded and flattened.

'Can you see anything?' Again, there was grandma's cautious signal. 'No, not yet.'

'Don't move your eyes away, you will see them now—look over there, look here they come.'

'Yes, running towards us.'

'Where are they now?'

'Inside the house through that hole.'

'Yes, inside the house. Come, come inside. See if they are within.'

'No, they aren't, grandma.'

'They are, inside the clay urn. Saro[1]... Kotkoti...'

While the vestiges of the words still floated in the breeze, those creatures that we had glimpsed running a little while ago, emerged from the barrel: an adult and two medium-sized jackals. I was the third of the group whose presence, position and role was rather negligible—I was merely the one who pulled the rope when asked to. I listened to them, saw all with my own eyes, and took everything in.

Parameshwar was not one to keep mum and he spoke up, 'Grandma, you had spoken only of one.'

'Yes, I did, but the story has not come to an end. Listen, the foundling of that day is now the mother jackal.'

'The pups are hers?'

'Yes, they are. Are you surprised? I had said I understood within days that she was a jackal's young, but she did not desire to go out into the courtyard anymore. What could I do? I fed her rice and vegetable curry inside the house. You must know that dogs are very clever hunters by nature; they sense everything by smell. As the days passed, I saw them running about, barking around the house the whole day. She always stayed inside, afraid to venture out. Then, one night, I found her busy scratching at that hole. I understood her conduct. Have you?'

'No, we don't, grandma.'

'You are grown-ups now; you have married and begotten children, what is the use of secrecy, better to speak outright. I understood she had grown into an adult; she had matured. Then what I did was to take up the crowbar and

---

[1] Abbreviation of Saraswati. The she-jackal is so named because she was found on the morning of Saraswati Puja.

widen the hole. And you see that heavy lid? I got that made too. I saw her going out, but she didn't return that night. The whole of next day went by, evening came, night fell; still, she did not come. I felt sad; still, I thought— the wild animal has returned to the wild, let it be, may she be happy. Oh, dear! As I was getting ready for bed the following night, I found her calling me near the mouth of the hole. I can understand her. Since then she has never stayed out in the night, but always returns to the hole in the evening. I take off the lid for her to go out before the first light of dawn. She doesn't stay at home during the daytime.

'Why doesn't she stay during the day?'

'Didn't I say, because of the dogs' mischief.'

'What about her meals?'

'Everything happens here at my place. They leave at dawn—where will they get food in the woods in the daytime? Earlier she would feed alone, now there are the two young ones. Like children of humans, they too love to eat *kotkoti*. One day I was eating kotkoti while they were snooping about my lap. I gave them some; they ate them all. So, I named both of them Kotkoti. Do you still think I am lonely, son? They are my daughter, my grandson and granddaughter. My two sons are as good as non-existent. They work far away and come home once a year.'

'Do they know about this?'

'You make me laugh. Everybody in the neighbourhood knows. I don't eat fish; I make somebody cast the net when my sons come home but fish with my rod every day for these three as they can't eat vegetarian food. I worry about them.'

'Grandma, you had said that day you would tell us the story of a jackal, what we have heard is hardly a story!'

'This is so, dear boy. In today's world, it is stories that are coming true; the realities of human lives are turning into an empty talk, lies.'

'I hear that this homestead, the pond, the orchard, the wetland amount to ten-twelve *bighas*.'

'More than twelve. Which is why I cannot visit my sons' place. This is my husband's birthplace, as well as my sons'. Many a time have I made King Yama go back. It is a deep attachment. On top of that, now they're here. Who will look after them!'

'The houses are scattered far and wide; don't you feel afraid in the night?'

'Afraid of what, of thieves and robbers? Stay back a little while and see how many dogs gather about.'

'Why do they come?'

'Praised be your intelligence! They come here for them. Otherwise, why would the dogs come every night? There are other neighbourhoods and other houses in the village but they are unconcerned about them. You know, son, humans are treacherous, but not the birds and beasts. There is peace in loving them, in caring for them. They are now like my biological offspring.'

In this way, grandma narrated their way of life through the night. No one slept; we did not even feel inclined to sleep. She finally paused for a while.

I took the opportunity—'Grandma, we have bothered you the whole day; we did not let you sleep in the night either.'

'No, you have given me peace. If you think it a bother, do bother me in this manner once a month, son. You will stay tomorrow, won't you, Dhumketu dear?'

'No, we will start at the break of dawn.'

'Are you on Saro's side, afraid of dogs?'

'No, of humans.'

'Go then, but let us meet before death takes over. I will wait for you.'

'We promise, we will come again, grandma.'

The jackal family went out from the back, us from the front. Grandma watched with tear-filled eyes. We could not walk steadily; it was as if our hands and feet were chained, our waists bound with ropes. We walked slowly and kept looking back like the bride alighting from her palanquin at her in-laws'.

The dark night has a unique attraction for me now. Night comes, darkness descends, and I venture out on some pretext or the other. I glance at the bushes in the darkness to see if I can find in them someone like the Saraswatis of Bawaali.

Translated from Bangla by Naina Dey
Originally published as "Bawaalir sheyali" in *Badaboner Kotha o Kahini*, 2007

3

Dokhno

PANCHANAN DAS

Neither Soma, nor her mother or father could ever have imagined such a thing, but everything does not always happen according to one's wishes. Joy can suddenly visit a family of humble means, just as sorrow can suddenly overcome a prosperous one. Not only did Viswanath Gupta get overwhelmed by his serious ailment, but his small, happy family had to suddenly weather a terrible storm. For a year and a half, he had no income. His savings were exhausted; the hospital doctors gave up on him. Since then, Viswanath Gupta stayed at home. Soma, on the other hand—apart from the time she spent bathing and eating at home—was out the whole day, often till ten o'clock at night. Her conversations with her mother over dinner were the only interaction they had. After eating, she would go through a few books or magazines, and then rest.

Today, while she was eating, Sarbari Gupta told her daughter, 'You won't listen until you fall ill. What will happen then?'

'Are we very well now? Where will the medicines come from?'

'We'll eat once a day.'

'We already eat once a day. The difference is that we eat it across two meals.'

'I fear that something will happen to you…such sorrow.'

'I'm used to it, ma.'

'I used to think—if only you were not born a girl.'

'And what do you think today, now?'

'I was wrong, these are wrong ideas. Boys can do many things, and they do so too, but they're selfish. I don't understand why people still want to have sons. Today I've understood my mistake. The two are not the same. The position of the girl child should be much higher.'

'Your thoughts are still wrong; you alone think this way. Forget it, let's wait and see what happens.'

'What will we wait for?'

'That school teacher's job.'

'You have to pay a bribe there.'

'I've heard. Let's see.'

'I've also heard from your father that it is very important to get the police on your side in order to get employed. Despite good marks, several certificates, and a healthy body, everything will still fall apart if you don't bribe the police. Your father didn't get a good job because he couldn't pay that bribe. So, he joined that private company. That's why I'm worried, dear; we have suffered before. Don't keep running around so much.'

The mother and daughter could still find a ray of hope. But Viswananth Gupta was not too optimistic. A live mound of flesh is not meant to be affected. The only sad thought amidst the joy was that she would have to go to a small school in a remote part of South 24-Parganas instead of working in Kolkata. At present, the only job was as a subject teacher there.

No, Soma did not have to bribe anyone for this job.

On that very day, she packed, and with new dreams, she set off, imagining a web of likely problems that might befall her in an unknown place. The place wasn't too difficult to find. She had not imagined that the roads and communication channels would be so good at Patharpratima. On arriving at the school, she headed straight for the headmistress Molina Maity's office. The jovial lady gave her a broad smile and said, 'Do sit down. You are Soma, aren't you?'

'Yes, bordi.'

'Where do you live?'

'It's about twenty-five minutes from the five-point crossing at Shyambazar.'

'I have a very good feeling about you. The girls will love you. Come, let me take you to their class. You don't have to teach today. Just a question. Do you want to go back home today?'

'I'm wondering what I should do.'

'You can go, or you can stay. It won't be such a problem. The girls are looking forward to meeting you.'

She introduced Soma to the students, showed her around the school, and brought her back to her room. 'I was telling you earlier—I'll tell you about where you can stay later, but do you see that pink house in the distance? Go there and talk to him.'

'Why? And with whom should I talk?'

'That is the residence of the school's secretary. He is always at home, either there or here in the gardens. That is his work. He will be happy to meet you and you'll also enjoy the experience.'

Soma listened to the headmistress and left. Just as she stood at the school secretary's door, a well-built middle-aged gentleman half jumped out of the verandah and came laughing towards her. 'Come, my dear, come. I knew you were coming in a day or two; come and sit down. So where do you live?'

'Kolkata.'

'This is what I wanted. A teacher from Kolkata to come and transform the school. Where will you stay?'

'Let me see. I haven't thought about it yet.'

'Oh. You aren't married. Then you have to stay with me. Look, my dear, I don't have any children and my wife is also no more. A widow stays with me. I manage things for her. Now her son is here too. You can stay here without any problems. What do you think?'

'Let me see. I haven't thought about it yet.'

As the conversation progressed, Soma felt a bit disheartened. Inwardly, she was rather angry with the headmistress. A bit distracted, she greeted the secretary and took her leave. 'May I leave now, kakababu?'

'No, that won't happen. No one has ever left this place on an empty stomach. Don't get up; please remain seated. You have to accept atleast a morsel of food! You can sleep here if you're tired. The school has some rules—take note of them. Look, my dear, in the beginning, I'll pay you as temporary staff for two months. After that, I'll make full payment and release you from this deduction. Don't worry. I've done the same with your headmistress and with everyone else. Most didn't agree to this in the beginning, but with time they understood the reason.'

Upon hearing this, Soma's eyes reddened, her face lost colour, and she began to sweat. The secretary noticed these changes. Amused, he said, 'What has happened to you, my dear? What is bothering you?'

She felt compelled to smile and say, 'This place is very far away.'

'Think of this as your home—your eternal solace.'

'I shall leave now, kakababu.'

'Come back to the school tomorrow—I'll come and meet you there.'

Soma returned and stood quietly in front of the headmistress. She looked at her for a while and then said, 'What has happened to you, Soma?'

'Nothing.'

'Uh-huh. A lot. That's what it looks like.'

'I might not return, bordi.'

'What suddenly happened? What's the problem?'

'Well, let's just say it's very far from home.'

'You knew it was far when you came—I can't accept that. Why don't you tell me the real reason, Soma?'

'No, bordi, it isn't possible to tell you everything.'

'Yes, now you're right. One can't tell a total stranger everything.'

'That's not what I meant. I just can't tell you.'

'If you consider me a friend, you will be able to tell me. An elder sister is like a mother.'

'How do I tell you?'

'If your mother asks you, would you say the same thing?'

Soma had no other option. She discussed her complaints one by one, and opened her heart to the headmistress. After listening to the whole thing, she burst into laughter and said, 'You crazy girl, then listen to the complete story. This school was built by him; he has given the school everything. Fifty *bigha*s of land and many lakhs of rupees. He loves the school so much that he never got married. He has provided shelter to an orphaned widow and when he heard that she had a son in an orphanage, he brought him here and took on the responsibility of educating him. It is as though the entire responsibility of the school is his alone. And you want to know more?'

'Tell me, bordi.'

'He is illiterate. He has done all this and more using just his thumb impression. When he heard that you were coming from Kolkata, he was thrilled. He distributed sweetmeats all around.'

'Why?'

'He said, "I must have done some good in my previous life that a teacher from Kolkata is coming to teach here." He has learnt many English words just by hearing them, but their application and pronunciation remain incorrect. It's not possible to learn them correctly, so he makes mistakes. You're a teacher from Kolkata, so he could not resist the temptation. You will be surprised if you listen to everything else. He is very serious about our salary. Oh, dear, why are you crying?'

'I didn't want to cry, but you made me.'

'Wipe your tears before someone comes. Listen to another funny thing—in the first six months, he will not give a new teacher the whole salary.

Actually, he feels that he will be able to retain teachers this way. He doesn't believe in the law. Later, not only does he pay the amount but also adds interest to it. How much he pays depends on him. And for these six months, in his mind, the teacher is temporary. Now tell me what you will do.'

'What is there to do, bordi, you have cleared my doubts and dispelled all darkness. Now I am in the land of the midnight sun.'

'Then go home now and tell your mother everything. I am sure she will understand.'

'You, too, are like my mother. In Kolkata, people say that the people of the south are unlettered, uncultured, unsocial and self-centred. How wrong the genteel people of the city are! There is so much to learn from the people here.'

'But you have come to teach.'

'I'll do both—learn and teach.'

'So what have you decided? Where will you stay?'

'Where there is an uncle, why will the niece have a problem? I have heard of simple people, but I didn't know that their words could be so straightforward. In these parts, there must be many people like him.'

'Of course—countless. All of them do not have financial wealth, but they are genuine people, people of the soil. When you live here, you will get their love, cooperation, closeness. They are called Dokhno.'[1]

'Tell me, bordi, isn't it possible to educate kakababu and free him from using his thumb impression?'

'Why not, but someone has to take that responsibility. You are there. But you know there are many illiterate people like him around. You will be able to help them, won't you? I think you will.'

Saying so, the headmistress instantly got up and hugged Soma.

In the gentle wind floating in through the open window, unnoticed by them, their flowing *anchals* caressed each other innumerable times. In the distant western horizon, one could make out an exquisite, clear green pattern like a strung bow. Nearby, the river was brimming over thanks to the untamed southern wind. Molina Maity told Soma, 'Open your eyes and look, Soma. See how happy the undulating waters of the Shibua, Mridangabhanga and Pakhinala rivers are. Innumerable small and large waves are dancing and playing restlessly. Just look at it. What are you thinking of?'

---

[1] People of South 24-Parganas or Dakshin 24-Parganas

'Bordi, similar waves are splashing in two small rivers nearby. Who will watch those waves? Who will keep track of them? I am thinking of them.'

Translated from Bangla by Arpita Chatterjee
Originally published as "Dokno" in *Badaboner Katha o Kahini*, 2007

4

The Museum

PANCHANAN DAS

Flashing nearly twenty-two teeth, Ghonteswar said, 'Hello grandpa, so sorry for being a bit late!'

'A bit late? Late by an hour, which is not a bit at all.'

'It is; I usually come before time.'

'Did you fall asleep?'

'No, my wife's been behaving erratically.'

'Fight?'

'Sort of. She's keen on managing something from me, I suppose.'

Rolling his eyes, Prankeshto said, 'What is she trying to manage, dear?'

'No, no, grandpa, it's not what you think. She's keen on going to God's altar.'

'Then what exactly do you need to manage?'

'A bundle of notes! To add to that, she intends to take one kid with her, leaving the other in my custody. A bundle of notes has to be parted with, and my daily wage has to be compromised—that doubles my loss!'

'Did you part with it?'

'She has big demands, as I said, grandpa!'

'You could've given it to her!'

'I'll have to resort to robbing then.'

'Just borrow, then.'

'I've tried that too. Hardly ever can I manage to get money when I need it.'

'You could've knocked at your grandpa's for once.'

'I'll keep that in mind.'

'Fine. Now hold it, we're already late. But one thing I must say, she's a good woman, she has faith in religion. You could've given her the money, you know.'

'Good? Not at all. Very stubborn.'

'As if you're somebody! Let me see.'

'That you're saying and seeing for the last three years.'

'I could visit your place, but this or that comes in the way. A lot of work!'

'Again, that same excuse.'

'What?'

'I just referred to what you usually do. Just dilly-dallying, all day long. I've never seen you working, grandpa!"

'Do you mean to say that I don't work at all?'

Ghontey nodded.

After calling out for Prankeshto a number of times, his wife said to herself, 'Oh what a relief! At least, I can cook in peace today.'

After making all the arrangements, Ghonteswar started with his work. After an hour of trimming this and sizing out that, he flashed his twenty, twenty-two odd teeth and said, 'Come, give me the nails!'

'Wait!'

Getting busy, Prankeshto ran to the adjacent cubicle. He thrust the plastic envelope and a bundle of sheets, all a mess, in front of Ghonteswar. It did not need to be untied. A host of pins and nails were disgorged, tearing off the entrails of the envelopes, papers, ropes and threads. Flashing his teeth in the same manner, Ghontey said, 'All rusty things, grandpa!'

'But these are antique pieces, dating back to my father's times!'

Screwing his eyes up, Ghontey said, 'Are these antiques?'

'What else?'

'It would be better if some of them were from the British or the Mughal eras!'

'A few are.'

'I'd asked you to get new nails, hadn't I?'

'Oh! But I found these nails instead!'

'And what about the blocks of wood?'

'Those may date back to the days of my grandfather or even his father! Even the grandchildren would love to bear the legacy.'

'Yes, that's possible. All are either teak or *pashu*.'

'You seem to be the great-grandfather of teakwood! Come on, hold it.'

Ghontey touched his forehead in reverence and got down to working. Prankeshto stirred a bit and sat firmly. The hammer went once and Prankeshto's heart started pounding; he could hardly stay calm. In a broken voice he said, 'Ghontey, you have left me undone. You failed to impale even one of them.'

'So what? I myself am undone! Look at my fingers, all smashed and crushed. . .'

'This is not a matter of being undone, I tell you!'

'No! Keep these with you, you can either get a good price or you can deposit these with the museum; you will earn fame!'

All of a sudden, he seemed to startle at Ghontey's words. Controlling himself, breaking into a smile, he said, 'Are you joking? Don't you see that my bamboo is being wasted?'

'Only a matter of ten-twenty rupees, but for me, it means the waste of a day-long work, of some hundred rupees or so and you are blind to that! It is almost noon.'

Prankeshto sprang up, 'You wretched chap, couldn't you tell me this earlier?'

'What's there to tell? Everything is happening in front of your eyes! You are busy keeping your account straight, you are outwardly penny wise, but actually pound foolish'

'Are you adding insult to injury?'

'No, this is for your own good.'

Scrambling up, slipping on the shirt hurriedly, he said, 'Let me take your leave then!'

'How can one leave one's house at noontide? It would be better if you leave after having a morsel or two.'

Prankeshto turned back to say, 'Oh, you nincompoop, what are you saying? Am I to be served as a guest in my own residence?'

'No, I simply asked because you are leaving in a huff.'

'Oh, you fool, I'm going to bring you your nails!'

'You're unable to make sense of what I'm saying! Such tight accounting can hardly help, grandpa!'

'No more wisecracks! Work your tools. Let me come back!'

Placing two low, wooden stools, Mayna's mother cried out, 'Lunch is ready to be served!'

Ghontey followed Prankeshto, close at his heels, to sit for lunch. He appeared restive, looking for something or the other. Prankeshto asked, 'What are you up to now?'

'I'm feeling so bad; I'm about to eat, without even starting with the work.'

'What will you get to eat, anyway? I couldn't even go to the market. Only dal and rice!'

'Fine! That's what the king takes. The poor cannot even buy that.'

Both hands held two platters of rice! Hot rice was pressed and shaped in the form of a beautiful pyramid. At one end was a bowl of dal, while on the other lay fried leafy vegetables, beside which a rotund ball of boiled potato lay, resembling a *kadam* flower in appearance, pepped up with finely-chopped fried chillies and thinly-sliced onions. The air was redolent of the sweet-scented fried red pepper issuing out of the boiled potato. Putting down the plates, looking Ghontey in the eye, the mistress of the house said, 'Don't be ashamed of asking for more, brother!'

'Absolutely, you don't need to say that!'

After all, they were grandfather and grandson; in this manner, light-veined conversation continued. Ghontey said, 'No rice, granny, just a little more dal will do.'

'Wait, there's another curry—egg-curry!'

Taken aback, the master of the house raised his eyebrows and said, 'Was there any need of dal then? Why did you cook it?'

'The thought came later. A guest is about to eat with us, how can I serve him just rice and nothing else?'

'Did you have eggs?'

'Did you bring them at all?'

'Then?'

'I brought them from the shop.'

'Each egg costs an extra fifty paisa, are you aware of that?'

'Will you then serve this kid only rice?'

'Dal-rice forms the king's menu; this grandson is a member of our household. Mind your words, my wife! We were almost full, this came as an added item, an exaggeration, do you understand me?'

'Keep your accounts to yourself!'

'You could've asked for it, I could've gone to buy it from the market.'

'You were busy with rusty nails, I called out to you and regretted it.'

Ghontey's siesta had by now been disturbed being with Prankeshto. Taking up the hammer in his hand, with sleepy eyes, he suggested, 'Grandpa, a little lazing on bed would be apt for now.'

'Just a kid to me in age but triply doubled in years! Relaxing is not that good.'

'I have overeaten and am feeling heavy now, grandpa.'

'Why did you eat so much then?'

'Would I give the egg a miss?'

Laughing boisterously, he said, 'Okay, so be it; the way fish is getting dearer these days!' Looking askance, smirking, Ghontey rejoined, 'Granny had to give it a miss!' With a solemn face, Prankeshto admonished, 'Shut up, take the tools in your hand, you chatterbox!'

Ghontey grew busy working the hammer. Prankeshto kept gazing at him. An extra nail beside one. Prankeshto fidgeted and sat firm. One, two, three, four, stood one after another and at this end, one nail was beefed up by an added one. Screwing up his restless eyes, Prankeshto roared, 'What have you done, my dear grandson? You left my wooden planks all cracked with random holes!' Flashing sparkling teeth, he said, 'You own a melon-garden, don't you, grandpa?'

'But it had never happened before, my dear son!'

'Those are light, fragile slats! They gave way to cracks and holes even before I could make a hole!'

'Now, what's the way out?'

'These are to be kept submerged in water.'

'For how long?'

'No question of hours and days. You have to soak them for months. Say, for two–three months. Unless they are drenched enough, the nails have no chance of getting firmly set in them.'

'You are letting me down again!'

It was as though a sliver of moon kept peeping through the clouds! Ghontey was looking on placidly, a smile dangling from his lips. Prankeshto nudged him, 'Hey, you have not nibbled at the "bait", have you?' Ghontey kept glancing at him while rejoining, 'The clump of bamboo is yours. A couple of them, to be precise. How can I let you down? I am afraid; what if you attack me with them?'

'What do you mean by "a couple of them"?'

'Right in front of you! Old slats of wood are your clump of *gente* bamboo, while the old nails have all turned spongy like cotton-balls, grandpa!'

'Illusion, all are illusory bonds! Neither can I burn them down, nor I can sell them off.'

'But you could come out of your lifelong bond with your parents; you could even sever all ties of illusion with your daughters!'

'I can't hold them back! It is impossible to hold them to myself once they come of age, given the rapid growth of a girl-child! Again, I fail to stall death, at ripe old age!'

'These have attained age as well! To quote you—three to four generations old!'

'What can I dispose of, Ghontey? Tell me. If I keep throwing all these away, the room will stand vacant! Everything has to be thrown off, then.'

'What significance do all these things have?'

'Look yonder, the things are aplenty. Though I do not possess cows for tilling the land, I still treasure the plough, yoke, ladder, everything! Threadbare drawing-net, *khebla, phoot, ghoni*—all are here, they come handy in the hour of need. While the ponds overflow during monsoon, and when the trees in the orchard are laden with fruits, I surround them on all sides by these curtains. Four antiquarian earthen barrels, nearly a dozen big and medium jars. Earthen pots, pitchers and platters will amount to almost two–four scores. There are four hookahs too! The bowls of the hubble-bubble pipe, including fresh and stale nicotine would be two–four scores too. Four hookahs! One iron safe is stuffed with shoes, sandals and flip-flops. Large, broken bowls, winnowing trays, sifters, bamboo-containers—all will count to twenty, twenty-five in number. Ordinary broomsticks too are two–three scores! Two-three rolls of *jhentla* mat are also there. And glass vials and bottles are almost ten–twenty scores in number. Besides these, the bundles of rope and coconut skins are in two sacks, again the jute sacks and nearly fifty low, flat wooden stools appear for count. Where to look for these stools, tell me, they are offered to our relations and friends to sit, on their arrival. And this husking-pedal as you see, a couple of this variety are there inside the room—of yore, of the bygone times of grandpa and great grandpa!'

'Have the husking-pedals gone bonkers?'

'No, they are quite weighty. Previously, the women used to husk, now even the men would find it difficult.'

'What more have you preserved, grandpa?'

'What more can I say? Come and see on your own.'

'Not today, grandpa, let it wait for the next visit.'

'Oh yes, why would you see now? You'd rather run to the city, spending money; you would spend your money just to have a look at it.'

'What's there to see, why are you bringing the city into it?'

'Why, that museum of yours? Everything there is the same as the things here, but this here is "junk" we hoard. There, all are old things, traditional items. Pots, pitchers, bricks, stones, pictures, paintings, bones, pitch-black, rusty broken exhibits, dating back two–three thousand years.'

'The Calcutta Museum is in possession of a line of valuable items, grandpa.'

'Oh-ho! These too will turn priceless, once they reach there, "Ignored at home, worshipped abroad". There, in the museum and here, in the storeroom. One day, you would find people coming in droves to this courtyard of your Keshto grandpa, here at Jagadishpur.'

'Shall I get to see that?'

'Your grandpa would get to see … these couple of racks are made for this only!'

'I shall make one for you, grandpa, according to your choice.'

'Please come! If all of us join hands in completing a piece of work, it is sure to be the best!'

'But many a thing is needed for it, grandpa!'

'Again, it will take many days to complete the work. The beehive cannot be made in a day—it is the result of the tireless effort of hundreds of thousands of bees. Everything is just here; they are to be kept in an organised manner, that's all. Please come, stand by me!'

'Me? An ordinary man of family, me?'

'Yes! I can depend on people like you! Come!'

While walking along, Ghontey cast his glance at both the ends of the path. All seemed to be priceless to him today—the pebbles strewn around, bricks and stones left in negligence, left-out toys, thrown off bric-a-bracs, everything, everything!

Translated from Bangla by Ketaki Datta
Originally published as "Jaadughor" in *Ali Galir Golpo*, 2014

5

Shaplas

PANCHANAN DAS

That canal of Gazi has robbed me of my night sleep. Its water increases and decreases ever so slightly—the tenuous relationship that it had shared at one time with the Piyali river has vanished. It is more of a Milky Way on ground than a mere canal, as it stretches from the north to the south, the carrier of thousands of *shaplas*. From early morning the market starts, this market of shaplas and *shaluks*. Bees come, so do the bumblebees, they all drink honey. There are more takers of the shaplas and shaluks, as the poor of the ten or twenty villages strewn around come crowding in.

Every night before I go to bed, I urge my mother, 'Ma, don't forget to wake me up before the dawn breaks.'

'Of course, I will—I do wake you every morning; do you have to remind me every day?'

'I won't get anything if I am even a wee bit late. That would be such a sad thing. The day will then stretch on without end.'

'You are sad if I don't call you, but it hurts me so much to wake you up.'

'What hurts you, ma?'

'You're too young to work, I tremble when I wake you and I am torn by anxiety when you leave.'

'What makes you worry so much?'

'How would you understand? Be careful while you pick them up. There are poisonous things around.'

'Do you mean things like snakes? There are none, but the bees have stung me a few times. What do you think they're up to during the night?'

'They do their job—they drink honey.'

'Shaplas have honey?'

'All flowers do.'

Ma never fails me. From Bhadra to Agrahayan—the autumn months—I run to the canal early in the morning; the water is too deep in the middle, so I pluck the smaller shaplas growing by the edge of the water and suffer looking at the bigger ones being picked by the others.

The dawn of full moon nights is so much fun, there is nothing to fear. I can count from afar the number of shaplas picked by the others from various spots. Gradually, a red light spreads to the eastern sky, the stars fall asleep, the Milky Way dissolves, and the shaplas also play hide and seek. Shaplas have so much fun! They travel to the village carried on the heads of some, on the shoulders of others, and the shaluks remain bound in the *gamchha*s around the waists.

The service of a maid is not needed in the countryside; all poor people suffer the same condition. I don't have any siblings, ma does not have any money, the only help she gets is from me. I do not recall my father. Two or four times each month we manage to have full-grain rice, two to four times we have broken rice, and the rest of the days we have hot or cold leftover water, boiled leaves of yam, watercress, wild *hinchey* and *notey*. Bhadra and Aghrahayan are the months that are kind to us in terms of providing food, even if it does not fill our belly. If you put dry leaves and twigs in a burning oven, the fire leaps up, turning them into ashes in no time. The stomach behaves the same way; if you put food into it, it turns it into ashes and one's hunger becomes more intense.

There is a house a few yards away from ours, familiar to us as the house of the short-tempered old man whom everyone knows as a miser. He does not employ any help. He makes us run the errands in his orchard, in addition to guarding it—the paths by which thieves and stealers of the leaves, or the cattle enter, are all made impregnable. Apparently, the old man is a relative by virtue of being our neighbour, so we call him dadu ('grandpa'). The path is lined by papaya trees. One day, I happened to stumble upon dadu on this path and was subjected to severe and multiple pulling of the ear. I failed to understand where I had gone wrong, but I did not want to know it either.

The next day, as I took the same path, I remembered what had happened the day before and happened to look up at the orchard. There was no escape; dadu's voice came lashing out, 'Hey there, you, *batkey*, wait.' Secretly, I was happy because he was calling me and this made me lose my fear of yesterday. Fearless, I also spoke out, 'Dadu, you mean me?'

'Yes, you; wait, don't run away.'

He put down the spade and stepped carefully but swiftly in front of me. Stretching out his right arm he held my ear, 'Listen, never look upward, it is a bad habit. Don't cast your evil eye on the fruit, if you want to eat something, just ask me, and I'll give it to you free of cost. But I warn you, never steal things.'

Hearing about the free gift, my mouth started watering. I was licking my dry lips when he said again, 'I hope you'll be able to run a few errands for me?'

'I will.'

'Always take the right path. If you work hard, you will never run out of means. Do you understand?'

I nodded at his words and smiled. I also saw him smile for the first time in my life.

'Okay then, come tomorrow morning. It is nice to work in the mornings during the summer, tell your ma.'

'I shall be here.'

Next morning I was there as promised. Dadu was happy. I asked him what work I was supposed to do and he said, 'Weeding, digging, watering the plants, putting up fences, repairing—easy things. You don't have to know black magic or be a scholar to do these things; do you think you can manage?'

'Yes, sure.'

I am older now; I have to dig the ground with a spade. I flop down on the ground, breathless as I work. Dadu caresses my head and says, 'I will give you an extra papaya today and a couple of bananas as well. Men have to work hard; they have to work hard all their lives. You're lucky that you're getting your training totally free. Go on, dig up the couple of *jhellas* in front of you and then you can go home for the day.'

Dadu again put his hand on my head; I remembered ma. The last few months have been tough for us. The canal does not have any more shaplas, and one can only find the few shaluks that are left after a great deal of searching. No one visits the canal anymore; I too have given up hope. This job, though hard, is helping us survive somehow. I think as I dig. Dadu comes back after a tour of the orchard and says, 'Let it be for today. You can take it up tomorrow. Take the papaya and bananas with you. Listen once more; the earning that comes of hard work gives one much happiness. When you eat these fruits, you will realise how wonderful the taste is; stolen goods don't have that taste. Let me repeat, never look upward.'

'Why, dadu?'

'You are only in Class 7—let another six or seven years pass, then you'll understand why. What's your name?'

'Madhu, that is Madhusudan. But everyone calls me Madhu.'

'*Bah*, I have got Lord Madhusudan himself in my orchard, no one can steal anything from here now. I want you to know that Narayan mistri never lies.'

I am now grown up; four or five years have passed already. Now I get the full amount for working in the field. The employer plans to cheat me and says, 'The same amount cannot be demanded by kids and adults, my lad. A boy of fifteen or sixteen and a man of thirty or forty, are they the same?'

I argue, 'I work all day, the same amount of work as others. I can do everything, I have learnt everything—to prepare the soil for farming and also to work as an assistant to a mason, as a mason and a thatcher. I work sincerely, I don't cheat while working, I don't work in a slapdash way, I don't care if I have to work long hours, I consider the job given as my own. Why should I be paid less?'

The man goes silent; he does not want to lengthen the argument.

Things changed all at once. My fees went up, sometimes by one rupee, sometimes by two. I come back home late at night after a day of hard work. Ma comes and sits beside me and brushes her hand over my body lightly and fans me. Between conversations, she says, 'Lord Narayan is showering his kindness on us finally, Madhu.'

'Yes, dadu started showing kindness four or five years ago.'

'Since when did he become your grandpa?'

'You won't understand, ma. If he's your father, isn't he my grandfather?'

'God is everyone's father. See how things changed over just a few years! Everyone else looks for jobs, but employers come looking for you. Earlier, if you wanted ten rupees, you had to put in twenty rupees' worth of labour, you had to sign for your fees and look for someone as security—now nothing of the sort is needed.'

'Because they trust me, because I am trustworthy. One cannot learn wisdom or intelligence in any school where you have to pass tests, but one can learn that when in poverty. It is poverty which purifies and matures you and shows you the right way.'

Our household keeps changing colour every day. The way youth changes hues, our household is changing too; tiles instead of thatch, brick walls instead of fences, proper roof in place of simple tiles. Mosquitoes and flies are on the wane and friends keep increasing in number. One day there is a flower garden in the courtyard and flower pots on the terrace. A narrow path stretches up to the front door, bordered by rows of flowers on either side, exactly like tiny and narrow Milky Ways. I have filled the small pool next door with shaplas, blood-red shaplas like the red hibiscuses in the white slots; I make time to gaze at them.

Mother asks me as she looks on, 'Weren't the other flowers okay? They are so pretty; why are you obsessed with the shaplas, *khoka*?'

'They will drink honey from them, that's why.'

'But the other flowers have honey too.'

'But they won't come for the other flowers. I want to see them.'

'Who are they?'

'The bees and the bumblebees of the shaplas of the canal. They are my inspiration, my secret to life, ma.'

'You still remember them?'

'They are engraved in my mind. When I look up at the night sky, I have no idea what the stars say. The Milky Way reminds me of the canal of Gazi. I recall the shaplas and shaluks; even today in the darkness of dawn, the crowd for the shaplas and shaluks has gathered. Every dawn, the memories of all those mothers waking up their children at the crack of dawn return to haunt me. I think of the pain and marks of suffering on their faces as they wake up their children and the happiness in the child's eyes as he wakes up acknowledging the mother's call. I understand everything now, ma. I want to go back. Once you finish school and establish yourself in life, you never have time to even take a peek at the school you have left behind; once the necessity is over, you never get time to revisit.'

'Yes, my boy, without suffering, greatness cannot be attained, but one also has to rely on oneself. One ought to have faith in God; He gives strength and courage.'

'Yes, ma. My human-god is still alive. It is he who had given me my strength and courage. Dadu blesses me every time he sees me.'

'Don't ever forget your dadu. You have a long way to go.'

'Indeed, I've progressed just a little bit; the rest of the way is tough. Look up, ma, the sun is rising. We only have daylight now, as the arctic people do for six long months. The whole earth is gleaming. I've got what I never even imagined. I had no dreams, but now I see around me, and I think. My dreamscape is crowded by these images—a canal with a host of flowering shaplas, bees humming among the flowers, naked children gathering the shaplas and shaluks, the early morning sky, the helpless mother with the child in her arms, the faces of those hungry people, their rib cages visible as they stretch, more like these...'

Translated from Bangla by Sucheta Bhattacharya
Originally published as "Shapla" in *Badaboner Katha o Kahini*, 2007

6

The Father and the Mother

Prasad Kumar Mandal

The Sundarbans is a gold mine in itself. It is overflowing with wealth, and goddess Bonbibi keeps calling us and visiting us in our dreams. We cannot hold ourselves back; we have to go. That world of honey, honeycomb and fish keeps tugging at us like an addiction. You can get as much as you want from that sacred forest. It is our life, our heartbeat.'

'Aren't you afraid of the tiger?'

'Of course I am. But that doesn't bother me. I enjoy the fight. They're very fond of human flesh, you know.'

'Human flesh?'

'Yes. Tigers are masters of stealth. They wait in hiding and pounce upon the unwary human for an instant kill. The tiger can pick the victim upon its back and disappear. But most often it loses a frontal battle.'

Raghu was surprised. Fighting with a tiger, what a feat! Bhulu Gayen, a farmer in his fifties, is a dauntless fighter. When the harvest season is over, he generally moves to the forest in search of honey and fish. He has a bagful of stories to tell. Raghu shows his interest, 'Heard the forest is full of poisonous snakes—a variety of cobras, the green tree serpent and others—aren't you afraid of them?'

'Oh no! Bhulu doesn't care about those', he wrinkles his nose in utter disdain. 'I know a lot of medicines and magical remedies. Many of us are experts in magic, but people die every year, oh yes, they do. How can you escape destiny?'

'Oh, so you believe in destiny?'

'Yes, we have to. Snakes and tigers show up quite often. Then we have to make offerings to goddess Manasha, the patron goddess of snakes. And if somebody dies, the dead body has to be left afloat on a *mandash.*'

Raghu was surprised. 'Why on a mandash?'

'That's the rule. Just in case the dead person comes back alive like Lakhinder', Bhulu continues in his local dialect. He keeps puffing at his hookah—'Sir, we have to give the king Dakshin Rai the tax that is due to him.'

Raghu cannot contain his surprise. 'Why so? Why do you have to pay tax?'

'That's the rule of our forest. Nobody knows whose turn could come next. But nobody really cares for their life.'

'Oh yes', Raghu agrees. 'I heard that the bandits are also very active in these forests? How do you people handle that?'

'We fight! They are actually cowards, you know. They simply take things away by force. They are afraid of the snakes and the tigers and hence, survive by stealing.'

Raghu is beyond words. What an undaunted spirit this Bhulu Gayen is—a man made of forged steel. As a farmer too, he is quite well-off. Moreover, he has additional income from his ventures in the forest. Hence, he neither knows defeat nor agrees to retreat from life's everyday battles. As a result, other traders respect him. Bhulu lets go of his hookah for a moment and says, 'Sir, we are not afraid of the humans or the animals. The biggest challenge around this place is the river embankment; it is like a killer arrow.'

'Why do you call it that?'

'Just like the arrow with which Ravana killed Lakshman by stealth, the embankment also kills.'

Perhaps he is right.

'The river dam keeps out salt water. If that is breached, we're doomed.'

Raghu is shocked.

Bhulu goes on to say, 'The waves are monstrous. The Raimangal river has extremely swift currents; it is more like an extension of the sea. What can the dam do? After all, it is made of mud. When the high tide rages in full force, we have to live on the extreme edge, lucky to be alive. On one side of the dam we have sweet water—that's where we live. We till the land and raise a golden harvest. The land is very fertile; it is flat land, but we can harvest only one crop per year. If that dam breaks, it becomes pure hell. All the cultivated land is laid to waste.' He continues, 'The embankment is a trickster, we cannot foresee when and where it will become unstable and break.'

'But you know all about these waters; so why does a dam break?'

'The Phantom of the water is the whirlpool, here we call it *ghol*. It continuously weakens and breaks the dam.'

Raghu was taken aback, 'What is ghol?'

'It is a sort of reverse current among the waves. It is an eddy, spins like a top. It eats into the riverbed as well as the embankment. Firing up with every spin, it moves under the water and hits the embankment at its base. This way, the embankment gradually wears out.'

'My god, what happens then?'

'The erosion compresses the dam as the tide rolls in and ultimately it breaks.'

'That is terrible!'

'Sir, these are killer whirlpools. The Raimangal is full of such deathly traps. Boats and rafts capsize very often.'

'How do you avoid that?'

'We have to keep our eyes open and avoid the eddies.'

Men like Bhulu are totally helpless. They blame their own luck but never blame others. They are, after all, veterans of this land and understand the dangers of the embankment. One has to recognise the behaviour of the land, water and current well in advance. But they still cannot prevent anything. So much pompous spending on planning and engineering takes place to prevent the dam from breaking. Still, it continues to breach. Projects go haywire. It would be prudent to consult these experienced people before the implementation of any project. In the meantime, Bama, the village headman turns up. He seems very busy. 'Uncle, have you heard the news? A ring dam is going to be built in the Sardar locality.'

Bhulu is dumbstruck. 'Again? A ring dam?'

'Oh, yes. From the sluice gate till Natobar Ghat.'

'Goodness me! A good deal of land will be lost because of this contraption.'

Bama is in tears. They are scared of the ring dam, scared of losing their land. He wipes away tears with the back of his hand. 'Uncle, let us go to the meeting. The contractor has come. The panchayat *pradhan*, Phani, will also be there. Let's go.'

Raghu wants to know what a ring dam is.

Bhulu takes a deep breath and explains, 'It is a new kind of dam to prevent erosion. They build the dam a couple of hundred feet inland. This way, much of the land is lost in the river, never to show up again.'

'But you get compensated, don't you?'

Bhulu exclaims, 'Compensation, come on! The government builds the dam out of its own funds, isn't that enough?'

Raghu feels embarrassed. In this land, there are no set rules for compensation. So, they have no idea about it. Bhulu is quite jittery, he requests Raghu, 'Sir, please come to our meeting.' Raghu concurs, 'Okay, let's go.'

About seven or eight hundred people are sitting on their haunches in the grounds of the local court. The village headman, the farmers and the busybodies—everyone is in attendance. People would have to move at least six to seven hundred feet inland from the main embankment; a ring dam will be built. This news has already reached them, so nobody utters a word. They are busy calculating how much of the fertile, crop-yielding land each one of them has to give up. There is no apparent reaction from the mass. The contractor is busy with his charts, explaining how much of the land will be taken over at every bend of the river, every nook and corner. This land yields food crop for the people, naturally they are emotionally attached to it. There seems to be no way out but to give up. The dam is essential.

'To hell with the dam! If the land goes, what do we eat?' A few in the crowd are outraged. They snatch the map, tear it up and continue to hurl abuse while shouting. 'We are not giving up our land. Get lost.' The presiding officer, panchayat pradhan Phani, is furious. 'Are you out of your minds? You all are going to drown in salt water. If ten people lose their land now, it is going to save the lives of ten thousand.' But the crowd keeps shouting. 'Down with the ring dam. Save your land!' The pradhan tries to pacify the crowd and explains, 'With great difficulty, we got this dam sanctioned.' But his pleas fall on deaf ears. Chaos rules. 'We know this is just an excuse to dupe and starve us. Down with the ring dam!' The crowd speaks as one, 'Repair the old dam and spare our land. You can erect a proper fortification with sal logs, bring boulders and strengthen it or lay out sandbags—you can easily keep the land and water in their proper place.'

The mob gets encouraged, and everybody starts shouting; resentment starts spreading like wildfire. The landowners are desperate and a fist fight ensues. They are not ready to forfeit an inch of their land; the fighting intensifies and results in total chaos. The contractor takes a bad blow to his head. The president of the local body is not spared either and he gets his share of blows too! Raghu is speechless. He had never expected the simple village folk to turn into a violent mob. The meeting gets busted, even the sanctioned plan goes down the drain. Now the high tide is bound to hit in full force. But nobody has any idea how to handle that.

After dusk, pradhan Phani is sitting alone on the cemented steps leading to the river. Raghu joins him and utters a few words of sympathy. Phani retorts angrily, 'The dam is sure to give way. Let the idiots drown when the high tide strikes or when the flood comes in.'

'You're getting angry for no reason. The villagers have indeed made some good suggestions to save the dam.'

'Do they understand our waters or our dams? All the sanctioned money will go down the drain. They are going to rob us left, right and centre.'

Raghu squints, 'Stealing?'

'Oh yes, the contractors do. If they have to repair or strengthen a weak dam, they always misappropriate funds. On record, they will show additional expenditure.' Raghu nods in agreement, perhaps it is true. The government always gets the work done through some contractors, that's the rule. But he does not understand the nitty-gritty of skirting responsibility and wants to know more. Phani continues like a know-it-all, 'The contract would specifically mention the use of sal wood, but they will use bamboo; that too instead of the specified ten feet deep bore, they will stop at four feet. Boulders and sandbags will also be used sparsely. They will even show twenty- or twenty-five-times escalated cost of the labourer, the dam inspector and the man who measures the water level at various points.'

'But don't you see all this with your own eyes?'

'That I do for sure, but they will convince us that materials have been washed away by current or high tide. They doctor the records; that's how they steal.'

'You seem to know a lot about this.'

'Yes, indeed. I have been duped a number of times for protesting against this. But you can prove nothing. You can never produce a witness. On the contrary, you are humiliated in front of everybody.'

Phani seems to be evading responsibility; he is hiding something. He doesn't seem to be as genuine as he appears. He knows so much, yet, he is unwilling to come clean. Precious land and crops are lost because of the misdeeds of a few. Why are they spared? Why cannot they be uprooted once and for all?

Raghu goes out for an early morning walk all by himself. He strolls along the dam and looks at the sandbanks; it is the high tide of autumn. The Raimangal swells with the gushing tide. He keeps a look out for eddies and whirlpools. His eyes are focused on the mangrove trees—*geon, bain, goran, keora*. While walking along the sandbanks, he pushes aside the branches of *hental* and casuarina bushes and watches these eddies playfully spinning in the water. He is alarmed at the sight of deep trenches in the mud made by these eddies. Do they really damage the embankment? Raghu is unable to fathom what Bhulu so easily can. He spends a long time there, puts his ears on the ground and tries to listen. But he cannot foresee any danger from the undercurrent eating into the dam.

It is midday. The overhead sun is bright and hot. Strong winds howl over land and water. The water level has now risen to the neck of the dam. People run out of their homes and head towards it—not out of fear, but joyous at the prospect of a good hunt. The women become busy with *thopa*, a simple trap to catch crabs. They use small frogs and fishes as baits and hang them at the end of a rope to lure the crabs. The young men prefer to use the *done*. A dozen or so hooks are attached to a long twine with small snails as baits, which is thrown into the river at least five or six hundred yards away. They can easily haul a variety of catfish—*kanmagur, pangash, gagra, tangra* and *boal*. The dam very often has breaches along the lower part; salt water seeps in through these breaches. The hole through which the salt water gushes inland is enclosed with makeshift mud walls and fitted with indigenous traps called *atol* to catch small fishes like *guley, parshe* and shrimp. The flooded paddy fields are teeming with fine *patna* nets to catch parshe, *koi* and *khoira* fish. Some use stronger and bigger *gopa* nets to catch bigger fish like bhetki and large catfishes.

Raghu is spellbound. This is a fun kind of livelihood. After crossing a stretch of thorny bushes, he stops in his tracks. The inland trenches, now filled with water, are teeming with atol and *kholla* nets, while the gaps in between are fitted with *lafa*, a bamboo platform covered with mud placed across moving water. The feisty fishes, instead of heading towards the net, leap up on the platform and get stuck there. You can have a good harvest of fishes like *shoal*, koi and a variety of catfishes. The *bora*, a non-venomous snake, sneaks in and gets its favourite snack, stealthily laying its claim on the platter of the humans.

When Raghu reaches the place where the river takes a wide bend and bifurcates, he cannot hide his surprise. Old man Jeebon, Pencho, Kelo, Bhuto and the lot are hiding among the mangrove trees catching *kamoth*, a killer dolphin-like riverine animal. They are using thick ropes attached to a sturdy bamboo pole with live bait of cats, puppies, baby goats, mongoose and water monitors hanging from the hooks. The entire device is held atop the running water. The greedy animals leap up to catch the bait and get caught on the hooks. Serves the man-eaters right! Now man is taking revenge by cooking and eating their flesh. The fat content makes it quite tasty too. Bishu uncle says, 'Sir, we're not afraid of the erosion, the storm or the flood. The snakes bite, the tigers keep haunting us, yet we do not leave our village and go away. The Raimangal makes up for all of it, even the Sundarbans do. Sometimes a deer or two are found floating in the river having been chased by the tigers. Then the joy of these people knows no bounds. They chase and somehow catch the animal and share the meat among themselves. They call it the royal meat because you can eat as much as you want without ever falling sick.'

The day moves on. Raghu's artistic mind is moved by the scenes he has witnessed—the river, flood, people, the ebb and flow of tides and the joyful life. He seems to be carried away by the strong winds and keeps humming to himself. He is brought back from this reverie as someone touches his feet. 'Greetings, respected sir.' Raghu stops in his tracks. It is a middle-aged woman with her head partially covered with one end of her sari. 'I am Kushi. Please come to my house, sir, I will be honoured.' Raghu is speechless and a bit hesitant. She is clearly from a poor family. Kushi catches hold of his hand, 'You are God, and you're my honoured guest. Since early morning I've been waiting here, for I know my God, my Narayan will come this way.'

'I am Narayan?

'Oh, yes, you are. My husband went to the forest around this time last year. He has not yet returned. I keep praying to God to keep him safe. Please come in, sir.'

Oh! So, she wants to serve a guest as a good deed. Service is good, but to accept that is difficult. But Raghu cannot ignore Kushi.

'Where is your house?'

'Over there, next to the dam', the woman starts leading him by hand. She moves down a path marked by footmarks. It is a small thatched house. Poles made of *goran* (a kind of mangrove tree) hold the rickety house with flimsy walls. It has a single room, but it is very neat and clean. Kushi gets busy as she brings water in an earthen pot to wash the guest's feet. She does not heed his protests and spreads out a mat on the porch—'Please sit, sir.' It is a very small house, enough for a single person, and she lives peacefully in spite of the dangers posed by snakes and tigers. 'Sir, please have some fruits', she says, offering some wild fruits on an aluminium plate. Raghu is surprised. A variety of tubers, *kau*, *keora* and other wild fruits are on the plate. 'This looks like the stem of banana tree—what is this?' 'Oh, no! It is made from the *hetal* tree, just sprinkle some salt and have it; it is actually quite tasty.'

'Why is the salt so coarse?'

'I made it myself, you can have it.'

Raghu looks around and understands. She has a place to make salt, next to the dam. A square piece of a wooden plank is placed on a large hole. On that, she has placed a couple of baskets filled with river water. The age-old way of filtration. What we know as an ancient method seems to work fine here. She leads a pastoral life, fully dependent on nature. Life in this pollution-free, clean, natural environment makes one envious.

The lunch menu is even more interesting. A whole lot of rice-like substance called *dhyab*, made from seeds of water lily, somewhat like mustard seeds, is served on a platter of lotus leaf. A bitter, green leafy vegetable is the starter.

'Taste a bit; you must.'

'But it is so bitter.'

'Doesn't matter, eat it with dhyab. It will help keep all ailments at bay.'

This is followed by more local vegetables and small shrimps. Curries made with stems of water lily, and more wild leafy vegetables follow. Then there is a curry made with small crabs, without oil or spices, yet so tasty. Finally, there is a sour preparation of kewra.

'Please have it, sir; it will help with digestion.'

What an indigenous menu in the land of rice! She has no expenses, hence, no worries. The general rules of the outer world do not apply here. Sustainable food is available in plenty among the water bodies, in the mudflats and along the dam. It is a never-ending source of food; take as much as you want, eat your fill. Small fishes are everywhere, all you have to do is plunge your hand in the water, take some and cook.

Dear reader, for a change you can visit the Sundarbans and the dam of Raimangal river. There are many villages hidden among the trees. You may even come across women like Kushi. There are women who would welcome you as a guest and serve food. The men work in the forest for their livelihood, and the women love to serve guests as a good deed to keep their men safe.

It is an age-old lifestyle, yet so unique. The barter system works well here. They have an alternative for soap and detergent too! Dry banana leaves are burnt to produce ash; this is used to wash clothes and it cleans very well. The mud is used as shampoo. The ash helps to get rid of lice because it has medicinal properties. The mud from the riverbank is used to treat a variety of ailments from stomach ache and headache to minor injuries. The feats of science have come to a standstill in this land. Why spend money without reason?

Tribal folk eat snails, oysters, rats and frogs. People like Kushi look down on them, taking pride in their own culture. The tribal women are very strong; they work with men as equals. They drink toddy and local hooch, beat the drums and sing and dance. But the likes of Kushi are modest, keeping their heads covered and prefering to stay indoors. Many communities happily sustain themselves in this pastoral life, but they are experts in polarising people based on caste and culture.

Kushi sighs, 'The father and son duo left for the forest, it is almost a year now. Let us see when they come back.' Raghu is suspicious. Nobody spends more than two or three weeks at a stretch in the forest. He either dies of snakebite or is killed and eaten by a tiger. But Kushi does not understand all that; her days go by in endless waiting. Evenings give way to nights. Days, months and years are spent in hoping and dreaming.

The day goes by. Raghu wants to leave. He takes out a wad of money and offers it to Kushi. She happily takes those and looks closely at the bundle from every angle. 'So, this is money?' Raghu nods his head. 'Wow! The paper is so beautiful.' Kushi is beside herself with joy. 'Sir, I have heard a lot about money. I know everything.'

'What do you know?'

Like an experienced person, she offers, 'Money can be used to buy and sell things. It can buy happiness; it increases your property and eventually gives rise to court cases. Even murder can happen.' Raghu concurs. In a moment, Kushi becomes sad. 'Sir, money is not all good, it has its faults. I am not going to touch it', saying so she returns the money with utter contempt.

Raghu is taken aback. They barter fish and vegetables; one is ready to even offer physical labour in exchange for something. But they never exalt money. Kushi clears her throat and speaks in a clear voice, 'Sir, would you please honour a request of mine?' Raghu is surprised. Kushi, like the divine Mother, has no greed for money. She is only interested in giving something to the world. He is prepared to give her anything she wants. 'Okay, tell me, what do you want?'

'I heard that the lakes and mudflats of Bok Char, Koi Jola, Shona Jheel, JonkaBil are all going to be auctioned?'

'Auctioned? Whose property is that?'

'These are private lands. Please explain this to the people from the government. Ask them not to go ahead.'

'Why?'

'This place—the marshland and water—is our life, she is our mother.'

Calling the marshland your mother! That is curious; who would believe that? Kushi's voice is trembling with emotion, 'This mother feeds us, we go to her every day; save our mother, sir, please.'

Raghu is surprised. Who will accede to such an unearthly request? But he takes her request seriously and replies with conviction, 'Let them go ahead with the auction, how does it affect you?' Kushi shakes her head, 'I am a childless woman, I'll be able to survive. But all those living around the dam will perish. The people of Buno Para, Bagdi Para, the fishermen and all communities would be orphaned, they will starve to death. Please save them.'

Raghu is perplexed. She is advocating on behalf of her neighbours. He tries to shield his own weakness and replies sternly, 'Kushi, you are unnecessarily worrying yourself. This river, the mudflats, forests—there is an unending supply of these. Why are you afraid?'

Kushi agrees, 'That's true. But the sea cannot compensate for this plentiful supply of sweet water.' Raghu is at a loss for words. Kushi is a mother to the core. Her heart cries out for these people who live by gleaning the marshes and fields. Her sad eyes are filled with tears and they start streaming down her face. Why is she so attached to this land and marshes; what is there for her?

There are stagnant pools of water and canals full of algae, wildflowers, water lily and lotus, along with small fishes, snails, frogs and turtles. There is no dearth of shrimps, crabs and tangra. Under the hyacinth cover on top, there is a plentiful supply of shoal, koi and other variety of fishes. The bigger ones come during the rainy season. The western flank of the marshes is lined with rows of date-palm and ordinary palm trees. There is a huge cremation ground under the big acacia tree. Everybody knows that the place is haunted. On the eastern side, there is a dumping ground for dead animals, which is frequented by cobblers, looking for animal skin, and dogs waiting for carcasses to be dumped. Crows, hawks and vultures keep circling the place constantly. They swoop down at the first sight of a dead body.

The swampy lake of Shona Jheel is lined with many shrubs—mostly wild local plants *geu*, *jhau*, *dhanighash*, *chencho*, *hogla* and reeds used for making mats. There are green vegetables—*kolmi*, hinche, notey, *chhanchi* and also many fishes. Then there are *dheres* (a kind of rabbit) and also jackals, wild cats, leeches and poisonous snakes. The snakes bite and people die; still, they keep coming to this place. The gleaners from all communities—fishermen, weavers, even the lower castes, all congregate here. They spread fishing nets, use traps and pieces of cloth to collect food. Entire days are spent groping and looking for food among the marshes.

Even the birds are busy—birds with curved beaks, egrets, cranes, kingfishers, seagulls; little cormorants and teals. There is a huge expanse of grassy fields where the cattle graze calmly. The cowherds play catch, kabaddi and indigenous games. They use coconut shells tied to a stick to husk grains of paddy lying around. They also trap egrets and have a picnic. Herds of boars dig the ground near the lake in search of tubers. It is thus a peaceful co-existence of humans, animals and birds.

If the auction and distribution of land really take place, it will spell doom. This plentiful natural resource will soon disappear, so will the rights to use them. There used to be rumours about that. Now the activities of the businessmen make Kushi extremely scared. She is close to tears when she sees them measuring the marshes and lakes. When they sit around the fields and make charts and drawings, she feels the pain to the core of her heart. Enemies, they are all our enemies! Isn't there anyone out there to save this holy land and its forests? Kushi cries, 'Oh god! What is going to happen to the people who live by gleaning? They are going to starve to death. Have mercy. Explain it to the government people.' Will anyone come forward to wipe the tears and calm the heart-wrenching cries of this inconsolable woman?

Translated from Bangla by Banya Datta
Originally published as "Janak janani"in *Mohomukti*, 2009

7

The Second Death

JAYKRISHNA KAYAL

A re they fleeing? Or are they returning home, basking in the joy of a fresh victory!

There are seven men altogether—one among them, with his right hand wrapped in a *gamchha* placed on his lap, sits silently, as if he has suddenly slipped and fallen into a daze. The rest sit around him, trying to make him come out of the daze by chattering among themselves.

The Matla roars indefatigably as the small boat makes its way through the river. It is full to the brim with logs of freshly-cut *garan* so it does not rock much. In the distance, the intoxicating wind playfully ruffles the leaves of the forest trees. Underneath the boat is the restrained swelling of the high tide—a true representation by nature of the roaring presence of the Supreme Being. In the midst of this, like a room within a room, these men have rigged up for themselves an invisible canopy of exultation and excitement.

The man sitting in silence is called Chhibas. Only a short while ago, he has literally come out of the tiger's mouth; his entire right hand had gone inside the tiger's mouth. But *boro miyan*[1] had probably made a mistake in his calculations. Thus, apart from leaving a mark of his teeth on Chhibas' flesh, he was not able to harm him much. Chhibas now scrutinises his hand, turning it this way and that. He cannot see the wound as it is wrapped in a gamchha, but he can smell the blood from outside. He has a bewildered look in his eyes and is yet to say anything.

Kailash leans over him from one side, and Sanatan from the other. Sarat nudges him gently from behind, 'What is it? What's the matter with you? Say something!'

Chhibas gives a tired look. His lips tremble slightly—or is it the faint curve of a smile? The votary, Dinataran, asks, 'Why are you looking at your

---

[1] The tiger is often referred to in the Sundarbans by this name.

hands repeatedly? It's nothing much; medicines will heal it. Now turn around and let's talk about other things. Want a smoke?'

Niranjan holds the hookah close to his face as Sarat passes him a glass of water. But Chhibas turns his face away. Seeing this, Dinataran says, 'Let him be! First, let him breathe properly. He has returned straight from the devil's mouth! Oh, to even think of it gives me goosebumps!'

He shudders as he thinks about what happened.

They desperately want to erase from their memories the horrible sight they witnessed just a short while ago, but it is a futile endeavour; it continues to make its way into their thoughts and words. They want Chhibas to return to normalcy by making him talk. But after a while, they forget about it and leave him alone, becoming engrossed in their own fear and excitement.

Chhibas remains seated in silence alone. The faint sunlight of the dying day is reflected in the river water. The sight reminds him of a dreadful yellow tinge and two equally dreadful eyes.

Three days ago, they had gone into the jungle with their empty boat via this very route.

Mangale usa budhe pa
Yatha ichhe tatha ja

('The dawn of Tuesday, looking forward to Wednesday/You are free to go wherever you want')

The instructions are very clear about *usa* (dawn):

Dake pakhi na chhare basa
Khana[2] bole tar nam usa

('When birds sing but do not leave their nest/That is *usa*, Khana says')

They had started on a very auspicious moment on the dawn of Tuesday. Their votary for this adventure, Dinataran Baole, had picked up the anchor with his own hands.

Of course, there was a reason for taking such precautions.

Despite their best efforts, they had failed to get a pass sanctioned for either garan or any other precious timber this time; they got the pass to only collect *hetal*. The reason was obviously paucity of money. But all of

---

[2] Refers to the legend of Khana; it is believed that whatever Khana said came true.

them had made up their minds that they would stack the boat with precious timber. Then, they would camouflage the timber with some hetal logs strewn above to fool the patrol officers of the forest department. It was not that they were not scared. They regularly ventured into the territory of boro miyan, risking their lives; surely, they could not be daunted by such trifles! Besides, due to the commencement of the journey on such an auspicious moment, they felt from the beginning that there had never been a more hassle-free environment before. Whether in the river or on land, it was as if someone had cleared away even the smallest of obstacles beforehand, in anticipation of their arrival.

That was indeed the topic of discussion on board last night. Sanatan remarked, 'No one was even pricked by a *kacha*. The moment of commencement of the journey was indeed auspicious!'

The base of the trees that have been cut down in the previous years rot, dry and remain hidden beneath the grasses and leaves like pointed sharp teeth. These are known as kacha. It rarely happens that one comes to the forest to cut wood and escapes getting nastily pricked by the sharp-edged kacha. But this time even that did not happen.

Taking the cue from Sanatan, Sarat said, 'Yes, it was indeed an auspicious moment. On top of that, this time, Ma Bonbibi[3] is pleased with us, don't you understand? Otherwise, could we imagine finishing the haul in just two to three days!' Indeed, one cannot think of returning home before seven or eight days after embarking on such a venture; it takes a number of days to find good timber.

But this time, on the very first day of the mahal, they had struck gold.

Dinataran had anchored the boat at the edge of the forest and alighted from it. Out of habit, he had chanted the appropriate mantras to check whether the soil was warm. This is a technique unique to the *gunins*; they can sense things by touching the soil after reciting certain chants. The possibility of any danger or the presence of boro miyan around makes the soil feel

---

[3] Bonbibi is considered to be the guardian of the forests. She is worshipped by the residents of the Sundarbans in West Bengal as well as in Bangladesh and is called upon by woodcutters and honey gatherers before they enter the forest for protection from tigers. Honey and wood are the primary sources of livelihood for the people in the region. It is believed that Bonbibi's arch-enemy Dakshin Rai takes the disguise of a tiger to attack men in the region as a means of suppressing Bonbibi. Dakshin Rai is considered a forest god in some parts of Sundarbans.

warm; otherwise, it feels normal to the touch. That day the soil felt normal. Dinataran happily set his feet on the soil and with his hands cupped, he collected water from a pond and cleaned some area at the base of a tree with it. The others were still eagerly waiting on the boat. After completing the ritual, he drew a mark with the drenched soil on everybody's forehead and tied the leaves of that enchanted tree in their gamchhas. He then gestured to them to come down.

The deep silence of the green forest was shaken for a moment. Wearing tied-up *lungi*s, axes and scythes in their hands, the enthusiastic young men jumped onto the soil of the forest one by one. Their voices trembled in a prayer—

> *Naye theke bone dichhi pa*
> *Rokkhe koro go Bonbibi Ma*

('We are setting our feet on the forest from the boat/Protect us, Mother Bonbibi')

They knew every inch of this forest—the trees, shrubs, grass, soil, everything. Yet the forest seemed alien to them. The bush of *bogra* over there or the shade of a few *gomo*s here; no one knew where the yellow death lurked. One shuddered to even think of it. But Ma Bonbibi would protect them. Hence, they shouted at the top of their voices to make their prayers for security heard, bowing their heads and touching the soil of the forest. Then, through the bushes and thorns, avoiding the pricks of the kacha, they made their way deep inside.

It was not long before they stopped in surprise and joy. Nobody had expected this and they could not believe their own eyes. It was a jungle within a jungle—rows and rows of deep, dense garan trees. It was as if no one had come to that part of the forest with an axe or scythe in the last ten or twenty years. It seemed as if deep within the forest, Bonbibi had kept her precious trees preserved only for them to discover.

Some of them had doubts. Sarat asked Dinataran, 'What do you make of it kaka, shall we start cutting?'

Sanatan expressed his doubt, 'Is it meant for us, or does the timber belong to somebody else?' Even Dinataran was unsure. On several occasions, people had come into the forest and not found suitable trees to cut. There were others who had failed to take back the timber with them even after cutting the trees. Ma Bonbibi visited them in their dreams and warned them—"This timber does not belong to you; I have kept it for so and so..."

What if something like that happened this time too after they cut the trees! Dinataran thought for a while and then declared, 'Start cutting. We spent the last night by the side of this forest. Ma would've let us know if she had such intentions.'

The others were eagerly waiting for these words to be uttered. At once, five axes started hacking and creating havoc. It was as if each tree they felled earned them the security of another day's survival. The men had forgotten that sudden death could be waiting just two feet behind any one of them. They were oblivious to the faces of the troubled relatives they had left behind.

Dinatran advised, 'Do one thing boys, there is no need to shred the branches off the trunk today. Just cut down the trees. Let the night pass, we will wait and watch.'

Sanatan agreed, 'Just another day and our boat will be full. Leave them for one night, no harm in that! Tomorrow morning we can shred the leaves and fill up the boat at the same time.'

Chhibas had not been able to suppress his happiness, saying, 'If not tomorrow night, we can return home latest by the morning of the day after tomorrow.'

It is customary to not think of home while in the forest, particularly of the women left behind. Yet, as soon as he uttered these words, everybody understood that he was thinking of home and in particular, a pair of sharp eyes hidden under a half-drawn veil. Dinataran looked up in suspicion. That made Chhibas bow his head guiltily. As a result, he could no longer see the ones in front of him, but that only made Himani's memory more powerful.

No one could sleep properly last night. By dusk, they had already finished cutting enough logs to fill up the boat. Then they returned to the boat and finished their dinner. But sleep evaded them. On the one hand, there was joy and excitement on having been able to stock the boat with precious garan timber; on the other, there was fear of an ill omen rocking the boat or the shadow of a familiar person appearing in the wind to let them know that the wood was not meant for them.

Amidst this tussle between fear and joy in everyone's minds, Himani and Chhibas were having an extraordinary romantic conversation.

'Shall I say something? But only if you allow!'

'What is it?'

'Will you buy me a nose-ring?'

'Why, all of a sudden!'

'See, women are not supposed to remain bare-nosed—it brings loss. Everybody says so.'

Chhibas remained silent. Himani's voice, deep with passion, spoke out again, 'The child came and died even before having my breast milk—if God is kind enough and gives another chance and the same thing...'

'Do you know how much it costs?'

'Two hundred rupees should be enough. Will you buy me one?'

Chhibas had not been in a position to commit to anything then. But tonight, he could clearly see in his dream the boat filled with garan meandering inevitably toward the *haat* of Jamtala...the timber godown of the Marwari...then dislodging the timber, collecting the money, counting and sharing it among themselves...Rasamoy's jewellery shop. He enters the house with a small package wrapped in a thin dark purple-coloured paper... He calls Himani aside and says, 'Give me your hands, Himani.'

'What is it?'

'See for yourself!'

The flame of the kerosene lamp quivers... The shades of light and darkness on Himani's face... Her thin fingers tremble... The purple paper is unfolded... Her excitement is clear from the way she is breathing heavily.

'O dear, you are too much! You actually bought the thing and then entered the house!'

'Put it on!'

'Why don't you help me put this on?'

Was it the fleshy warmth of Himani's breath or the morning sun that made Chhibas come out of the previous night's daze? Waking up with a start, he could hear Dinataran's voice, 'No, boys, there is nothing to be afraid of. Ma had kept these logs for us only. Get off the boat, shred the leaves and quickly stack the boat with the dry logs. If you work fast, I think we can start before dusk.' He then proceeded to ask them, 'Have any of you dreamt of any ill omens?'

They look at each other's faces. At last, Sanatan spoke on everyone's behalf. 'When did we sleep, let alone dream! To be honest, I was constantly tugging at the logs of garan throughout the night. How could one sleep!'

'Exactly!' Sarat agreed with him. 'None of us can be at peace until the logs have been dislodged at Jamtala haat!'

The morning light was shining through the leaves and the trees of the forest; it shimmered in the waters of the poina and in the muddy black soil.

A flock of parrots flew past, and almost at the same moment, the fearful cry of these men was heard once again on the second day—

Naye theke bone dichhi pa
Rokkhe koro go Bonbibi Ma

They alighted from the boat and stepped on the soil of the forest. After they had stretched a bit, they started trimming the branches of the trees that had been cut down last evening. Shredding the leaves and branches, they stacked a few logs at a time; then carried them over their shoulders to the boat. They walked in a group guarding each other, and Dinataran walked along guarding all of them a heavy wooden stick clasped firmly in his hand.

The boat was filled almost to the brim; not many trees were left to be cut. They would be done after carrying the remaining few to the boat. Chhibas, Sarat and Kailash were tugging at a big tree, Niranjan was wiping his lips with the leaf of a tree after having a smoke. Suddenly, Sanatan shouted, 'Watch out, boro miyan!' He was pointing towards the other direction, but before he could finish he had collapsed on the ground. Chhibas looked straight ahead. Just a moment ago, he had held his scythe high to cut off a branch; but before he could understand what was happening, he felt a yellow blur lunge at him.

No, not exactly at him—he did not know what made him embrace the *sheora* tree beside him with his left hand. As a result, his body moved and suddenly his right hand carrying the scythe was inside the beast's mouth.

How long did this last? Chhibas couldn't exactly remember; he was stunned but instantly realised that the beast's mouth could not shut itself. The upper edge of the scythe was stuck in its upper jaw. A sharp-clawed paw shattered the bark of the sheora tree into pieces, and lunged at the other side.

After that, Chhibas did not remember anything.

He continues to sit in that stupefied manner. The rest are creating a row by recalling the sequence of events. Dinataran said, 'Did I look anywhere else? At once, I struck him on his head with my heavy wooden stick. Then he turned towards me—Oh, what eyes!'

Sarat said, 'We wouldn't have abandoned you, kaka, even if he had cornered you. But what can he do, he needs some space to jump. On one side, I stood with the axe and on the other, Niranjan, Kailash, Sanatan; all were armed. Perhaps on seeing that...'

'What if he had actually turned around and pounced a second time?'

'Then nothing could've been done.'

'Actually, our senses were not working at the moment! Did any of us do anything consciously?'

'Had Chhibas not fallen unconscious, we could've chased it away, what say?'

'Enough of your bravery! Such good logs we'd already cut but had to flee, leaving them behind, and you think we could've chased the big cat—rubbish!'

'But we're bringing a man alive from boro miyan's mouth! Just think about that!'

In this manner, by collectively recalling the incident, perhaps they wanted to invoke Chhibas' memories. Maybe they thought it would get him to talk again. But there was no response from him. As soon as boro miyan had let him free, Chhibas had fallen unconscious. They had pulled him up to the boat and set sail without daring to wait another moment. At first, none of them could pull the scythe out of Chhibas' hand; it was as if the clasp had frozen. It was an equally arduous task to bring him back to his senses. Now that he could sit up, he could probably even hear some of their conversations. But none of them had been able to make him talk despite their best efforts.

Kailash expressed his fear, 'Hope he hasn't lost his mind!'

'Poof! Nothing of the sort!', Sarat protests. But there is not enough conviction in his voice. Chhibas' dazed expression and silence have made everybody consider the possibility that Kailash may be right. A short while ago, these men were cackling with the joy of victory. Now everything has come to an abrupt halt. Cold and icy fear was creeping in, much like the silent and invisible wind blowing around them.

The sun is about to set and a faint darkness descends on the surrounding forest line. The waves of the Matla are now flowing towards the sea in the opposite direction. The sound of the oar cuts through the waters as an unnatural silence continues to devour these men.

Suddenly, Sarat nudges Dinataran, 'O kaka, isn't it the patrol boat?'

He points at the white boat ahead. Dinataran looks at it, so do the rest. As soon as they see the boat, they hurriedly get up. The metal hoop of the boat is still in Kailash's hand. In a nervous voice, Niranjan tells him, 'Turn the boat around, Kailash; enter into the narrow strip of water on the left side.'

As soon as he hears these words, Kailash starts to steer the boat away. Sarat and Sanatan scramble for the oar. Like the wriggling tail of a snake whose head has been firmly caught, the water of the river has embraced the land here with a vice-like grip, tying it up on all sides. Such areas are known as *suti* or poina. Through such meandering poina, they want to get lost in the cover of the forest, but cannot. Perhaps the men on the patrol boat have already seen them. In a moment, the boat comes from behind and stops them. These men who fought with a tiger just a short while ago, suddenly feel drained. A few men from the other boat jump onboard. 'Hey, show us your pass.'

Dinataran was the first to come clean, 'We don't have a pass, babu.'

Sarat corrects him, 'He means we don't have the pass for hetal. We couldn't find hetal, so...'

From the other boat, an order is issued in a grave voice, 'Bring all of them aboard, Ganesh, and tie their boat behind our boat.'

Perhaps they want to say something; their lips quiver but no one makes a sound. One of the men snatches the metal hoop from Kailash's hand and throws away their oars. Then he pulls up Kailash onto their boat. The others follow Kailash in silence.

Only one of them does not get up—Chhibas. The men gaze at him sternly. One of them tries to pull him up by his right hand but this leads to a sudden explosion. He springs up, holding an axe with both his hands—an aboriginal body carved out of black stone. The lungi worn by him sways at his feet, his curly locks wave wildly in the wind and his eyes seem to bulge out of their sockets. He is wobbling and making the 'cooi' sound—this is a signal through which someone in sudden danger inside the forest lets others know about his situation and spreads the news outside. Everyone, including the surrounding trees, leaves, soil and water is startled. Those who had tried to pull him up step back in fear on seeing the axe held high in his hands.

Of course Chhibas cannot make the sound for long. Before the axe in his hand can come down, there is the sound of a firearm. The axe falls to the ground. Still continuing with his 'cooi', Chhibas falls back into the intoxicating spiral waves of the Matla.

The water smeared with the hues of the setting sun now flows drenched in red towards the sea.

Translated from Bangla by Swagata Bhattacharya
Originally published as "Dwitiyo mrityu" in *Nabhimul*, 2015

8

The Shrimp-catchers of the Mangrove Forest

NIRANJAN MONDAL

It was a dark and silent night. One could hear the sound of the water lapping along the banks of the Raimangal river in the salty breeze and the tedious chirping of crickets; the air was heavy with the scent of the *bain* flower. But the silence of the night was shattered by the sudden noise of agitated commotion from the riverside locality. These were the shrimp-catchers of Gayenpara.

'Hey son, get up! Wake up! Don't you hear me, Rakhal? The ebb tide has set in. You need to hurry if you're to catch shrimps. Get up and get going! Wake your wife up and light the lamp!'

At Gayenpara, situated right on the bank of the Raimangal, it was Rakhal Gayen's mother waking up her son. The old woman suffered from gout and could not sleep well at night. She had started nagging her son and daughter-in-law even before daybreak. Rakhal retorted in anger:

'Why are you making such a row in the dead of the night? The first cock hasn't even crowed yet, it's dark still. It's backbreaking labour through the long day for me, and after that I can't even sleep peacefully at night! You're counting your days, you old hag! Won't you ever have some sense?'

The old woman was sleeping in the courtyard of the thatched hut. She sprang up from her bed as she heard Rakhal speaking:

'Don't abuse me in this old age. I'm saying this for your own good. The river is ebbing. At this time you'll be able to catch a lot of shrimplets with your dragnet. Such a large family—four sons and two daughters—you need to feed them, don't you? No one else would feed them if you sit back at home. The more shrimplets you catch the better you'll be paid. As the old saying goes, "It's money that makes the world go round".'

Rakhal's wife got up in the midst of this chaos and lit the kerosene lamp. Meanwhile, clear light was visible on the riverside. Broken words and the sound of the casting of fishing nets came floating through the silence of the chilly night.

Rakhal told his mother:

'You and your daughter-in-law carry on with the fishing dragnet and the large vessels. Look there, our Jata Gayen is leading with a light. I'll bring the large net and the bamboo poles.'

Rakhal's wife was counting the pin-sized shrimplets of the previous day. The old woman held the lamp high. When Rakhal reached the river bank with his net she said, 'Rakhal, now cast the spell. These days the water is infested with crocodiles and sharks. Throw three clods of earth in three directions of the river. It will bind the jaws of the crocodiles and the sharks with a magic charm and then you can safely get into the river and haul your net. It's your father who taught you the mantra. He was such a renowned *gunin*! People would come from far-off places to get a token of the magic charm from him. How he was revered! Chhidam Mandal of the *malla*s was a dedicated admirer of your father. It was none other than your father who saved his snake-bitten son. Such a gifted gunin! Still, he went to the forest with the honey-collectors as their fortune-teller and never returned. My heart breaks when I think of it … my heart breaks to pieces …'

Rakhal said, 'What's the use of lamenting now? Let me remember the words.' He waded into the river and standing in the knee-deep water of the Raimangal uttered the charm:

Across seven seas and thirteen rivers
If the crocodiles and sharks
With the ebb and flow
Come and go,
Between the ebb and tide
Let fast, very fast,
Their mouths be shut fast.
Whose order is this? It's the
Order of our presiding *Bonbibi*,
It's the order of the Lord of the jungles,
It's the decree of the supreme Mother Goddess,
Of Ma *Kamrup Kamakhya*.
Let the river be shut.
Fast, fast, really fast!

Afterwards, Rakhal planted a small stick on the bank at one end of the bamboo-fastened fishing net and tied a cord to it. 'Hold the rope and stand on the sandbank. I'll cast the net straight into the water.' He jumped into the water and started spreading the net saying, 'The tide is high today. See how the salt water is glistening in the dark. Looks like there will be a lot of shrimplets today.' His wife replied, 'Yes, Amulya's mother was saying that Amulya caught a lot of shrimps last night.'

Casting the large net carefully, Rakhal reached the riverbank smeared with salty slime to the knees and told his wife, 'Give me the dragnet. I'll drag it along the sides of the sandbank. Meanwhile, you change the water of the big vessel containing the shrimplets.' But his wife cut him short, 'You don't have to get into this waist-deep water in the middle of the night to drag the net. You can never trust the salt water. Remember the saying "salt water, dark night/wife, vulture and raven" should never be trusted. Don't you remember that poor man of Jairampur whose leg was bitten off by the shark? He bled so profusely…Oh, I still remember the anxiety and helplessness. Those charms and spells no longer work these days. This is Kalyug. Unwed girls are giving birth to children these days, widows are remarrying. Those old charms have lost their efficacy. That's why I won't let you get into the water and to drag the net.'

But did anybody pay heed to what she said? Rakhal had already moved far along the riverbank dragging the net in chest-deep water. Changing the water of the vessel of the shrimplets Rakhal's wife called out to her mother-in-law, 'Ma, go home and bring my elder son Nuno and elder girl Phuti to help me sort the shrimplets. You won't be of any help with your poor eyesight.'

The old woman started for home, obeying her daughter-in-law.

By now the riverbank was resounding with the cacophony of the shrimp-catchers. Jata Gayen of the neighbouring house started singing at the top of his hoarse voice, dragging the net—

Shrimp is my bread-giver, my son,
Shrimp is my grandchild,
The money-making insect floats in water
And we try catching it day and night.

Rakhal shouted, 'Why, that's a nice rhyme indeed! You seem to have a knack for it. It's not easy to come up with such verses.' Ranga, who was standing next to him said, 'Jata, the other day you made a rhyme on our village folk. Why don't you let Rakhal hear it?'

Jata said, 'But where's my incentive? Give me a *beedi* at least.' Ranga gave him a beedi and he started reciting in a loud monotone:

…Kanchan of Kalkhali is broken
Binod Hauli has bloodshot eyes
Tall Kailo shits standing up
Bhuban Bachhar sits thinking
Punni's son Dhiren is a hookah thief
And Durgo the boatman is a *ganja* addict.

'If I continue to come up with such verses about the village folk, Punni's son Dhiren will get real angry!', said Jata. Others burst out in wild laughter. Such light-hearted talk lessened to some extent their painful drudgery of hauling the net through the salty muck in waist-deep water.

Rakhal called out to his wife, 'Come here with the large vessel and separate the shrimps.'

He plodded upward from the knee-deep slime and shook the shrimplets from the dragnet into the vessel.

His wife started sorting the shrimplets with the help of an oyster shell from the heap of muddy waste. In the light of the weak kerosene lamp, she started putting the reddish-brown pin-sized shrimplets into another vessel and counted 'One…two…three…one-twenty…two-twenty…' She continued counting them in this fashion. The shrimplets would be sold on this count—sometimes a hundred rupees per thousand, sometimes barely fifty.

By then Rakhal was back with his dragnet in waist-deep water. There was no break for him, no rest. The cool breeze of dawn continued to blow. Dawn was breaking. The soothing early morning breeze lent melody to Rakhal's voice as he sang, 'O my sailor mind, take up the oar/I can row no longer/I rowed the boat throughout my life—O yes! I rowed the boat through this whole life… How long shall this life be…' In the semi-darkness of early dawn Rakhal's mind travelled down memory lane—to the long-lost past, to the times of suffering and privation.

He belonged to the village Amtali. But it did not offer much scope for shrimp-catchers as the river there did not attract too many shrimps. So, he shifted with his family to the village Hemnagar, on the other side of the river Raimangal.

Images from the past gradually clouded his eyes. That year Aamtali did not receive enough rain during the months of Ashwin–Kartik. The lush green paddy fields dried up in front of their eyes, bereft of even a drop of rain. As far as one could see, long stretches of parched paddy fields with the corn dried up lay desolate like the desert. Losing his last resort, he turned destitute. He alone knew the suffering and privation that he had endured from the tilling of the land to the planting and nurturing of the paddy. He used to work at a local household in the morning and tended the paddy in the afternoon. With time the plants turned lush green. When the soft breeze of Bhadra blew through the youthful cornfield Rakhal felt as if young girls were swaying in the exuberant high tide of youth. He used to be overwhelmed at the sight. After that came the month of Ashwin and the untimely drought. Fiery heat waves descended from the skies, burning and devastating the green fields.

After that life turned even more difficult. All the villagers were affected by the drought. There was no work in the village. Then came the shrimp-dealers from the Malancha-Ghushikata area. They lured everybody with money and showed them the trick of catching shrimplets with nylon nets. Since then, life had been a constant struggle—catching shrimps to earn a livelihood. Would you call this a life? A long sad sigh emerged from Rakhal's broken heart.

Thoughts of misfortune carried him away to a new world in the cool breeze of the early morning. The branches of the *bain* and the *garjan* on the sandbank swayed in the salty wind. Amidst the silence you could hear the sound of the yellow leaves shedding. From across the dense wood on the other side of the Raimangal came the early morning twittering of birds. Dragging the net along, Rakhal came close to his wife and shouted, 'Hurry up! Finish off the work quickly. Don't you remember—the dealer will come this morning? If we can't sell our shrimps to him we won't be allowed to sell them to anyone else later. Remember that Muslim dealer from Mollakhali who bought a hundred rupees' shrimplets from me on credit the other day? He never paid me back. You can't trust people these days. As the saying goes, a person with a head of dark hair is nothing but a scoundrel. Look at our ill fate! Here we spend days in this sluggish saline water disregarding the threat of crocodiles and sharks. And there goes the dealer. He tricked me of my hard-earned shrimps! This is our fate.'

Arranging the cast net properly Rakhal started off with his dragnet in the eastern direction in chest-deep muck. It was almost morning by now. Rows of nylon net set up along the sandbank swelled like peacock-blue sails against the silvery breeze of the dawn.

The charm of the morning continued to spread. Yellow Indian cuckoos sang, sitting on the caraway branches—'Talk to me dear wife! Oh talk to me!' But its wife had fled in anguish never to return. Bank mynas were warbling. The morning was flooded with white herons and the charm extended through the sweet call of the open-billed storks. Ducks were diving into the water and resurfacing. Spreading flowery white wings, it appeared as if they were deep in meditation seeking the soundless dawn of the soul. But Rakhal paid little heed to all this. Dragging the net along, he went on speaking to himself.

They were poverty-stricken. And hunger had driven them to this troublesome life where they had to earn a livelihood by shrimp-catching. But the profit of their pains was reaped by the fishery people of Kalinagar, Nyajat and Chaital. These fishery-babus were now filling their ponds and reservoirs with thousands of shrimplets bought at a throwaway price. When the shrimps grew they would fetch crores of rupees. And the babus would then enjoy life to the lees with wine and women. Fragrant wines would intoxicate their enchanted nights. But the poor, hungry villagers with large families—they would never taste the bliss of a fistful of white well-cooked rice in the afternoon, just the way they would never enjoy the luxury of basking in the golden sunlight descending from the blue sky. Shrimps used to fetch good money earlier. But the market had declined since. The fishery people too were no longer offering good price. The prices had now slumped to a mere four to five rupees per thousand. Still, you must run the family. Nothing could be done. Hunger was merciless. This tough life, so much of physical labour through day and night—Oh god! Would our days of privation never come to an end?

Rakhal dragged the net along, whispering to himself. His inner dialogue continued, 'With the breaking of the dawn, the crow and the bank myna have left their nests with that indomitable urge to live their life anew. The dove's prayer for the golden sunlight can be heard. The eastern sky has turned crimson; that marks the end of all fear. The salt water is tinged with the colour red. The day is not far away. Look, the red round ball-like sun has already galloped up the sky like an energetic horse. The sweet allure of the morning light creates waves in the sky and the air all around. The dawn of happiness is approaching. A yellow-striped sari with a golden border for his wife, brown trousers for Nuno, milk-white shirt for him, brick-red frock for Phuti—a fistful of rice two times a day, a piece of green paddy field tilled by plough and oxen—'

What stupid dreams were these! Dragging the net along, Rakhal grew almost senseless and nonsensical thoughts started to play hide-and-seek in the deep recesses of his mind. What was that? A bite on his leg? His right leg suddenly felt weightless... The salt water was suddenly turning red. Gradually the golden dream seemed to engulf his mind completely and he was unable to remember anything. Rakhal's head was reeling.

Jata who was nearby threw away his net and ran to Rakhal—'Dada, what happened?' He jumped into the water and dragged Rakhal onto the bank, 'Why so much blood, Rakhalda?'

When he was brought onto the shore it was found that a shark had torn away lumps of flesh from below his knee. The sandbank flooded with blood. These saltwater sharks were so ferocious and their teeth so sharp that one couldn't gauge the danger at first when attacked. Rakhal too had been unable to fathom it. Rakhal's wife was sorting shrimplets attentively. As Jata called her, she came running and tumbled down—'Oh god! How could you do this to me? How could you ruin my life like this?'

By then, Rakhal's blood had coloured the salt water red as if it was Holi. But the suffering and devastation of these poor, victimised, subaltern people did not shatter the golden sun, nor did its golden fragments splinter and dissolve in the salt water of the Raimangal.

Translated from Bangla by Baisali Hui
Originally published as "Badabaner bagdamara" in *Badabaner Padabali*, 2019;
English translation reproduced from *Janajati Darpan*, 2020

9

The Crocodile

SHYAMAL KUMAR PRAMANIK

A crocodile in the Matla River ate Buri's mother. Kailash Morol[1] came running to the village early in the morning to bring this news. Everyone in the village rushed to gather around his house on hearing it. He was still panting while streams of sweat ran down his body. His eyes were bloodshot.

'A terrible thing has happened. You will not see Buri's mother ever again.'

A howling Buri was sitting near his feet. She was a girl of about thirteen or fourteen. Her father had already passed away. Now even her mother had been dragged away by a crocodile, leaving her with no one to call her own.

'What will happen to me? Who will look after me?' Anxious questions about her future poured out of Buri as she wailed.

'What is the point of crying, little girl? Is your Kailash *khuro* not still alive?'

'But khuro, how did Buri's mother get dragged by a crocodile? Only last evening khuri came to visit our home. She chatted with our Puti's mother for a long time and even said "Why don't you find a good match for Buri? So quickly has Buri become of a marriageable age! A girl in bloom like her should not be sitting in her mother's home!"' Kuber rambled without a pause.

'How can I say how Buri's mother ended up in the crocodile's mouth?', Kailash defended himself impatiently. 'Listen, Kuber! I had gone to Sridharpur market town. Stocks of goods were supposed to come to the godown there. I was sitting on the bank of the Matla when all of a sudden, in the hazy, gathering darkness, I could make out a woman getting into the water. After a while, she cried out—"Save me! Save me!"—and I realised that a

---

[1] Morol/Mondol is an honorific title given to the village headman.

crocodile had caught her. But in an instant, everything was again silent over the dark Matla waters.'

Kuber persisted with his queries. 'But why did the woman enter into the Matla waters so late in the evening, and what proof do you have that she was Buri's mother?'

'I don't know all that. But I'm certain that it was Buri's mother. We lived next to each other for so many years; you say I wouldn't be able to recognise her? I could tell that it was Buri's mother as soon as I heard her voice.'

Buri's crying had become more intense as she listened to her Kailash khuro's dreadful descriptions. Tears were pouring from the very depths of her heart. Buri's father had passed away when she was a mere child of five years. There had been some altercations with Kailash khuro over farming a two-*bigha* plot of land in the Gobindopur fields. Buri could not recollect all the details. She could only remember the blood-splattered corpse of her father lying in the field in Gobindopur. It was a horrible sight. Someone had crushed his head. Not a single bone in his body was intact.

Buri had been sobbing all this while but now she became quiet. A tight knot formed in her chest. She shrieked, 'Kuber kaka!'

'What is it, child?'

'Can you take me to the banks of the Matla once? A crocodile could never have killed my mother.'

Kailash now bellowed with rage, 'Am I lying then, you slut!'

'Shut up, uncle. Why are you abusing Buri? You're the headman of the village', Netai cautioned Kailash, stepping forward from the crowd.

'How am I abusing her?' Kailash immediately toned down his aggression.

. . .

It was the season for the rains. Dark clouds covered the entire sky as winds rushed in from the south-eastern corner. Would it rain today? The turbulent waters of the Matla were dashing at the banks like intoxicated cobras. Fishing boats were plying these turbulent waves with their nets in search of the hilsa fish. The boats of Ramjan Ali and Kuber floated next to each other.

Kuber shouted from his boat, 'Ramjan bhai, have you seen the sky? There might be a storm coming this evening. We should fold our nets soon.'

'Yes, Kuber bhai. I think so too.' The wind seemed to be getting stronger and clouds were rushing through the sky like dark giants.

The fishing boats milled around the piers of the Sridharpur market town. In this market, Kailash Mondol was a wholesaler of fish; he had been the only big trader of fish in the market for a long while. But Ghanashyam Das had recently set up his shop in the market. The man was able to buy all the stock from fishermen by paying high prices. Kailash Mondol found this insolence on the part of Ghanashyam Das quite intolerable. But the man obviously had money from the time he used to smuggle goods to Bangladesh through the deep forests of the Sundarbans. Kailash Mondol was not a novice at this game either. He too had lots of experience in the smuggling business.

Kuber's boat soon reached the market pier. Many other boats crammed close to his. An inky darkness had spread over the entire sky. So intense was the darkness that you could not see anything even a few feet away. The wind had also started to pick up by now. The Matla seemed to be seething.

A large brick room with a double-gabled roof stood adjacent to Kailash Mondol's shop. A hurricane lamp with a low flame was casting a faint glow in the room. A window had been left open in it. Through that window, the inside of the room could be barely made out in the low light. Kuber could see Kailash and Biharicharan discussing something as they stood facing each other.

Sometimes Biharicharan would roar with laughter and the strains of that laughter would reach Kuber's ears. He somehow felt suspicious. Kailash Morol should not be in his shop so late in the evening. He must be plotting something; the man was rather crooked.

Darkness seemed to be descending with the approaching wind at an alarming rate. Maybe a storm would soon rise. Bolts of lightning were ripping the pitch-black sky apart while the clouds roared like lions. Kuber sat quietly in his boat. 'What are you thinking so intently, boatman?', Golok asked him. Golok had worked in Kuber's boat for a long time. He was approaching his fifties but his hair and beard had already turned white. He had no family to call his own, neither had he married. His life revolved around Kuber's boat. Kuber had tried to convince him to get married and start a family but Golok turned a deaf ear to all his urgings. All he would say is that it was better this way as there was no one to hold him back in life. Kuber had also stopped pushing. Sometimes, however, even Golok felt that it would have been better if he got married—maybe he would have had some peace in his life. He still remembered Kusum's pretty face although it was such a distant memory. Golok was then a young man of twenty and Kusum had been just fourteen. She would often come to Golok's house with her mother. God alone knew what she chatted about so incessantly with Golok. He remembered one particular day often. Ranihati's Charak fair was very popular. People from dozens of villages would come to participate in it. One day, Kusum suddenly came and asked him to take her to the fair. Golok vividly remembered holding hands with her as they walked through the fair... rode the Ferris wheel. After suffering from fever for three days, the same Kusum had passed away. Golok pulled himself out of his reveries. Why was he having all these thoughts?

Kuber was still sitting silently.

'What are you thinking so deeply, boatman?'

Kuber did not answer. He was still trying to understand what Kailash Mondol was plotting so late at night. Kuber would often have anxious thoughts about his wife Lokhkhipriya at home. She would be waiting with her children anxiously for him to return. The times were not very good. Everywhere there was fear and dread. No one could foresee what would happen to them. Kuber thought about Buri's mother. How did she end up getting eaten by a crocodile? He still could not believe it; it seemed impossible as though this was a story made up by Kailash Morol.

It had been raining for the last two days. The monsoon season was at its peak. Ceaseless rains had flooded the surrounding piers and open fields. Netai had gone to the market town for some work. It was already dark and the whole town seemed to be deserted. Only two hurricane lamps burnt dimly in the two large shop buildings owned by Kailash Mondol and Ghanashyam Das. Netai was, however, startled to see a boat preparing to leave from the pier at this time of the night. The sight baffled him. Where would the boat go on such a stormy night? No boat ever braved such dark and terrible conditions. Why would they do so? He hid behind an earthen mound to observe but from such a distance he could not make out anyone inside. It was still raining and squalls of gusty wind were blowing. Netai tried to shield himself with his umbrella and waited quietly despite the rain. He saw someone alight from the boat and approach the embankment. The man soon reached the embankment and started looking all around. All of a sudden, he spotted Netai and let out a threatening cry, 'Who is there? I will kill you and throw your body into the river!' Something glinted in the man's hand.

Netai did not linger there a moment longer.

A few days later the monsoon season was finally on its way out. Autumn was getting ready to make an appearance with its bouquet of blooming *kash* flowers. The music of the approaching Durga Puja filled the air. White tufts of clouds floated leisurely through the blue sky. Boats were also floating gently through the Matla river. Some of them were going fishing while others were travelling in search of commerce or to visit a town.

Six or seven women were in Rashid Ali's boat. Kailash Mondol and his accomplice Biharicharan were also present amidst this small crowd. Rashid Ali's face seemed to be sterner and more serious today than usual. He had travelled with Kailash Mondol, Biharicharan and flocks of women a few times in the past as well but no one had ever seen him with such a grave face before. Kailash Mondol took out and lit an expensive cigarette. Then he turned towards Rashid Ali and asked, 'Mian—why do you look so grim today?'

'Crocodile. I have seen a crocodile, khuro!'

Kailash Mondol shuddered. 'Crocodile! Where did you see it?'

Rashid Ali fell silent. 'There is a crocodile somewhere close, khuro.'

Kailash Morol came out of the boat's awning. 'You have lost your mind, Rashid.'

Rashid Ali did not answer. He was thinking about something.

'I will not go any further, Morol. I will drop you off at the next pier.'

'What are you saying? Did I not pay you all that money?'

'You take your money back, Morol.' Rashid dug out some money from his tin of beedis and threw it at him.

'What are you doing, Rashid? You're disrespecting a senior!', Biharicharan cried out.

'When did you people show any respect to anyone?' Rashid's eyes glared. 'Do you think I don't understand anything? I too have a wife and kids at home.'

Kailash Mondol was startled. Had Rashid caught onto something? Kailash took out a gun. In a trice, Rashid had unleashed the boat's rudder and hit Kailash Mondol hard. He crashed into the river.

Biharicharan let out a scream. Rashid's strong hands clutched Biharicharan's throat. Then he roared, 'I will also throw you into the Matla's water, you bastard!' The women in the boat suddenly shrieked, 'Crocodile! Crocodile!'

Rashid Ali released his hand from Biharicharan's throat and looked at the river. A fearsome crocodile was looming towards Kailash Morol, its mouth wide open.

Translated from Bangla by Saikat Maitra
Originally published as "Kumir" in *Akalmegher Kotha*, 2002

10

Kshantoburi's Family

Shyamal Kumar Pramanik

'You scoundrel, you devil's daughter! Why don't you die?' Kshantoburi's grumbling grew louder. Waking up, the old woman had called out to her son's wife, 'Get me a cup of tea, Nami.' Ghosh's wife had called for Kshantoburi immediately through a messenger. She would have to parboil about two sacks of rice; this was an entire day's work.

Kshantoburi's daughter-in-law was Namita, commonly called Nami. On hearing her mother-in-law's order she stoked the fire over dung cakes and made tea. How she managed to stumble and fall down while bringing her the tea was beyond Kshantoburi! Moreover, of all things, she shattered the new porcelain teacup! It was quite natural for Kshantoburi to get furious over this; she had bought the cup from Dewangaji's fair after a lot of deliberation.

Kshantoburi used to work at Gopal's house in the village. Steaming the unhusked rice, drying it, husking the rice by the machine at the Ray household with the help of servants, all of this was a lot of hard work. The salary was fifty rupees every month for all this labour. She had been working ceaselessly for years here but the pay had never been increased.

Kshantoburi's husband, Nagen Mondal, used to work at the Ghosh house too. One rainy day in the month of Shravan, Nagen was returning from their fields, having ploughed their lands. It was evening when he started. Darkness had descended and the way was unclear to the eye. Shooing the two cows walking ahead of him and carrying the ploughshare on his shoulders, Nagen made his way home. The land and fields were inundated by the rains. As he waded through the accumulated rainwater, walking along a narrow path, a krait bit his leg. All its venom spread through his body. In excruciating pain, he somehow managed to drag himself home but died that very night. Kali *gunin* from the village had come to see him but could not save him. Nagen Mondal was set afloat on a raft of banana stems.[1]

Kshantoburi looked at Namita's face. She was standing despondent as if she had committed a great crime.

'So, you broke the teacup?'

The woman kept quiet and did not reply.

Kshantoburi's voice grew louder. 'I will not get to eat today. All these women bearing ill-omen, they do not pay any heed to their household!' Saying so, she left for her work at the Ghosh house.

Namita concentrated on her housework. She had not been feeling well recently and felt oddly weak. She had informed her husband Panchugopal of this. He had called Kali gunin, who had performed some occult rites. He had said, 'Panchu, your wife will completely recover in a few days. Don't worry. Give her this *jolpora* three times a day. No spirit can possess her after that. There is a *brahmadatti* in this bamboo grove, his evil gaze has fallen upon her. But he doesn't know of my powers yet! He can do little else.'

Kshantoburi returned home in the evening. She had steamed two sacks of rice and dried them at the Ghosh house. Her waist felt as if it were broken from extreme exhaustion. She could no longer drag her body. In the afternoon, the Ghosh mistress had given her a few handfuls of spoiled *panta bhat* from the previous day to eat. It had not satisfied her hunger, still, she silently endured all this for her pittance of a pay. When she returned home after an entire day of drudgery to find Nami lying in bed, all her frustration came pouring out at the son's wife. 'As if no one else feels unwell in this house! Is that a reason to lie in bed so early in the evening? What an ill-omened woman!'

On coming close and touching her forehead, she noticed Nami was burning with fever. Her anger melted and she exclaimed, 'What kind of a man is Panchugopal? His wife's burning with fever but he's paying no attention. Not home the entire day, who knows what work he has gone out for. Granted, one has to work. But that does not mean one doesn't take care of the family! What can he be thinking?'

Panchugopal returned home late at night. He had gone to the city in search of some work. Raju Mondal from the village—who pulled a rickshaw

---

[1] People who die of snakebite are often not cremated or buried, but set afloat in rivers on rafts made of banana stems; the convention can be traced back to the story of Behula and Lakhindar in *Manasamangal*.

in the city—had taken him there, but Panchu did not get the job. He returned disappointed and empty-handed. On top of that, Nami was unwell. So he had had to borrow ten rupees from Raju.

No sooner had Panchu returned home than Kshantoburi started venting all her anger towards him. 'So the hero returns after midnight. Have you noticed the condition of your ailing wife? When you went to the city, you could've taken your wife with you and visited a doctor. What does Kali gunin know? Can his black magic cure any illness?'

Panchugopal was aware of these things. But one needed money to see a doctor. How would he consult one without any? So he kept quiet.

Kshantoburi continued, 'This didn't cross your mind when you got married, did it? I had repeatedly urged you to first stand on your own feet and marry only afterwards. Now that you've brought a girl from another family, do you have the capacity to feed her? Did you not remember this when you were having an affair with her?'

Panchugopal had married out of love, against his mother's wishes. He was quite obstinate by nature since childhood and never listened to his mother's pleas. When he was all of ten years, his father had died of a snake bite. His mother toiled in different houses to raise him. Kshantoburi had wished he got an education, that he had at least been educated at the village school. Her husband had had the same dream, that his sons get an education and earn a name for themselves. He had also believed that educated people did not get exploited easily.

Nagen Mondal had two bighas of land. He had inherited this land as ancestral property but could not hold on to it. The elder Ghosh landlord, Gopal Ghosh, managed to grab it in his clutches. This was after he had married and brought Kshanto home. Nagen's parents had died early. He had no one in the family to advise him. Kshanto had once fallen ill with kala-azar. There was no money in the house. Nagen had gone to borrow some money at Gopal Ghosh's house who laughed heartily at his request, 'Nagen, I cannot just lend money to people like you without any security, can I?' Nagen had fallen at his feet begging, 'Master, I shall plough your fields and repay every penny. I will work at your house.' Gopal Ghosh had replied, 'Do one thing, Nagen, mortgage your two bighas of land and take the money. Repay the mortgage and release your land whenever you can.'

He could never get back his land. He had failed to understand how the two hundred rupees incurred interest to become two thousand in a few years! Gopal Ghosh had made a lawyer write something on a piece of paper.

Nagen had put his thumb impression on it. Some time later, Gopal Ghosh called him to say, 'Nagen, since you cannot repay your debts, surrender your land to me. I cannot possibly leave my money with you for eternity.'

'But sir, I tilled your lands for such a long time.'

'How long was that for? That is hardly enough to repay your debts. Besides, you kept borrowing money from me every now and then.'

Nagen Mondal felt lost. He tried to recall for how long he had been toiling at the Ghosh house. Gopal Ghosh had said, 'Nagen, half of what you earn from working in my plantations will go towards repaying your debts and the rest you will take home.' He had agreed to this arrangement. He worked in their fields for years after that and willfully endured poverty in order to comply with this arrangement.

He could not repay his debt—Gopal Ghosh gained control of his land. Nagen was utterly miserable. That land was not merely soil! It was his mother; it was Lakshmi, Annapurna, Divine Mother. But it was now someone else's. Let it be, Kshanto was alive! What would he have left if he had lost his love?

Kshanto understood her husband's misery. She used to tell him now and then, 'Your two bighas of land is now owned by another, all because of me!' Nagen used to laugh and say, 'So what? Control over land is not permanent. You survived. What would I have lived for if I were to lose you?'

Nagen loved Kshanto dearly. Once, he had taken her to the Dewangaji fair. This fair was held in Narayanganj the day after Poush Sankranti, the last day of the month of Poush. The old and young from the village of Gajipur visited this fair. It lay beyond Gajipur and Mukundapur, a path of three-four *krosh*. The distance was not a deterrent, though. They were young and able-bodied and paid no heed to the distance. Holding hands with Nagen, Kshanto took her first ride on the Ferris wheel. It was a time of bliss. Evening fell as they roamed about. They bought two *papad*s and two *beguni*s to eat. Kshanto lovingly demanded, 'The babus have tea in porcelain cups. Why don't you buy me one?', and Nagen had done so.

That was the same teacup Nami had broken and this was why Kshantoburi had been furious. It was not just a porcelain cup! This cup carried the memory of her husband's love for her. She glanced at Nami's face now. Her body felt as though on fire with the fever.

Kshantoburi wet the *anchal* of her saree and gently wiped it across Nami's face, forehead and body; this seemed to cool her down a bit. She told Panchugopal, 'Sit beside your wife. I shall light the hearth and cook some food. We have to do something for her.' She then made for the kitchen, grumbling.

Panchugopal had not acquired an education. When his father died, Kshanto admitted him to the village school. However, he had little interest in his studies. He had accompanied Suresh to Kolkata instead. There was nothing of value in this village. Kolkata was full of various things—wide, tarred roads, different kinds of shops, big houses and cinema halls. Suresh was a bus conductor in Kolkata. His mother used to work in a wealthy household. He had found work for Panchugopal in that very house—taking orders and running errands for the babus, washing the car, going to the market for fish and vegetables.

Another girl worked in that house, cleaning the house, washing the utensils, cutting fishes and grinding the spices, while Suresh's mother did the cooking. When the girl was done with her work, she went to his mother to sit by her; she was just like her own daughter.

Panchugopal had heard that the girl's family was from somewhere in the Sundarbans. Crossing the river Matla, one would reach Sonakhali, and then cross another river to get to Basanti. Gosaba was still a long way from there. Panchugopal had never been there. He had only heard that those places were remote. The waters were infested with crocodiles and the lands were the habitat of tigers. The people there survived despite these dangers. This was their lifelong fight to earn a livelihood. Countless lives had been lost in search of honey or during fishing. Still, they did not fear death—they did not have the luxury of doing so. Namita had lost her parents in the same way. Her father, Poran Das, used to enter the forest to break beehives to extract honey. He was a *mouley*, a honey collector. He used to go into the forest every day and return home before evening. Of course, he did not go alone. There were many other mouleys like him who had to cross a river by boat to reach the forest. On that fateful day, he had entered very deep within the forest in search of beehives. Death was lurking for him there. The tiger was very close, yet he did not sense it at all.

After Poran Das' death, Namita's mother Shashibala moved to Kolkata, accompanied by her daughter. They used to live in a slum in Behala. Suresh's mother lived there too. Shashibala worked in the homes of gentlefolk. Then, one day, Shashibala felt a fatal pain in her chest. Holding the hands of Suresh's mother, she implored, 'Look after Namita. I will not survive this.' It was a plea of a dying mother for her daughter. The city was hardly safe. Many a person roamed about with ill intentions. Misfortunes dogged females at every step. Moreover, Namita was vulnerable—hapless and without any support.

Suresh's mother had kept her word. She loved Namita like her own daughter and always kept her close to herself. Who knew how Namita got involved in an affair with Panchugopal? Suresh's mother did not hold Panchugopal in high regard. He appeared flighty to her and seemed to have little interest in his family. However, he belonged to their village. His parents were good people too. Suresh's mother was ill-fated, her husband was addicted to alcohol. He also had a roving eye. This caused a lot of rancour between them. Women ill-fated in their matches lead lives of utter disharmony—this she had learnt from her own experience. Loving Namita as her own daughter, she wanted to ensure a pain-free life for her.

White clouds floated in the blue sky of autumn. It was the time of Durga Puja, the most important festival for festival-loving Bengalis. The city of Kolkata was bedecked with lights, and *dhaak*s were playing all around. Suresh's mother discovered that Namita had eloped with Panchugopal.

She went to the village of Gajipur in search of Panchugopal but never found him. Kshantomoni had retorted, 'How could you not keep her close, Suresh's mother? And what sort of a girl is she to run away with a man?' Kshantomoni kept grumbling, not the least since she had already sought the hand of Nibaron Mondal's daughter for her son Panchu. Nibaron's wife Taramoni was her childhood friend; they were from the same village. Taramoni used to say, 'I shall marry my daughter off to your son. Do you agree?' Kshantomoni would reply, 'I completely agree.' Her daughter was quite presentable, efficient in housework. It was better to marry among acquaintances. Otherwise, some strange female would marry into the house and destroy family peace. Kshantomoni was deeply troubled hearing the news Suresh's mother had brought her. Panchugopal had always been this indifferent; he never listened to anyone. The younger child Naresh was more responsible, he would surely make his family proud. He was studying in high school while working at the Ghosh farm to contribute to the family. How many in the village would do such a thing? He would fulfil his mother's dreams, study, get a government job and make his family proud, surely bringing affluence to his needy family.

Panchugopal came back to the village one day, bringing Namita with him. She wore *sindoor* on her forehead. Kshantomoni did not speak to him for a few days. Having no son is better than having one like this, she thought. But Panchugopal stayed on. He only set out here and there in search of errands. On some days, he worked in the fields of the Ghosh's. Sometimes he went to the docks to carry loads for the babus' warehouses and sometimes to the city with Babulal to work as a labourer. He did chores around the house as well.

A few years went by this way. Then Namita came down with something, it was not clear what. She became frail, ran a fever and did not have the strength to work. Kali gunin came, performed rituals, gave her jol pora. Panchugopal could not take her for treatment in the city. He did not earn enough; every day, he would go to the city in search of work.

Panchugopal came and sat by Namita's side. 'Are you in pain?' 'Yes, in my chest. It is a strange pain.' Panchugopal lowered his face and kept sitting. Kshantoburi brought a few rotis and called out, 'Have two rotis soaked in water, child.' She gave a few of them to Panchugopal too. 'How will you survive without eating?' Namita woefully stared at the warm rotis and tried to gulp down a morsel.

The boats of the fishermen were all engaged on the river during monsoon. Swarms of *ilish* had swum into the Ganga from the depths of the sea during this time of the year. They laid eggs deep in the sweet river water and were caught in the nets of the fishermen. Gopal Ghosh owned four trawlers. With nets to catch ilish, the trawlers sailed towards the confluence of the sea and river. There, swarms of ilish were to be found. Panchugopal got a job in one of the trawlers after talking to Ghosh babu. His trawler was rushing towards the confluence, where the fish would be abundant. The sky abruptly darkened without warning and a storm started out of nowhere. The waves suddenly rose. Such enormous waves! One of the waves drowned Panchugopal's boat in an instant. No one knows where a body goes once drowned in the sea. When it stopped raining the next day, Panchugopal's body floated on the river.

Kshantomoni was heartbroken. As for Namita, it was as if she had forgotten how to cry. She was pregnant with Panchugopal's child. What would happen to her now? Kshantomoni held her in an embrace and wept. She had no daughter of her own. If Namita had been her own daughter, what would she have done? Would she have let her disappear in the crowd? Would she be able to survive with lustful men around? Kshantomoni was brimming with maternal tenderness. Namita was carrying her son's child.

Naresh returned home that night. Having passed out from school, he now worked as an accountant at the Ghosh warehouse in Nabiganj. Kshantomoni sat beside her younger son lost in her thoughts. Suddenly, she took hold of his hand and said, 'Naresh, as your mother, I have a request to you. Will you listen to me?'

Naresh was taken aback. He had never disobeyed his mother. What could she be asking for?

'I am telling you, son, God will bless you. Marry Namita. As a mother, I cannot let her come to grief.'

Naresh stared at his mother, surprised. An old illiterate village woman with such a big heart! Her benevolence knew no bounds! Would he be able to make his mother happy? What would the village full of superstitious people think?

Let them think what they want to. They would live their lives the way they wanted to.

Translated from Bangla by Srishti Dutta Chowdhury
Originally published as "Kshantoburir shongshar" in *Rupnarayaner Majhi*, 1982

11

Pathshala

SHYAMAL KUMAR PRAMANIK

I was ten or twelve years old then. Standing in front of our house, Suresh Master would often call me, 'Gopal, are you home?' My name is Gopal Mandal. I used to be a student of Suresh Master back then. Nowadays, children cannot even imagine what could possibly compel a teacher to visit a student's house. I had not gone to school simply because I did not want to; this was the reason for his visit to our house. He had come to take me to his *pathshala*.

Our village was named Hirapur; it was located near the river Matla. Once upon a time, this area of the Sundarbans was covered by a dense forest. It was an abode of animals. During the rule of the sahibs, these forests were acquired. One of my ancestors, Nataraj Mandal, who came here from Khulna district, became the owner of a hundred *bigha*s of land after clearing some forest area. In those days, no brahmins or kayasthas lived here because of the lack of basic facilities. Though there was a railway track from Kolkata to Canning, the way beyond that was full of rivers, furrows and forests. In those days, to reach our village, one had to cross the Matla from Canning by boat, and then walk through a mud path for around five miles. During monsoon, the road became so muddy and slippery that one risked falling at every step on the way to our village. One had to cross this road to bring all the essentials from the town of Canning. I have heard that my grandfather, Brajmohan Mandal, went to the town once every month to get all the essentials. He used to start his journey at dawn and returned late at night. But he never returned alone. Villagers always accompanied each other. There were several reasons for them to journey back home as a team. In those days, there was always a risk of tigers attacking the village for hunting cattle and humans. Moreover, there was also the threat of dacoits and thieves. Frequently, one would find corpses floating in the river. My grandfather was not afraid of those things because he knew very well that if one feared death, they would not be able to live in that forsaken area of the Sundarbans.

My ancestors were independent then. Free. Physically, they were strong, and their mind was full of courage. They had conquered forests to become owners of the land. They used all their strength to plough the field with the help of bulls. The land was fertile and they enjoyed cultivating the paddy fields even as they got drenched in the rain. They utilised the spare land near their house by growing vegetables. They went fishing in rivers, streams and ponds. What else they could they ask for?

People like my grandfather, who belonged to the lower castes, started facing problems when some higher-caste people began pouring into the land. Earlier, these higher castes used to live on the other side of Matla—mainly Canning and Sonarpur. They had never had the courage to cross the river and invade the forest on the other side of Matla as they were afraid of tigers. Moreover, they did not have the prowess to turn a forest area into cultivable land. Poor farmers would do the farming and the beggarly fishermen would go out fishing, while the higher castes only enjoyed the fruits of others' labour. However, one needed to be crafty to savour these fruits. When intelligence made a man devious, he would naturally start to take advantage of the situation using unethical means. Religion was often used to rationalise such unethical behaviour. We come across many scriptures in the Hindu religion—those of Manu, Jagyabalkya, Kattayan, etc.—which endorse ruling over and exploiting the lower castes. In these scriptures, some facts about the origin of the world have been described in such a way that even the rich literates would be awestruck—forget about the poor, illiterate people. In the *Manusamhita* for instance, it has been said that this world was in complete darkness at the time of its origin, in a state of deep slumber. Nothing could be seen. Neither logic nor knowledge could help us understand this state. It was then that the divine power, which is beyond perception, created the elemental forces and other sensory things with an inexorable power of creation and then revealed itself, effacing the darkness of the world.

The wily tales start after this description. A narrative of discrimination is revealed—amongst human beings, the same human beings whom God himself had created—that divides human beings into standard and sub-standard men belonging to higher and lower castes, respectively. The story goes that for the prosperity of the world, the divine Brahma had let the brahmins, kshatriyas, vaishyas and sudras arise out of his mouth, arms, thighs and feet respectively, their responsibilities and occupations predestined to ensure a systematic functioning of the world. The brahmins would gain knowledge through their scholarship of the Vedas, performing rituals and collecting alms. The kshatriyas were assigned to the safety of men, the vaishyas would look after business, and the sudras would humbly serve all of them. These sudras are the farmers and labourers of today, involved in all the material productions of the world but detested, exploited and deprived. The scriptures made provisions for dominating the supposedly sub-standard section of people in this hierarchical system of society. If any sudra was found reading the Vedas, he could be beheaded. In the Ramayana, at the request of a brahmin, Ram himself beheaded Shambuk for the crime of reading the Vedas. One would be amazed to learn of many similar customs detailed in the scriptures. For example, a brahmin is considered the highest form of living being; it is his birthright to have authority and lay claim over every creation on this earth. His divine majesty is supposedly boundless, irrespective of his actual knowledge prowess.

Anyway, my ancestor Nataraj Mandal never had to think about all this because he had never read any scriptures. He was a labourer. His hard labour had made him acquire the forest, and while the village Hirapur was settling, he made his own house with mud for the walls and leaves for the shade. He used to cultivate his own land and this land would provide him his daily meals. At the time, the men who had settled here were all labourers.

Things changed during my grandfather's time. More areas of forests had been acquired by then. The area had started flourishing with fields and farmlands all over, and this attracted the brahmins and kayasthas. Jaydeep Chowdhury was the first among the babus to come to Hirapur; he was kayastha by caste. His family had a fair amount of wealth in the Sonarpur area. They had been educated in schools in Calcutta. Despite owning ancestral property, it is surprising that he settled in a remote village like Hirapur. But people say that he had an affair with a girl from another caste and eventually married her without his father's approval. As a result, he was deprived of his share in the ancestral property and then came to Hirapur with his wife. No one knows how he found out that this village even existed but surprisingly he acquired a considerable amount of land within a few years of his arrival here. The source of his accumulated wealth remained a mystery, but many can tell how he had acquired the land in Hirapur. At first, he started his business of usury. It is heard that when his father deprived him of their ancestral property, his mother, out of affection, had secretly given him all her jewellery. Chowdhury's intelligence must have given him the idea that living in such a village amongst the poor and illiterate farmers with his wife of another caste would be comparatively easier and would allow him to prosper at their cost.

Within a few years, Chowdhury became a *jotedar* of the Sundarbans area. His business flourished. During those days, famine and epidemics were common. In such times of penury, when the helpless illiterate farmers asked him for money, Chowdhury made them give their thumb impressions on agreements they would never understand. Within a few years, the lent money would sum up to a huge amount with the interests charged, and many of the farmers who had borrowed the money could not pay it back. As a result, they had no option but to give up their land to Chowdhury in order to pay off their debts. Problems arose when any farmer in debt did not agree to give up on his land.

Slowly, Jaydeep Chowdhury became an influential person in this locality. A large brick house was built. Footmen, sentry and stewards were employed. A Durga temple was established. A lower-class Rarhi brahmin, Sreepada Mukherjee, was brought as a priest for the temple from Sonarpur and given some land. The villagers also benefited from this. Earlier, there was no brahmin in this village. Seven villages away, there were two brahmin families, but they were too conceited and had to be paid extra money for performing pujas, last rites, and weddings.

To Sreepada Mukherjee, the remote place was like heaven because he was the only brahmin here. He was like a *gurudeb* to all the peasants and was the priest of Hirapur Durga Mandir as well as of Chowdhury's house.

Several years passed by. Jaydeep Chowdhury was now old. He decided that he would establish a pathshala in the village that would add to his glory, and so he did. But it was difficult to get a teacher. He appointed Sreepada Mukherjee as one but Mukherjee did not agree to teach the lower-caste boys and girls of the village. He said, 'Chowdhury babu, if these peasants were given education, they would no longer obey you; who would listen to you then? They will start advising you eventually and will not obey me either.' But Jaydeep Chowdhury was stubborn. In his youth he had arrived obstinately in this remote village accompanied by a woman of a lower-caste. The same attitude persisted. He became desperate to do at least one bit of good work. He said, 'Whatever happens will be dealt with later. Children of the peasants need to be educated.'

But then he suddenly died, and the school closed.

Suresh Mandal was the son of a lower-caste family in this village. He was a farm labourer by profession with a thirst for knowledge since his youth. With his own efforts, he had completed his primary education. His dream was to study in a college in Calcutta but unfortunately that dream remained unfulfilled. After the death of his father, Dharani Mandal, the entire responsibility of taking care of his widowed mother, his two young brothers, and two sisters fell on his shoulders.

After Jaydeep Choudhury's pathshala suddenly shut down, an idea crossed his mind—he would teach the lower-caste uneducated boys and girls of this village. He then started a pathshala in his own small mud house and began teaching with great care and love. He used to give books to the poor students; for this, he would have to beg for money from people. There were several people belonging to the lower-caste society who were landowners in the Sundarbans area. However, they did not have proper education. Suresh Mandal went to them to ask for money for the students. He did not limit his time for teaching the students; his door remained open all day. If a student did not go to school any day, he would go to their house to enquire. Thus, Suresh Mandal in this way became familiar as Suresh Master in the village of Hirapur.

Slowly, the number of students increased. His house could no longer accommodate his students and so he began to teach them near an old banyan tree in the field in front of his house.

Many days and nights passed have since then. After receiving basic education, I got a clerk's job in an office in the city. As a result, I had to leave Hirapur to live in the city. Here, in the city, I married and started a family life. My ancestor Nataraj Mandal had become the owner of a hundred bighas of land by clearing the forest. Generations later, I received some portion of that land. I sold it off and settled permanently in the city, having almost forgotten the name of Hirapur by then.

Suddenly, one day, my heart longed for my place of birth. My son was now thirteen years old. He also wished to visit his ancestral house. And so it happened, that after many years, I finally went to Hirapur with my son. The village was not the same. The Chowdhurys had left for Calcutta; they no longer visited the village. The descendants of Sreepada Mukherjee were settled in different places. But surprisingly, the people of Mandal para, where I was brought up, had almost remained the same—that same old penury and illiteracy still existed. I went to Suresh Master's pathshala. The same mud house with a thatched roof, bearing no signs of improvement, stood there as

I had seen it many years ago. The pathshala continued—students were loudly memorising that same old multiplication table in unison. I eagerly desired to get a glimpse of my Suresh Master. I saw that a young man of twenty-one was teaching the children. I enquired about Suresh Master, and the boy said, 'Father died a few years ago', and then asked, 'Are you coming from the city?' He continued, 'I too wanted to work in the city. But what could I have done! My father handed over the pathshala to me at his deathbed. Someone needs to teach these poor and illiterate children.'

'You are right', I said dazedly as the image of Suresh Master flashed in front of my eyes.

Translated from Bangla by Nirnoy Roy and Koushik Goswami
Originally published as "Pathshala" in *Chaturtha Bharatbarsha*, 2014

12

Suleiman Fakir

SHYAMAL KUMAR PRAMANIK

A communal crisis suddenly broke out in the Manohorpur village by the river Bidyadhori. Half of the residents of this village were Hindus and the other half Muslims. But all along, this region had enjoyed a bond of camaraderie and there had never been any communal tension. There were some reasons behind this. In this village of the Sundarbans, gods and goddesses like Bonbibi, Dewan Gazi and Satyapeer are worshipped regularly by people of both these communities. They all make offerings to them. All differences between the people are erased, be they Hindus or Muslims. They are all poor. To fill their bellies, at times they throng the Sundarbans to collect beehives; at times they go fishing in the river. This river, this forest—they are the ones that feed them.

The trouble first started in the Muslim locality. Early in the morning, Somed Ali Mondal was going towards the Bidyadhori for fishing. As he left his house, he saw that the tall palm tree on the bank of Jafar Naskar's pond had toppled over as the soil on the bank had eroded. The roots of the tree were now exposed.

As he came near the tree, he suddenly spotted a stone statue under the roots. The brick wall surrounding the statue was broken. Somed Ali hurriedly returned home and came back with a spade. The sun had not come up yet. He quickly looked around once and when he saw no one there, he started digging the soil with the spade. Next, with both hands, he pulled out a perfect statue; its face was indescribably beautiful. Pressing it to his heart, he stood up. Suddenly in the faint darkness, he saw four men coming in his direction. Bidhu, Madan, Haru and Ansar Ali of the Muslim locality had set out for the jungle early in the morning in search of honey. The boat had been anchored on the banks of the Bidyadhori. Seeing the stone statue in Somed Ali's hands, one of them exclaimed, 'Well, Somed chacha, what is that in your hands? This is a figure of our deity. Where did you find it?'

'It was there in the soil under the roots of this palm tree', Somed Ali stretched his hand and pointed in that direction. Ansar Ali saw that the soil under the roots of the tree had eroded and it had fallen into the pond, and on the bank of the pond, the ruins of an ancient civilisation were staring at the light of the world.

'Give us the idol, Somed chacha. We'll worship it', said Bidhu.

'It is I who found the idol. The statue is mine; I won't give it to you.'

'You're a Muslim. You have no right over the idol of our deity!'

The uproar brought the villagers to the spot. Zafar Naskar, on whose land the stone idol had been found, cried out, 'Stop this ruckus now. The idol has been found on my land, so it is rightfully mine. Only I have a right to it.' The people belonging to the Hindu neighbourhood thought this was a trick on the part of the Muslims. What would they possibly do with a Hindu idol! They would certainly sell it off. It was an idol made of stone; a relic of the past. It must be very costly. Occasionally, antique dealers visited this place. If they got word of the idol, they would pay a high price for it. The Muslim neighbourhood were believed to be poor, low-caste people. No brahmin or kayastha resided in this village. Only the Pode, Bagdi and Chandal people lived here. The people belonging to the higher castes did not even consider them Hindus. There were many temples in India where they were not even allowed to enter—being allowed to worship was a far cry. They would certainly sell this stone idol off. Why should the idol then be handed over to them?

Ultimately, the issue reached the elders of the village and a meeting was held to solve the issue. The elders of both Hindu and Muslim localities were present. Selimuddin Mondal of the Muslim locality said, 'The issue is very sensitive and both parties have presented very forceful arguments. If the idol is given to the Muslims, the Hindus will not agree as it would hurt their religious sentiments. On the other hand, the Muslims have a point as well. The idol is valuable. The poor, low-caste Hindus might sell it off.'

Ganesh Mondal, one of the elders from the Hindu locality, said, 'Well said Selim, you have a point there. But a way out has to be found.'

The discussion among the elders brought silence upon the assembly. The elders were clearly not supporting any one side. No one could solve the problem. Suddenly Haru exclaimed, 'Can we not bring the problem to the notice of the leaders of our party?' Haru believed in the philosophy of the Communist party. Ansar Ali said, 'Sujoy Bhattacharyya of our party is an idealist. Let us inform him.' Ansar Ali was a member of the Congress party.

'No, the issue will not be placed before any party. Perhaps you don't know, but the political parties seek their own interest in everything—they are only concerned about strengthening their power. They understand nothing but power and their own interest; for this, they create rifts among people, sometimes even killing them. They will set fires to homes on the pretext of religion, caste, language, region. This partition, the communal riots...it is all because of them', Selimuddin said all of this in one breath.

'Then what should we do?' Madan asked Selimuddin.

'A way out has to be found.'

Ganesh Mondal said, 'Dear Selimuddin, how about placing the matter before Suleiman fakir of Kamalpur?'

All those assembled supported this proposal. Suleiman was both a fakir as well as a family man. His family consisted of his wife and children, but he was not very family-oriented. His ancestors had been well-off. Even now, some land remained and the family continued to survive on the same. Suleiman fakir was constantly looking for something in the marshes and jungles of the Sundarbans. Along the roads and fields, he could always be seen searching for something.

When asked, he would say he was searching for the history of man. He continued to search for man's civilisation, his culture and his language. He had scoured the banks of Bidyadhori, Matla, Raimangal, Kalindi, Saptamukhi, Thakuran and Buri Ganga. Well, just a few years back he had gone to explore for something on either side of the river Mani. Standing near Tilpi, he had said that the civilisation of our ancestors is hidden here. How amazing! Right here, under the soil had been found so many archaeological specimens. All these were thousands of years old; they were possibly the ruins of the city of Tilogrammam described by Greek and Roman historians. Suleiman fakir roamed around, wandering from Chandraketugram to Harinarayanpur, in search for the history of their ancestors.

Suleiman was brought to Manoharpur for the arbitration. After reaching the assembly, he looked at the crowd assembled there. Addressing them, he said, 'Tell me, what is it that disturbs you?'

'Fakir saheb, you have already heard everything', Haru said.

'Indeed, I have. But could you not find an easy solution to such an easy problem? You had to summon me for this? All of us are poor people. This soil, this river, this forest—the Sundarbans provide you sustenance.

The stone idol is very costly. Couldn't you sell it and divide the money among yourselves?'

'The deity is to be sold off?', asked Bidhu.

'I understand what you say. This fascination with religion will always remain within your heart. The religion of the Muslims will be there for the Muslims, the religion of the Hindus will be there for Hindus. But there is also the religion of Man.'

All those who had assembled there looked at him. 'What do you mean?', they asked.

'That religion is the religion of man. All of us are human beings. Our religion is humanism. Look here, Haru, Madan, Ansar—all of you were going to the jungle in search of honey, to assuage your hunger. Just think, if anyone fell in danger, wouldn't the other run to help? When Haru Mondal and Madan Naskar were in trouble, Somed Ali and Jafar Naskar went to help them; again, when Somed Ali and Jafar Naskar needed help, Haru Mondal and Madan Naskar were there to help. Isn't that true?' 'True', answered all those who were present.

'The idol is made of touchstone. Apart from that, it has great antique value. Do you understand?'

'We understand, fakir saheb', Jafar Naskar answered, 'but...'

'I understand what you want to say. I merely made a proposal. See if you find it acceptable. Do only Hindus have an attachment to the idol? Do the Muslims have no attachment?'

All assembled there gazed in wonder at Suleiman fakir's face. What could this fakir possibly mean!

'I can see that this idol is 1500 years old. The Muslims had not yet arrived in this country. At the time in this Pundra and Banga, even Hinduism was not so widespread.'

'Then who was there in this country?', asked Ganesh Mondal.

'Our ancestors.'

'But then?'

'I understand what you want to say. Listen, it was human beings who first arrived in this world. Religion came later. It is human beings who created religion. So many religions now exist in this world. But 1500 years ago, Buddhism was here. The idol you see here is the image of Lord Buddha. We were then Buddhists. It is here that our ancestors had established the powerful Gangaridi state. Megasthenes, Diodorus, Pliny, the great poet Virgil, Valerius Flaccus, Ptolemy and so many other Greek and Roman scholars have written that history. You tell me, is that the history of the Hindus, or is it the history of the Muslims? That history is neither of the Hindus nor of the Muslims—it is the history of our ancestors. How ancient is our civilisation! Deulpota and Harinarayanpur over there are as old as the Egyptian civilisation. In those ancient times, traders from here used to do business with Greece, Rome and Egypt. In this territory were situated the port cities of Gange, Agga, Palura and Tilogrammam. Again, during the Buddhist era, for the pursuit of knowledge, Buddhist centres for learning and culture were established at Balanda and Hatiagarh. Later, following the natural progression of time, Buddhism declined and Islam arrived. Many people assembled under the Islamic flag of equality and fraternity. Yet, so many continue to cling to their ancient religion. It seems to me, religion is a personal matter, but humanism is something universal.'

'We had summoned you here to solve our problem. What about that, fakir saheb?', asked Haru.

'This supposed problem of yours is hardly a problem; it is purely your creation.'

All those assembled there stared at Suleiman fakir. All of a sudden, he appeared to be very desolate. He started reciting a few lines by Tagore,

Though the evening arrives slowly and at a leisurely pace,
At one gesture, all the music has ceased,
Though there is no companion in this endless sky
Though tiredness descends on this body…

Then he spoke to himself—'Oh my bird, Oh, you blind one, do not fold your wings yet.'

A faint shadow clouded Suleiman fakir's eyes. Many years ago, when he was a child, some people had caused a communal riot in his village. The country had not yet attained independence. Many people had lost their lives in that riot and many dwellings were burnt to ashes. So many families were destroyed. He did not know who had instigated these actions. He had only seen his dear ones die in front of his eyes. Even today, he has not been able to forget that day. Since then, he had taken up this life of a fakir. He had spent his entire life searching for ways to create bonds between people.

Suddenly he called out—'Give me the idol. Jabbar saheb has built a museum at Harowa. Much of ancient history and information along with many idols have been preserved in that museum. This idol will also stay there.

Our ancestors have built this idol. All of us have a right over this. Those who wish to could always go there and see it.'

Everyone agreed with him. That the problem could be solved so easily was beyond the comprehension of Madan, Haru, Somed Ali and Jaffar.

While leaving, Suleiman Fakir put on his *jobba* (a long robe) and picked up the long stick made of *betal* wood in his hand. Then looking around at the assembled crowd he said, 'It is man who has bound himself to the shackles of religion. Believe me, you are all free; man is free.'

Translated from Bangla by Suchorita Chattopadhyay
Originally published as "Suleiman fakir" in *Chaturtha Bharatbarsha*, 2014

13

Birds of the Forest

SHYAMAL KUMAR PRAMANIK

A breeze blows briskly. Through the vast bare land ahead, you could walk by on some dark night, penetrating the cold and the dense mist. When you cross the field, you will be standing before a bleak yellow forest. There, the serpent and spirits lie facing each other. If you walk on the path beyond, at the end of it, you will see a small hut at the edge of the forest. It is hardly a house—more like a bird's nest. The house is constructed of broken twigs and branches; its roof is of dry leaves. There, sit two primitive humans— a man and a woman.

In my story, these two characters have no social identity. They may even have forgotten their real identities themselves. No one knows if they think of these things any more. But when it is late at night, and when the man and the woman quietly lie on the clay floor of their hut, the man can be heard letting out a sigh.

'Do you remember those days, Kokila?'

'Which days?'

'Those days of gathering mangoes. The days when I used to come to pluck mangoes in your large mango orchard at the break of dawn. You'd come out too; we'd then look at each other surrounded by the morning mist. You looked very beautiful then. I used to keep staring at you, and you'd call me a stupid buffoon.'

'You've started with your ramblings again?'

'I feel sad, Kokila. You were so beautiful.'

Jotayi is riddled with excruciating pain when he glances at Kokila now. Her long hair is dirty, knotted and unwashed. She is clad in a torn saree, no other cloth on her shoulders. Only a part of the saree covers her breasts. Starvation has aged her far beyond her years.

Jotayi feels miserable. Sometimes, when he looks at her face, he finds it hard to recognise her—as if this is not the same Kokila, as if she hailed from a different planet altogether.

This region is a deserted forest in the Sundarbans—a vast stretch of barren forest land. There, in a tiny hut, they reside. A wattle fence surrounds it; the roof is thatched with *gol* leaves. There is nothing in the house; they have no belongings except for a few vessels and pots. That, and a torn *kantha*.

How old is Jotayi now? Forty. But he has aged already. His hair is matted, his face dirty and he has a white beard. He wears a very torn unwashed piece of rag. He owns nothing from the world outside, however, his inner world is rich. Jotayi sings. In the dead of the night when the world is wrapped in darkness, he stands beneath the sky holding Kokila's hand and sings in an elevated voice—'O *Sakhi*, you spent all your life with me, and yet I could not give you happiness...' His melody spreads like the soft hues of the full moon. Green leaves rustle to its call.

The vast barren land is dotted with shrubs and bushes. There is no society. The village of Mukundapur is visible far away. Here, only shrubs, canals and infertile lowlands exist. In the wetlands, only the water hyacinth grows. Fishes and water snakes roam freely in the water. Winds blow about making ripples in the water. The *sundari* and *geyo* trees stand smiling as the intoxicating salt breeze of the Sundarbans laughs to this melody of the trees. This breeze has a peculiar smell; no one can endure it. No one from the village who has wandered this far into the forest has ever returned. It is said that once Bonbibi leads them deep into the forest they are never to return.

How Jotayi and Kokila ended up here and built their home in the forest is an enchanting story.

Jotayi loved Kokila, and she loved him back. Kokila can no longer remember how this love came to be. She only remembers the dawn of their childhood when they would hold hands and go plucking mangoes early in the morning. The two would fly about from one tree to another in the morning breeze. On some afternoons they would come walking to the edge of this forest. The forest would beckon them, and they would run around, frenzied.

The neighbourhood women used to pass comments, observing such things, rebuking Kokila's mother. They would say, 'Your daughter has grown up, Kokila's mother. This behaviour of hers does not look good, roaming about in forests with Jotayi. Marry her off to someone.'

Their words affected Kokila's mother. The girl had grown up in these few years, right before her eyes. It was indeed time to marry her off.

However, her mother soon realised that Kokila did not want to get married to anyone other than Jotayi. They were in love and got married eventually. All of this had happened a long time ago.

It is afternoon now. Cries of incorporeal spirits travel across the wind over the vast expanse of land. In this abandoned landscape of forests and wetlands, Jotayi and Kokila's hut trembles vigorously in the wind. Kokila holds Jotayi for comfort. In this limitless solitude, the two souls yearn to have each other intimately.

People say this area is haunted by spirits and that one can hear their wails in dark houses. These spirits are said to be of dissatisfied souls—the bodies of those who die of accidents before their time and are buried by the edge of this forest by their family. The family members scatter *khoi* on the path as they return. Spirits cannot come near if they sing the name of God but after the people leave, the spirits come in large numbers. They befriend the newest member. Sometimes they have fights with the newcomer but they always reach a resolution.

No human has ever resided in this area of spirits. But Jotayi and Kokila built their little house in this abandoned piece of land. People think they are mad; why else would they build a home in the deep forest of their accord?

Jotayi and Kokila hold hands and wander around the forest all day. They seem to be in search of something but never find it. They spend the nights sitting quietly, facing each other. Myriad noises can be heard in the forest after dark. Some of them are male voices, some are female, and others are of children. They sit quietly and listen to this together. Kokila holds Jotayi's hand as she says, 'Hear, there, our son's voice.' Jotayi says, 'Quiet, quiet, Kokila.' And then, an unending silence descends.

It is pitch dark. Kokila and Jotayi come to the edge of the forest and stand, holding hands. Thousands of stars are faintly visible far in the sky. The world is in deep slumber. Five *krosh* from here is the village of Madhavpur. Jotayi's insides wrench in painful remembrance. Several memories overwhelm him. There, they saw the light of the world for the first time. They grew up holding hands. Their child was born there. They had their land and home there but they have nothing now, only memories.

Once, Jotayi had gone to the village market to sell vegetables. Kokila had arranged his wicker-basket. In the afternoon, Gopal had gone to pluck mangoes from their garden. It was the month of Baishakh. The severe sun rays had cracked the dry soil in the fields. Everyone had been desperately waiting for rain; the ponds had dried up. There was not a drop of water anywhere. Was that why the *gokhro* snake had bitten Gopal's leg to quench its thirst?

Kokila was in bed then, watching the sky. Where was the abode of gods beyond the sky? She was wondering about such things when suddenly she heard Gopal's loud cry, 'Mother, a snake!'

She had rushed like a lunatic straight to the garden. By then the snake was escaping through the fields. The boy was writhing in pain on the ground and slowly turning blue. In a short while, everything was over.

Kokila's heart-rending wails reached Tarini khuro, who came running. He had said, 'Gopal will live, daughter-in-law. Give him to me.' He laid down his body in a vessel of banana leaves and floated him on the waters of Matla. The ferocious stream of Matla had taken Gopal with her. Tarini khuro had said, 'Gopal will live. But he may never return.' Alas! Who knows if he had only offered this as a consolation to Kokila? However, Jotayi and Kokila had believed his words.

Time flows towards eternity. Everything that ages is gradually erased from the face of this world. The new is born. One day Jotayi and Kokila venture out in search of Gopal. Tarini khuro could not have lied. Gopal must be alive. They get exhausted in a while. But they do not wish to return to the village. They build a house far away from the village in this deserted forest. Who knows what they were yearning for? All this happened a long time ago.

The sky is covered with clouds today. A strong wind blows about. The trees in the forest dance joyously; it will rain soon. Jotayi comes out of the house and stands holding Kokila's hand. The stream of Matla is ferocious, the water restless. Jotayi's heart feels hollow out of some unknown fear. He starts singing, 'O Sakhi, I have rowed this boat all my life but could never find a bank.'

This is the last day of Chaitra. Out of the blue, a dark cloud appears from the northwest corner of the sky, bringing with it a dangerous foreboding. More dark clouds hide the sky in a moment and a violent storm commences. The Matla becomes furious. Jotayi and Kokila stand before its bank holding hands. The Matla's untamed waves lash out against the bank like a venomous snake. If the bank gives way, things will take a turn for the worse as the entire area will be inundated with water. Jotayi looks at the dark clouds in the sky as they dash across the sky with the stormy winds. Sometimes the clouds collide against one another and roar like wild animals. Kokila watches the violent waves of the Matla. The river swells like a vengeful snake wanting to avenge all the injustices perpetrated by humans. She continues watching intently. The pain in her heart dances to the rhythm of the waves. She had once floated her own child on these waters.

Slowly, darkness descends upon the world. Kokila sees it trickling down the black waters of Matla. A curtain of darkness appears suspended over the river. She also notices a small boat swaying violently in the waves. Alas, the boat is adrift in the middle of the river during such a storm! A number of people are aboard; it will capsize any moment now. The boatman is frantically trying to row the boat to the bank but is failing to do so. Violent waves crash against the little boat. Kokila feels as if she can see an infant hiding his face in his mother's breast in the boat.

The storm grows stronger and the waves turn furious. Suddenly a frantic cry from the middle of the river alerts Jotayi and Kokila. The boat has capsized and the people aboard are all drowning along with it in the black waters, the river swallowing the helpless lot in her blind fury. It all ends in a short while. Kokila is in great distress. She draws her arms around Jotayi for support.

The sky is clear the next day. The sun shines bright. Jotayi and Kokila see a group of people approaching the forest. Perhaps their loved ones are lost in the depths of the river. Maybe the relentless Matla has swallowed their land and country too.

Gradually the people gather around and sit close to the forest. They search for branches, leaves and scraps to build a shelter with. The place slowly turns habitable as they stake their claim to the country of Jotayi and Kokila.

Jotayi and Kokila maintain their distance and do not mingle with them. They feel ill at ease again. Then, one day they tie all their belongings together in a bundle.

Eventually it is discovered that the two are not in their hut. They have left for somewhere else!

Translated from Bangla by Srishti Dutta Chowdhury
Originally published as "Aranyer pakhira" in *Khilipaner Meye*, 1996

14

The Chronicle of Hariya Dom

SHYAMAL KUMAR PRAMANIK

Nibaran Chowdhury of Sonagaon was a man of enormous wealth and property. His mansion was as grand as a palace. A huge pond lay just behind it—it had a *ghat* erected of stone. He had no needs, no dearth in life, yet his eyes bore signs of greed like those of a snake.

Sonaga or Sonagaon was a calm, deserted and beautiful village in the midst of natural wonders in the Sundarbans. During colonial rule, this region was a remote and dense forest, the land of snakes and tigers. Eventually, the forests were cleared by the the Dom[1] community, who built small houses here and created a vast landscape of agricultural land where paddy cultivation was started.

Having been treated like animals for ages, this group of Doms lived quite peacefully in these distant lands infested with dangerous wild animals. But this happiness did not last for long. The government appointed *gomosta*s to collect revenue from this area.

Nibaran Chowdhury's father, Adhir Chowdhury, came to this village as a *gomosta*. He was a conniving man—his eyes were full of greed. He was not only lustful for more land but also for women. After settling at Sonagaon, Adhir Chowdhury got engaged in staking his control over the land, deceiving the simple-minded and illiterate Doms. Gradually, he was able to create a dynasty of wealth. The ones who had cleared the forests, cultivated crops in the salty soil and had made the place habitable were now turned landless. The world moved on as is its nature. Adhir Chowdhury passed away. But Sonaga remained the same, still. The evolution and advancement of the outside world had no bearing on the society here.

---

[1] A caste that is one of lowest in order of hierarchy of the caste system; historically, Doms have been responsible for cremating dead bodies.

Adhir Chowdhury's death escalated Nibaran Chowdhury to the position of the village moneylender. His earnings from his lands had decreased slightly. The Doms asked for higher wages and refused to work without it. They mostly went to the rivers to fish for Bagda seedlings since the earning was better this way. The fish tradesmen at Ranihat purchased the seedlings from them. Indeed, some Doms survived solely on cultivation and worked on Nibaran Chowdhury's land.

Danger was at hand everywhere here; death lurked in the shadows. Around this time last year, Nidhu Dom, father of Hariya Dom, was eaten up by a river crocodile on what had been a day of festivities for the Dom community. Dharma puja was to be celebrated in the village. No other Dom had gone to the river. Instead, many were busy cutting bamboo shoots, involved in their traditional occupation of making baskets and other everyday commodities. The sun had spread its warmth since early morning. That was the day he died. The crocodile had been close by. No sooner had Nidhu entered the water than the crocodile pounced on him and dragged him into the river's depths. His half-devoured carcass was discovered three days later in the forest of Kumirmari.

Hariya never returned to the river after that, restricting himself to the land since the incident. He had about ten *bighas* of land adjoining his house. There, he toiled hard to make a betel orchard for paan cultivation; paan had a good market.

Things were going well for Hariya and his days were passing agreeably. Trouble started all of a sudden one day. Nibaran Chowdhury's accomplice Neelmadhav came to say, 'Babu has called for you, Hariya.'

Hariya was taken aback. His relationship with Nibaran Chowdhury had soured since last year. Besides, he was a diabolical man. Not only was he in control of a lot of land, but he was also involved in a flourishing trade of smuggling; he was the ringleader in this place. Smugglers from Kolkata paid regular visits to his house as the Bangladesh border was not far from here.

Hariya was in deep thought. Last year, before his father's unfortunate passing, Nibaran had called for him and told him that he required ten bighas of land close to his place. He had plans for some project. The plot he had shown Nidhu had also included their own share of land for which Nibaran offered him a measly sum in exchange. Nidhu had refused the offer. Nibaran had gritted his teeth in blind rage and rejoined, 'Alright, we shall see how it goes!'

Nidhu had not lived long after that. Within a month, he had met his end and Hariya became the head of this house and family.

Hariya made for the Chowdhury residence as soon as Neelmadhav left. The sun was burning bright by then. A bird whistled unmindful of little else in the mango orchard of the Chowdhurys. Was it because she had seen Hariya? When he reached, Nibaran was fishing in the pond. Seeing Hariya, he stood up smiling and said, 'Come, Hariya.'

'Master, what could you possibly have to do with a lowborn like me?'

'What are you saying, Hariya? You are the people. We are nothing without you.'

Nibaran Chowdhury was known for his oratorical skills. During the last election, he had travelled around in the cars of different ministers, delivering speeches in various areas.

'If you could tell me why I was called here, master?'

'Hariya, you do know...', Mr Chowdhury coughed a little, 'I am planning a project. I will implement my plan in this village itself. But I need land. What I want to say is that I need the ten bighas of land you own at Dom-*para*. I have asked this of a number of people and they have all agreed. Now if you agree too...'

Hariya stood up immediately and spoke very slowly, 'Do what you have to with your own land, master! You have an extensive plot. Why reach for the tiny plot of ancestral land the poor have?'

Chowdhury was livid. Grinding his teeth, he said, 'Okay, I shall deal with this later.'

That night Hariya lay on his torn mat of date palm leaves silently. Sleep evaded him in the tiny clay hut. The broken door was of bamboo, the roof of hay. It was long since fresh hay had been spread over the roof. Every monsoon, rainwater would seep through the roof and wet the inside of the house.

It was late at night. The world was covered in deep darkness—it was quiet everywhere. Dewdrops fell silently while the moon observed the chill in the air from the sky. A vast expanse of land lay on all sides, in the midst of which the little village of the Doms was fast asleep.

But Hariya was wide awake. Beside him, his wife Lokkhibala was asleep with their four-five young children, covered in a torn *kantha*. Nowadays it was getting colder towards the end of the night. His children were stirring in their sleep, restless in the cold. Hariya looked at them and pondered over their lives and the society they would grow up in. Something had to be done. He could see clearly how the Chowdhurys had tricked them all to accumulate enormous wealth while the rest turned paupers.

The sun rose in the east. This was the beginning of winter. The north wind blew relentlessly. A jackfruit tree stood in Hariya's courtyard where a bird perched and whistled vivaciously. Hariya was listening to this. If only he had been born as a bird, he could have lived a happy life. Life as a man was one of immense sorrow.

No, he had to do something. One could not leave one's ancestral land this easily. An idea emerged in his mind. It had originally come from Babulal, a member of the gram panchayat. Hariya had voted for Babulal in the last election. In fact, he had voted for everyone in Babulal's organisation. It was Babulal who had explained to him, 'You know what, Hariya? We are *sarbaharas*, we who have nothing—our party is an organisation for the proletariat. We must mobilise. If we cannot, mahajans like Chowdhury will wrest everything from us.'

Hariya liked what he had said. During the elections, he had accompanied Babulal, travelling across the entire village to explain this to the people. 'We are the proletariat. Our party must be proletarian.' Now, he rushed to Babulal with this new problem. Besides, this was hardly an individual issue. Twenty families in the village would soon be rendered homeless by Nibaran Chowdhury.

'You should probably go to the panchayat head, Hariya. They will arrange something.'

Initially, Hariya had not paid any heed to this. He had replied, 'They never do anything for us, Babulal.'

Babulal hailed from Hariya's village, he belonged to his caste too. Besides, the two always rushed to rescue anyone in the village in times of trouble. The panchayat head was of a higher caste. He did let them sit when he visited, but what he said was quite incomprehensible to Hariya.

Hariya had visited the panchayat office two years ago. Nibaran had snatched a lot of plots from the village for fish farming. The villagers were united in their unwillingess to let go of their lands. There was a direct clash between the Doms and the people working for Chowdhury. The Doms had even banded together and lodged complaints with the panchayat. What came as a surprise was the way the panchayat had casually explained to them how the plots had to be released for Chowdhury; they explained how there were plans to create prawn cultures. These prawns would be exported to foreign lands and this would bring dollars to the country. The Doms hardly understood any of this. The panchayat had explained, 'All of you will get money.' However, they never received any money. From then on, the Doms had been suspicious of the panchayat as it was clearly in league with Chowdhury.

'No, Babulal, I shall not go to the panchayat head.'

'Why don't you first go and see, Hariya? We're the ones who elect them.'

Hariya went to the panchayat office that morning itself. The head was sitting and chewing paan. His close aides sat surrounding him. He was surprised to see Hariya.

'Hariya, there you are!'

Hariya fumbled a little before saying, 'Sir, the Chowdhurys want to acquire my plot.'

'Chowdhury, what Chowdhury?' the head acted surprised.

'Yes sir, Nibaran Chowdhury!' Hariya was polite.

'Understood now. Yes, Mr Chowdhury did mention it. You know what Hariya: he will execute an agro-based project over there. The produce shall be exported and earn foreign currency. You won't understand. However, acquiring ancestral property cannot be tolerated. This is completely unfair!'

'That is why I have come to you, sir.'

The panchayat head thought of something for a moment. Then he said, 'Now Hariya, if Mr Chowdhury offers you an amount, will you not be able to buy a house elsewhere?'

Hariya retorted, 'I know that scoundrel Chowdhury well! All our lives his ancestors have made fools of us and we have been impoverished.'

The panchayat head put another paan in his mouth and went on to say, 'This is a grave problem, Hariya. You do something—go to the MLA; it is impossible for me to solve this.' Hariya hastened to the MLA's residence. Even on a winter day, the sun was shining brightly overhead by then. Two eagles were soaring in the wind close to the horizon. He had not eaten anything since morning and was starving. He reached the MLA's doorstep in a while.

The MLA's house was an enormous two-storeyed building. The parlour was very crowded and there was a meeting going on. Hariya was able to recognise the MLA at first glance as during the last election the MLA had toured his village.

Hariya waited for a while outside the parlour. The meeting appeared to be important and quite intense so he thought it inappropriate to disturb the MLA at such a time. It could be an ongoing discussion involving work in the country. After some time though, Hariya heard a roll of laughter from inside the parlour. This made him think the meeting was perhaps not so important after all and he quickly entered the room. Bowing reverently to the MLA he said, 'Sir, I have a request.'

Everyone present was exasperated at Hariya for disturbing the MLA in the middle of a meeting. Although the MLA himself was quite annoyed at the unwarranted visit, he said nothing. He looked at Hariya and asked, 'What is your name?'

'Sir, it is Hariya Dom.'

The MLA felt nauseous hearing the surname; Dom was the lowest of all castes. He asked, 'So what is your request?'

'Sir, Nibaran Chowdhury wants control over my ancestral land.'

'Nibaran Chowdhury; Nibaran Chowdhury from where?'

'Sir, Nibaran Chowdhury from Sonagaon. You had been to our village during the last election, remember?'

Now the MLA said, 'Understood. They're all like that. They've become rich, oppressing the poor. They will no doubt seize all you have. That's why the poet Sukanta had said—what was it? I forget. I am forgetful these days.'

'Sir, you must provide a solution to this.'

The MLA thought intently for a while. Then he said, 'Alright Hariya, I have an urgent meeting to attend today. Why don't you come tomorrow?'

The next day Hariya arrived at his place early in the morning. But the MLA was nowhere to be found. He had left for Kolkata at the break of dawn. Hariya finally managed to meet the MLA after three days of repeated visits.

'Sir!'

'Listen, Hariya. I have been dwelling over your matter for a few days. Mr Chowdhury is not an easy person to tackle. You must go to the minister.'

Hariya did not waste a moment and rushed to the minister's residence. The minister's house was far from the village, in a mofussil town. Hariya kept running like the 'runners' of ancient times. The sun slowly set in the sky as he continued to run. Evening descended and darkness covered the world again. Hariya was barefoot and clad in torn clothes. Starving and utterly exhausted, he finally reached the minister's residence.

But was it this easy to meet a minister? He had gone to Kolkata on some important business and his return was uncertain. Hariya retraced his steps home like the runners once more. The night approached its end and the morning sun appeared in the sky.

When Hariya reached home, his wife was heating rotis on the clay oven. The boys were sitting around the oven and warming their bare bodies in the warmth of the fire on the cold winter day. Seeing Hariya, his wife called out, 'What happened? Some men working for Nibaran Chowdhury had come today to say we have to leave within this month or else they would bring people to evict us.'

'As if! The minister will definitely find a solution to this', Hariya's face glowed with confidence.

After a long wait and multiple trips to and fro, Hariya finally got a glimpse of the minister once more. But it was difficult to get to talk to him. After sustained efforts, he got hold of one of his servants and reached the minister's room.

Hearing everything the minister said, 'Look, we have to do big things for the country. How do you think I have the time to ponder over such trivial matters as yours?'

Hariya grasped the minister's feet and said, 'You are our father, sir. Where will we go if you do not look after us?' The minister was enraged and said, 'You are such a rascal! Scoundrel! Isn't my time valuable? Get out of here; such a nuisance!'

Hariya had to return dejected. But he could still not accept the situation so easily. That day he called everyone in the Dom community for a meeting and convinced them that they had to do something. Budho Dom even blurted out, 'That rogue Chowdhury tricked my ancestors into giving away their farmlands to him. Now he's planning to turn us homeless!'

Hariya listened to all this silently. As the night emerged, a kind of fervour grew within every Dom's heart.

Hariya asked them to return to their homes for the day. Everyone left. Hariya, however, stayed put. He slept in the courtyard of the Dharmaraj Mandir, where the meeting had taken place. As he slept, he dreamt of a beautiful garden with hundreds of *parijat* flowers, surrounded by mountains. Thousands of stars shone overhead. A rainbow path ran up and merged into a galaxy and multiple golden chariots rode down that path. Various gods were sitting in these chariots drawn by white horses. Hariya gazed at the gods, wide-eyed.

The chariots stopped before the parijat garden and the gods came out one by one. They offered their obeisance to Hariya and he was completely taken aback. The ones who had never been allowed to even witness the gods of clay in the temple now had the very gods standing before one of their people. He decided to complain against Nibaran Chowdhury, but before he could say anything, one of the gods said, 'We have come here for your help, O human.'

Hariya was dumbfounded; it was as if the gods were playing a prank on him. Even so, he heard them out. A deadly monster had conquered paradise. The gods somehow escaped his grasp. No god, *yaksha* or *rakshasa* could defeat him owing to Brahma's boon. Only a human could. This is why they were here making an earnest request to Hariya.

But could Hariya do it?

Without thinking too much, he told the gods, 'Give me a weapon then.'

One of the gods gave him a sword. Hariya brandished the sword and rode a divine chariot to the palace of the monster. A violent war commenced. Finally, Hariya emerged victorious after stabbing the monster in his chest.

Meanwhile, morning had broken out. While Hariya slept without care, people from the Dom community gathered together. Nibaran Chowdhury's musclemen had surrounded their village. They would all have to leave at once otherwise the goons would set fire to everything.

Hariya was still in a trance—returning from paradise basking in his glory. He woke up with a start as Budho shoved him. Thousands of villagers were gathered around him. He could also vaguely make out the men Nibaran Chowdhury had sent.

Suddenly he let out a loud cry, 'Go, bring everything you can find from your houses—lathis, large sticks, everything else!' He ran forward with a large stick himself, uncaring of everything else. Yelling at the top of his voice, with the gathering of thousands behind him, he said, 'You bloody rascals, I shall not let anyone return alive from here today!'

Chowdhury's goons had seen nothing like this before. Sensing trouble, they broke into a run. The people of Dom para were ecstatic in their victory. Nibaran Chowdhury was never seen entering their village again.

Translated from Bangla by Srishti Dutta Chowdhury
Originally published as "Hariya domer upakhyan" in *Khilipaner Meye*, 1996

15

Ghost Tiger

Utpalendu Mondal

[1]

The seedlings were all submerged under water. How could the water be drained out? There is still time before ebb tide. Farming will probably not yield much this season. The villagers had all left for the Andamans or for Bengaluru. Who is left behind to tend to the fields? Headman Binod sat on the open stretch in front of his house. A farm maintained for generations—maybe we are now witnessing its end. One can till the land, but there are no more seeds left to sow. Binod lit his *beedi* from the fire of the *shnajal*. Smoking the hookah had almost become an extinct practice now. The sweet tobacco from Champahati would have normally spread its perfume at this time of the year—one can't find even a whiff of it now. In our childhood, when we did not have any money, we would smoke whatever we could lay our hands on! And nobody smokes the hookah these days. What times have befallen us! These kids are also useless—the oldest just wanders around. So many people travel such long distances to earn some cash, but these kids do not show the slightest initiative. Apparently, if you go to Sonarpur or Jadavpur, there is money to be found everywhere—can these nincompoops not catch hold of any of it? They while away their time making excuses. One always finds them in the town centre, chatting away to glory. The Scheduled Tribe guys are found indulging themselves with booze and the kids trail behind them. Binod thinks to himself that it is good that there has been no farming this season—he gets to starve the kids that way.

The west wind carries with it the smell of rain. This thunderous rain was not likely to stop anytime soon; neither is the storm likely to cease. Gone… all of it is gone. This rain has not been brought in by monsoon; a depression has brought it in. The whole day has gone by without the faintest glimmer of sunlight. The Kurekhaali river looks ready to brim over. The dams are not maintained properly, how indeed is the water supposed to be kept in check? The fish have all left the ponds to swim over to the fields, and there is no one to stop them. Are these boys humans or are they little devils? They will readily forego the name of their ancestors; I wonder if they will even perform our last rites?

The tigress crouched beside Adhar Mistry's boat that had been tilted in front of the cowshed because of the fresh coat of tar. A black striped tigress beside a black boat. She was very hungry, and there were only tigers left in the forest. The trees had been felled to the ground by the storm. Not a deer, not even a wild boar was to be found anywhere. What would she survive on? One couldn't survive on wild fruits alone. That was why she was forced to cross the river, right through the Kurekhaali marketplace to land up here. Camouflaged against the boat, she lay holding her breath. Right at that moment, a baby goat walked past her in the rain. She simply couldn't let it go. She just grabbed it by its neck and was walking away when…a scream! Why were these apes even passing through this place?!

Natabar Raptan, Deben Mistry, and Nirapad Member were returning home. Seeing the tiger, Natabar fainted right on the spot. Deben Mistry jumped into the Kurekhaali, swimming and screaming. As he choked in the water, even the mere Kurekhaali seemed like the mighty Bidyanadi. The Raimangal joins the Kurekhaali stream here to increase its volume to such an extent that it cannot possibly be swum across. He kept thinking that the tiger would catch up with him mid-river but he was so scared that he could not even muster the courage to turn around and check.

Nirapad Member, whom people simply called 'Nirapad', entered his ancestors' names in the master roll; he had also been stealing for years. And yet, he was safe. He screamed, 'Tiger!' and some people gathered at the call, carrying lanterns and gas canisters. One could barely see anything in the dim light. In this confusion, the tigress slipped away. No one could find her now. Along the canal all the way till Sukhdev babu's ghat, the guest house and boat no. 652, there were people everywhere. Yet, she could not be found. Bypassing the net and the water and the river, straight into the forest she went. Nirapad Member gathered men to stay on guard that night. The panchayat elections are to be held soon—this is a time for serious discussions. This is also the aftermath of a massive natural disaster, time for money to come into their hands from the government. Money from the Centre, money from the State—all of it would be stored safely. Nirapad explained, 'Our land is the safest of all. No industrialist will come here to take it. So, we should have no trouble in continuing farming.' Manoranjan Raptan added, 'On top of that, it is full of tigers. Who dares come here? Everyone is scared for their lives. That's why I always say "Let the tigers come". You people should not get scared. At least the tigers won't take our land.' Hearing this, the bleak gathering cheered up. One group remained at Haatkhola, another near Sukhdev babu's ghat. Nirapad went to rest at headman Gyan's party office. Headman Gyan was not there at the moment, neither were his sons. His grandsons were there, but they were not members of the party.

Today the sky was finally looking good. There was sunlight this morning. The situation was the same as far as the eyes could see. The water would recede as soon as the ebb tide came. As of now, water levels still seemed to be increasing. If anyone so much as commented on this matter, Nirapad was quick to advise them to go check out the situation in Bombay. The movie stars were actually moving away from their homes in the city! 'At least you people are not having to sit around along the edge of the river', he said.

Sukhdeb replied almost immediately, 'If the wild tiger moves away from the forest into human settlements what are we supposed to do? We didn't ask for the rain or the flood to strike us like this.' At this, the forest official Manohar Baule chimed in, 'Killing a tiger means killing the forest. The forest has always given us so much.' Sure, it had. But did that mean that a tiger got to stroll in any time? Baule had been called in for consultation regarding the problem. They had been standing guard every night but to no avail. Yesterday, there was a tiger attack on Subhash Bachhar as he was driving the van. It was monsoon, and since there was nobody around, he was driving slowly to match his melancholic mood. Right at that moment, the tiger had attacked him! He survived only because he sped away. Thus started the tiger search with renewed vigour.

Binod had not been around for a while. He was here today because some of the boys couldn't make it. He had never seen or even heard of such tiger attacks in all his life. His ancestors had been heard to have beaten tigers to a pulp before sending them away on a raft. And look at the situation now!

'Are the tigers these days some kind of god, the Fotikir Shib?'

'I swear! Subhash has brought a weapon. We can now attack on sight.'

'Kill it, yes! We can't take this anymore—can't eat in peace, can't shit in peace. What a place this has become. From glory to nothing. Thank god Harihar Badyi isn't alive to see this happening.'

The team was moving forward. They were quite fearless because ahead of them lay the BSF camp. There, the men stood guard with their guns. The police had come earlier. But they had failed to find anything there either.

The tiger was certainly as evasive as a Fotikir Shib. She would appear one moment and disappear the next, that too in this darkness-engulfed land submerged by water from the Akash Bonya plantation—it seemed that she was quietly hiding alongside the water. The moment she saw the men, she would make a move. Where would they go then? Which way would they flee? There was water everywhere. Their limbs were flaccid; any effort to run would only mean that they would fall down. The dirt tracks had not dried properly—there were patches of slippery mud everywhere. Thus, they needed to proceed with caution.

There were big houses accompanied by large orchards on both sides of the road. The streets here were sub-standard. Every year the panchayat would promise concrete roads but that never happened. The houses on the two sides belonged to well-to-do people. They all used to belong to Congress; now they belong to Trinamool. The Congress in Kolkata could probably be bought. But the party cannot buy the people here. And for that reason, they resorted to curbing their livelihood from time to time.

'Look, there is no one here from Raptan's and Khajanchi's house. Is it certain that the tiger will not go to their places and take their goats and ducks? After all the goats and ducks are not like cows in sheds that are protected on all sides.'

'Look Binod—if a confrontation with a tiger or a snake is predestined, who can alter that fate?'

'True. Yet, see—we poor people are spending the night guarding. Should they not send at least one person? The entire village is in the midst of terror, and they are sleeping peacefully—this is unacceptable!'

'Yes, who will the tiger pounce on, what if a cow passes by, there are no saplings, everything perished under water. We are unsure of the future of agricultural activities in the region this time...'

There were no rice seeds in Binod's house. Who knew from whom he would borrow once again! On top of that, there was the threat of the tiger's attack.

No, something had to be done. Even though the tiger came only once in a while, it did manage to secure its prey and cross over to the other side unscathed. Another night guard said that yesterday the tigress had taken away Ramapada's black sheep. She was too cunning; it was proving impossible to catch her.

Nirapad is not there today and as usual, Binod was bossing around. After midnight another group would take over. The fields were still flooded.

On one side the land was lower; the water would take longer to recede from there. According to the shopkeeper Robi, the water would not recede until there was ebb tide. They continued to walk along the unpaved lane. Binod was talking about how the village has fallen into bad times—there was a need for a prayer to catch the tiger. The boys were listening to him attentively. Among them, Shoshanko, through a fishery business, had managed to buy some land. Whether the land would yield anything this year, who knew!

'I absolutely agree with you, Binodka.'

'If only it weren't for this, someone has been spotted standing and walking on water in Amoga, Boro Nodi, Raimangal, also the Kalindi rivers.'

Shoshanko solemnly went on to say, 'The ferry services stop after six. Just think about the hassle. The business will soon be over.'

Binod said, 'Everything will be over. Do you think that God is not with us? Have faith, this will be over soon.'

'Yes indeed, Kolkata has been completely submerged by flood. The other day, Ganesh and Kartik were ferrying across the river to the other side—a distance of hardly two hands remained before they reached the bank—and both of them saw someone walking on the river. Ganesh said, "I thought I was mistaken, but then I saw bhai was also looking at it!" Both fainted before they could reach the river bank. The people of Hatkhola rescued them. Since then, after sunset, nobody crosses the river.'

'A lot more will happen. A married woman goes to Delhi and gets married again. Unmarried girls come back after indulging in immoral activities, do you think that God is not watching all this...the almighty has His own judgments. For instance, this tiger—we have never had to guard our village against a tiger. It is our misfortune, but if I find the tiger...'

'What will you do?'

'You'll see. You, that Nirapad, Gour and even those *netas*—I will not spare him.'

'But what will you do? Are you going to kill her? Beware!'

'Then should I just sit back and prepare the seeds? And then start working in the fields? I don't even own a cow or a calf. I've sharpened the pickaxe...I will strike the head and then, whatever happens, will happen.'

'The police will not spare you.'

'So what? Am I like you? Do you not know what I have in my *konchor*...'

He could not bring himself to finish his sentence. After all, the boys were with him. Indeed, he was walking around with an axe and he would strike the tiger's head. Then he would mount its back. *Shala*, such a huge physique he had. The way he pretended to ride a horse during his childhood. . .just like that. . .

[2]

The field director of the Tiger Project had given his instructions—lure her with a goat, then shoot with a tranquiliser and drop her off deep into the forest. This news was conveyed to the group by Subol Roptan. He was a member of the Bonorokshya committee, a committee appointed to save the forest. There had been times when Subol had lost his head. He had sold off all his land. All that remained was a house; he earned enough to feed one mouth. His parents were no longer alive. He had married off his sister into a good family and now worked for the party. His wife had left him a long time ago. Subol accompanied the group today. Nirapad had told him, 'Convince everyone properly. If this fails, our party will get a bad name. As it is, we're not doing well. The Left Front may end up being the Right Front. The Nandigram-Singur incidents have already created trouble.' The senior members (of the Left Front) did not even consider them humans. They did not see Subol as a human being. *Shala*, good for nothing. He could not manage to even keep his own wife from leaving—squandered away all his land and property.

Subol has to face all the trouble. The field director had patted his back and said, 'If anyone can save the Sunderbans, it is you, the locals. The Sunderbans is one of the wonders of the world and its ecosystem needs to be protected—' and a lot of other things that he no longer remembered. He had tried to explain that to the villagers but would the village people ever understand? The school-going children laughed and joked about him. The field director did not mind as he had the party backing him—why should he be afraid? The forest needs to be protected at any cost. If tigers ceased to exist, how would the *ban*, *kewra*, *hetli*, *dhudhul* survive? Most of the trees had been cut. Some trees had been trimmed to such an extent that they looked bald. How long would they be able to protect the Sunderbans? If the local people did not realise it, how would the other people, the outsiders, understand the issue?

'The *gram-sadha* talisman needs to be brought to the village and tied at the Haritala temple.' Everyone agreed with Binod. The idol of the deity worshipped by Jyotish Gayen's family for two generations was really powerful. The deity had been brought only once before to the village.

Subol said, 'Do you think this will help?'

'What else will help? You've left your wife to become a big scientist; you tell us the answer!'

'The food chain is getting disturbed in the jungle, and I think that's why the tigers come to the village.'

'So do something about it. Why don't you rub mustard oil on the tiger's balls and request him—baba, don't come here again, please?'

The whole team started laughing as they moved forward in the darkness. The hurricane lamp has been set on the lowest lest it use up more fuel. Could the tiger see in such darkness? But then tigers were intelligent creatures. Binod recalled the time a tiger had come to Sunil Mridha's place in Kumirmari and killed one of their cows. Sunil's father was a hunter and had died in the forest; his hunter friends had probably killed him off during that expedition. Sunil died grieving for the cow. Binod kept up with his narration, but the tiger was nowhere to be seen. If the Kurekhaali dried up, tigers would be able to easily cross it. Binod's mind wandered away. He thought of the dismal state of the farmlands. There was no water in the fields. The seeds had been sown once again. The new seeds would take some time to grow. These plants could not withstand a flood; the small leaves and buds would surely be destroyed. The *akash-banya* trees had almost wilted. He tried his best, but could not manage any more seeds. His boys maundered in the town centre. One of them went gallivanting around Sardar *para*. But it was alright. He was now old enough to find himself a girl and get married. His mother was also of the opinion that everything had to happen at an appropriate age. But who would give their daughter's hand in marriage to the boy? What would he feed her? They had only a few bighas of land, and after paying the workers their wages there was not much left. They had to take loans if their houses got destroyed; they got loans if the crops went bad. Year after year, their land was in debt. If there were no jobs, they were compelled to go to Kolkata. Who would have the money then? The city-returned or the locals?

Dhiren Gharami was returning from Parghumti. He was wearing a fine dhoti, had a cigarette in his hand and a fancy bag on his shoulder. People like him had all the riches in the world. Binod had once dreamt that money was falling onto his laps like flowers from a tree. But not everyone has the money for paddy seeds; only the wealthy farmers had the lion's share. His grandfather used to say, 'Even if you don't have the money for food, you should always keep some paddy seeds. That is going to provide the food for us in the future.'

Binod had decided that he would no longer ask for paddy seeds from anyone. He would buy the leaves. Many people were not selling the seeds because they wanted to sell off the leaves first. His house had already been mortgaged to Bonjon Master. No, there is no dearth of money. He would have something to eat, as long as he lived. His grandfather used to be the *nayeb* of the zamindar; all these fields were managed by him. He had always had fish to eat with his rice. Now his family is not given any rice seeds. Everything certainly depended on fate.

Binod stood in front of the *ol* orchard. The trees had reached his chest height. All of these were *madraji-ol*, the south-Indian variety. He thought of all the fish dishes that could be cooked with ol: *ghusho chingri* with fried ol stem, *kyan* fish curry with ol. He could digest rich food at his age; he still had a lot of strength left in his body. He could even do all the household work alone. But what had he got after labouring all his life? Nothing. The lazy and the protected were the moneyed lot now and he had to ask these people to lend him some money.

Binod rested there with his eyes closed, waiting for the evening to fall. The tiger was in the ol orchard. It could catch whatever it wanted and cross the small *duni*. Binod sat admiring the ol trees. The madraji-ols had such beautiful leaves! And the trees were so tall that one could sleep underneath them. These days the skies were clear, but it was too hot. He went to sit on the ghat of a pond. All the fish had escaped. Now, they were hoping for the *bill* fish to enter the pond. Otherwise, what would his family eat all year? There was no money to buy fish. Only the Kurekhaali had fish in it. But all the locusts ate them up. He was about to take a drag from the *beedi* when the tigress came and attacked him, slipping away right after.

Darkness had not yet set in; there was also some faint moonlight. The people of the Kurekhaali were engaged in a brawl, taking on one of the neighbours. In the middle of this, the tigress swam across the river and took a shortcut across the settlements. She did not enter the market, rather went into the nearby forest, rested a while and then crossed another *khali*. Even the birds did not have an inkling; the ecosystem was not affected either. Only underneath the trees of *ban*, *kewra* and *gami*, some paw-prints were found. But those prints were soon washed away due to the ebb and flow of the tides. Only the ghost remained—Binod's ghost. He walked in the waist-high water of Kurekhaali. The locals were afraid of him. The BDO sent a report, Nirapad made the locals understand it. How astonishing, the tiger did not come back from that day onwards. But locals still got scared if they saw the ghost. They joined hands and bowed down to him. Binod's wife was not afraid; she saw him clearly. Her husband had not abandoned her. He still walked, the same way he used to earlier, across this para and that para but never at his home. So what had he gained by dying?

Translated from Bangla by Oly Saha, Sanghamitra Deb and Soham Sinha
Originally published as "Bagh bhoot" in *Golpo Ponchish*, 2008

16

Bhushon and his Family

UTPALENDU MONDAL

Bimol went out with a basketful of ripe *doira* bananas. Ma had given him a plate of *panta* rice, and that was now causing him to belch. He likes this time of the morning. In the wee hours, going past the *gomo* tree of the low land, one steps into the swamp and the pond called Shanti that has gone dry. He puts his basket down on this marshy land and relieves himself. Since there is dearth of water, he goes to Nibaron's pond to wash himself. Then, he strolls up to the footman's house and finds the mid-road, and then going across another marsh he reaches the ferry ghat. Bhushon has the ferry this year; he goes near Bhushon's house and squats on the fishery dam. Sudhonyokaka has come from the No. 5 carrying a handbag, the *haat-besti*. He lights a *beedi* and amidst bouts of cough calls out to Bhushon. Bhushon comes out with red eyes; he must have smoked ganja. Sudhonyokaka blares, 'His wife is dead, and so this Bhushon of ours is on the romp!' Bhushon has set up a shop on the verandah of his house, his son Chondo runs it. His son is a chatterbox just like his father, but he is good at studies. Jadob, the lame man, died last year; he is survived by his wife and two children and Bhushon guards their house. Bimol notices that the rows of shanties under the fishery dam no longer exist. It was here that he used to see Bhushon's father mending their large barge. The boat was in poor shape and water used to seep into it. He spotted an opening like a rat-hole in between two wooden planks, and the old man was plugging that chink with a piece of wood. Before applying tar, they used to jam the breaches between the planks with jute fibre. The young kids would gaze in wonder at it, but the old guy used to work in silence. Bhushon and his father possibly hailed from the neighbourhood of Bosirhat, and used words like 'jabane', 'khabane'. One winter night, that old man passed away. The previous night, he had eaten a bellyful of tortoise meat, inspired by Bosudeb the carpenter (who was then working on mejojyatha's door), and maybe that was why he went to meet his maker. Bhushon's father is no more, and his large barge is nowhere to be seen. Now a modest dinghy is all that Bhushon is left to ferry with.

When he studied in Jogendranath High School at Taranogor, Bhushon was no ferryman. It was Petambor, the forest guard, who used to ferry his boat. Petambor smelt of sour jujubes. After he left school, the settlements around slowly vanished. Some buntings can still be seen fluttering about—here was the hovel of Bosudeb the carpenter; there the shack of Baghanoto. They have all shifted to other places, maybe to some areas in East Pakistan. Bhushon pulls his boat out and pushing it into the water says, 'Careful! Move slowly, or else the prow will veer away.' He rows as the flow tugs the craft towards the house of Baburam Sordar. Bimol steps down on to the fishery dam and starts to hotfoot it with the basket balanced on his head. Mollakhali is now a daily market and unless he reaches there on time, there will be no prospect of sale. The shopkeepers and the teachers are his buyers. While passing through the *para*, he bumps into Porimol. Porimol used to study at a school near the market, but he too has dropped out like Bimol. He asks his questions, and Bimol answers in monosyllables. Porimol's elder brother once studied with his elder brother. Porimol notices his basket, smiles and walks up to a distance by his side. He then sees an idol decked in sola and tinsel at a public altar and instructs Bimol, 'Do the *pronam*.' But Bimol is carrying the basked on his head and cannot do so. He instead speeds up. As he nears the hospital, he steps on to the brick-laid footpath. To the right side there are a series of quarters, inhabited by nurses who certainly are not from this locality—they have plump arms and legs and reek of Kolkata as it were, wearing blouses all the time. A woman calls out to him, but he does not respond. These people do not want to pay—all Kolkata people—and only plead with him to take his payment on the way back. But on the return journey, these women will not be around, for sure.

In a series of sheds on the left side, people were binding beedis. Who knows where these beedis were exported? Possibly to Bangladesh. He goes and squats in the vegetable market; the cottage of *kobiraj* (a doctor who prescribes Ayurvedic medicine) is on the right. Originally this room belonged to sejo jyathamoshai, and kobiraj is a tenant there. The kobiraj is an old man, he writes a stylish hand, and his company gladdens Bimol's mind. The man does not have a good practice here, but even then he does not move out. Today, nobody has come from his house. Customers are scarce, Bimol is late, and what is more, doira bananas are not in high demand. One or two leader-type guys take an interest and buy a couple of bunches. He gives two to an old beggar woman. That dark bloke from the goldsmith's shop comes and takes a bunch, and says that he will pay him when he packs up to go home. On another side, near the fish shop, a big castrated goat is being chopped off for sale. He gets to eat meat only once in a while; sitting beside his basket of bananas, he inhales the tang of mutton. Some beedi-binding men, carrying tobacco in sal leaf, haggle over the price of bananas, and he gives them bananas at a concessional rate of a pair for five paise instead of ten. The sun beats down fiercely and he ties his *gamchha* around his head. If the bananas are not sold, it will be rather trying to carry them back, especially when his neck is already aching. Ma had told him to take home a container of Gouri balm. The shopkeeper at the station area is Raja the Marwari, and he stocks two types of Gouri balm, one genuine, and the other fake. Raja is a crook; he simply disdains the people of his settlement. Once this had even triggered a furore, and Raja's shop was vandalised but later mended by the members of the Haat Committee.

Today Bimol has not got a single paper note, only coins. Now he will not refuse the customers, he will oblige everyone on every offered price. The pockets of his English pants are brimming with jingling coins; these may even spill over or rip his pocket on his way back home. Feeling parched, he advances towards the tap near the fish market. He asks a boy to sit by his merchandise, but when he comes back after drinking water, he finds him eating bananas himself. Okay, eat your fill, honey. This boy is from Mollabari and had come to the market to sell vegetables. He lives near the ferry ghat at Palamari.

'Would you give me a bunch of bananas?'

'What for?'

'My nephew will be happy. I cannot buy lozenges for him but may give him a bunch of bananas.'

This boy does not go to school. What an easeful life! In all probability, Bimol too will be asked to give up studies. But if he did not study hard now, when would he? A couple of bunches still remain to be sold but Bimol does not wait any longer; he wends homeward. Those fair girls are cooking something and the smell is really mouth-watering. The beedi-binders are listening to Radio Khulna and swinging to the tune of music.

'*Ki go*, need bananas?'

The old man adjusts his glasses on the bridge of his nose and glances at him. Then he says, 'Rubbish! We don't eat those seedy bananas.'

We know very well what these Pakistanis eat, thinks Bimol. He puts his basket back on his head and starts walking. On the right is a government building in which an irrigation officer lives. This man consumes a lot of tobacco, for sure. Tobacco has been spread on a dish in sunlight, and its flavour is so very enticing! Ma had asked him to buy some Motihar tobacco which he has not been able to procure. A fistful of that tobacco could jolly well serve the purpose. But he dare not. After all, the person concerned is a government official, he must have some clout. Doctor jyatha had once told him to meet that man and inform him about the erosion of river banks. What was jyatha thinking? How could he be that optimistic? That shorts-clad man would not be the least bit bothered about what he, a mere banana-seller, had to say. However, he had met him and informed him all the same. The officer had enquired about his village and the river, and then declared, 'That is not mine. Well, do one thing—write an application to the superintendent engineer at Free School Street. Then the dam will be built, and there'll be *payelling* on it too.'

The sun had become quite oppressive by now so Bimol took a shortcut to the vicinity of the old lady's house. This house is inhabited by none except one old lady, who spreads dried mangoes and jujubes in the sun. The house reminds him of Horihor's ancestral home in Bibhutibhushon Bandyopadhyay's novel *Pother Panchali*. From the shade of the mango tree here, one gets to see Rosik Mondal's house on the other side. He has a pucca building with cemented ghat. In that ghat, he had once seen a half-naked housewife washing vegetables in the pond water. The old lady sits quietly in the verandah; at the backyard, a bitch, the well-known brass-coloured Khenki of the locality, lies idly. In the cowshed of Modhu Biswas, a cow from Bhagalpur is chewing the cud. The cow looks at him with dilated eyes, and the moment he holds a couple of bananas to its muzzle, it gobbles those down pronto. He scratches the cow's dewlap as it eats. Modhu Biswas's wife comes running and demands, 'Hey, what are you up to?' He takes to his heels and hides near a tubewell beyond the canal till she goes back to her shed. Biswas owns a shop in the market and is quite a lout. While walking back home, Bimol runs into Santosh Bagh, the moneylender. When dams are built in the area, this man becomes the contractor. Sushil, his son, is Bimol's classmate. Santosh is the brother of their teacher Shantibabu, and this Shantibabu has one serious vice—he is extremely crabby and beats Sushil black and blue every time he goes off the handle. Santosh walks with long strides and chews paan like a goat. The sun is relentless overhead, the loo wind is blowing, and Bimol's whole body feels like it is being scalded. Santosh says, 'Come under my umbrella, please', but he cannot keep pace with him.

Santosh, however, has a scandal to his name, news of which has spread in his locality. Taramama has two wives, one hailing from Mollakhali, and the other from Bionod Houli. Once, Santosh got benighted while working on the dam project and was forced to put up in Taramama's residence. Since then, the local people have started pulling his leg. The street urchins pester him by yelling, 'Paramour of two wives!' Bimol too feels tempted to get his goat by repeating those words, but in this sun, when even spittle is being reduced to dust, he cannot quite manage to blurt it out. Santosh is, after all, a companion on his journey. The two cross the Bilan field, but cannot see the dam. He has cramps, the panta rice he ate in the morning has long exited his system. The overcast sky continues to be scorched by the sun. Once they enter Mistry para, it becomes a little cooler and more shadowy. A few teenage girls were walking ahead of them. Santosh tells them, '*Ei khuki*, hey girls, would you give us water?' The girls rather coyly reply, 'We will, if you come to our house.' But Santosh does not stop, he walks apace. The girls look back only to find them walking away. Bimol must make haste; if Bhushon stops ferrying, he will have to stay back on this side of the river bank and there will be no other way out. Going near Baburam Sordar's house, he hollers, '*O majhi, o majhi!*' He sees the boat packed to capacity on the other side, but Bhushon is not around. He must be smoking ganja somewhere. Suddenly a bloke comes out of nowhere and boards the boat. He must be in a tearing hurry, so he rows it fast to this side all by himself. As the boat nears this bank, Bimol steps on to the stern and gets into the craft. The dhoti-clad man, who is extremely foul-mouthed, gets down. Bimol now squats, ties his gamchha tightly around his head, holds fast on to the stern, and leaps into the boat. He has really grown up, hasn't he, he thinks, chuckling to himself. He spreads saline water over his head and wets his shirt in order to cool off. Since the river now has an ebb tide, he keeps the prow to his left and floats downstream. Bhushon's mother stands in the distance and asks him to bring the boat to the ghat. He rows on, skirting along the bank, and once the boat reaches the ghat, he lands on the beach. Bhushon's mother demands money, but Bimol refuses to pay. Why should he? He had to row all by himself, after all. Bhushon's mother softens and looking at his sun-burnt face, asks him, 'Whose son are you? Which one is your house?' Bimol cites his jyathamoshai's name, and the old woman looks at his basket. She takes all the unsold bananas, some of which are already rotten, into her hands. She wants the whole lot for ten paise. Bimol demands twenty, but the old woman stands her ground stubbornly. At last, the bananas are exchanged for ten paise and the woman has the last laugh. Bhushon's son hangs around his grandma; Bimol delivers all the bananas into her hands and sails across the marsh.

Postscript

I came across the name 'Bhushon' in Achintyakumar Sengupta's poetry. Before that, I only knew of the Bhushon of our village, a strapping figure with a bare breast, always rowing the boat. The estate under the fishery was his abode; the ferry ghat was by the side of his house. When I was a boy studying in Class 5, I used to wait by his house for the ferry. On the other side of the bank was my school, Taranagar Jogendranath High School. At the time, Petom Majhi was the ferryman; he used to live on Rohis Khan's land, who was the forest leader. The Muslims and Adivasis lived around that land. Petom used to smell of sour jujubes; from time to time he used to blurt out, 'Oh! Disgusting! I won't ferry today.' Petom's son was my age, but he was not in school. Bhushon at that time used to turn their boat upside down and smear tar on its bottom. His father was then pretty old and he used to patter away on his boat, wedging bits of wood in between wooden planks with a tiny chisel, so that water did not seep through. Chondro, Bhushon's son, was younger than me; he used to run his father's shop and I also found him reading books at home. Chondro gradually grew up, came to Kolkata and wandered about; he looks older than me now. On a few occasions, I bumped into him and learned that he has a clerical job; yet, he calls me advocate. This is the way of the villagers, they lionise everything, but that day when in my office I saw Chondro on the news, crying (watching television is part of my job) I was flabbergasted. None of us is Tagore, I have suffered much sorrow in this little life of mine, and am also suffering from high blood pressure and diabetes. I no longer have the physical agility that I had thirty years ago. I was looking at the TV, nonplussed. The more I tried to convince everybody that he hailed from our village, the more rigorously the peons, clerks and my colleagues refused to believe me. A physician's wife, who happens to be my colleague, was rather surprised. She told me sympathetically, 'Sir, don't watch such stuff, your heart will turn heavy.' From what I could see, that little boy Chondro had come to Kolkata, bought a plot of land and built a house on it. I knew his father; whenever he chanced upon me, he used to ask, 'Mama, are you okay?' I keep no track of Bhushon these days. Once I had asked Chondro, but he refused to answer. Or, he answered, but spoke certain words which were useless. This Bhushon too must have been a refugee; why else would he have squatted on the government plot under the fishery. Beside Bhushon's hovel, there were the shanties of Baghanoto, Basudeb the carpenter and Bhupen, the tall guy. Later, Baghanoto hanged himself, Basudeb, the carpenter came to settle in the frontal part of our land, and Bhupen and family moved elsewhere. In this transitional period, our locality looked really deserted. In my teenage years, I used to wonder at the fragile wall of oven clay of Basudeb's cottage. I was even more surprised to look at Bhushon; he had never appeared depressed. The village folk, of course, are seldom depressed. After his wife's death, he had not remarried. I never saw Bhushon intoxicated, but did see a ganja plant in his house. In the indifferent wind of Chaitra, wearing a tulsi garland round his neck, when he called me 'Mama', it was with a touch of tenderness. I was then employed elsewhere.

In my summer vacations I used to go home and also had to visit market places. And so, Bhushon's ferry service was absolutely essential. As he ferried, I asked him about his son a couple times, but he answered, 'Mama, don't ask me this question'. The ferry charge was five paise, but he did not accept money from me. His father was a lean man, but a clean man all the same, often found mending their big boats. He had died suddenly one winter night. Basudeb, the carpenter, told me smilingly, sporting his decaying teeth, 'Last night, both the father and the son ate such a large quantity of tortoise meat, that the old man died.' Basudeb was then working in our house. I have seen Bhushon's mother too, she was swarthy, with rows of healthy teeth. Every year, we used to steal paddy, and in exchange for that, would bring puffed rice from their house.

One fistful of paddy with one fistful of puffed rice—its taste is ethereal. In the last century, urea was yet to arrive in our village and Folidol and Dimecron (popular pesticides) were also not known of. But one or two people still hanged themselves and committed suicide even in those days.

We had to go on and off to Mollakhali daily market with vegetables from our house. No, it was not because of poverty, but because there was nothing else we could do with the surplus things except sell them off. On one occasion, I had two bunches of ripe seedy bananas, which in the Sundarbans parlance is known as doira bananas. The ripe doira bananas are very sweet, but they rot quickly. I had to carry a basketful of these bananas to the market by Bhushon's ferry. I had to travel a long way through barren fields with no paddy; in fact, paddy was not being cultivated then. I crossed one field after another and reached the daily market at Mollakhali. Half of my bananas were sold, and the other half remained unsold. To reduce the weight of my basket, I fed Modhu Biswas' Bhagalpuri cow a couple of bunches of those bananas. The cow munched on them happily wide-eyed. I would have fed it the whole lot, but Biswas's wife came chasing, and I had to beat a hasty retreat. At the time, poor cobblers of our village used to kill cows for their hide by poisoning them, so Biswas's wife had reason to be alarmed. She chased me alright but did not raise a huge alarm or call people. In case she had, I would surely have been lynched that day. Anyway, carrying the leftover bunches in the basket balanced on my head, I once again travelled back across Bilan field and ghat, and boarded Bhushons' ferry once more. It was noon; Bhushon had finished his lunch and was having a siesta. Unless a babu-type dhoti-clad man brought the boat back to this side, I would have been left out in the open with a hungry belly under the seething Chaitra sun. I embarked on the boat and had to row it all by myself. The tide was ebbing then, so the boat did not quite touch the ghat. I had a good mind of leaving the boat there and going away, but Bhushon's mother intervened. She emerged as a shadowy figure in front of their hovel and forced me to push the boat up to the ghat. I paid the ferry charge to that old lady and showed her the contents of my basket seeing which she flashed a smile.

I did not see Bhushon that noon. But during those days, Bhushon used to praise his son to the skies. Dhiren Sardar had not passed his matriculation exam—he was a non-matric who loved to flaunt his English-speaking skills among illiterate people; he had memorised his subjects, objects and verbs. It was this Dhiren Sardar who taught English to Bhushon's son. In the eighties and nineties, English-educated people did not find it difficult to get a job though I don't know why Chondro did not get any. But he was surely in the queue. We, who have left our childhood back in the village, and have become accustomed to messy lives in the city, are more or less established now. We are married and some of us own cars. This author is no exception. But still, there is a lingering sense of loss.

After his wife's death, Bhushon did not remarry, but villagers used to say that he lived with the next-door widow. When a body needs another, neither society nor inhibitions come in the way. Nonetheless, nobody bothers about how many women some Hemingway or Marquez lived with, but a village is a village; in rural life, one gets shamed for his father's sexual promiscuity. When I got a job, I was the third from my village to do so, thereafter many got secured jobs in banks, and some became doctors and lawyers. But, under the rule of the Left Front, the autochthons had to move out, and the party cadres became all powerful in village administration. They were so autocratic that many villagers had to leave their village. The job market was quite open then, and Chondro took this opportunity to graft himself within the suburbs of Kolkata. Satyajit Ray had once said that people came to Kolkata to eke out a living. We too came with that purpose, but in the process of finding a living, we lost quite a few things.

Losing and finding is part of life, there will forever be hidden sorrow and tears, just in the manner in which Chondro wept, and I was perspiring in my air-conditioned office chamber. Did we make the right choice in coming here? Was it really necessary? One uncle of mine, who was a school teacher, asked me, 'Why have you come to this desert land?', and I could not answer. Had Chondro not come to this city, had he not taken care to disseminate his ambition among his sons, would his son then have committed suicide? Progress of this sort seems to be pointless. Now jobs are scarce, but that has not prevented rural folk from migrating to the city. My father and my uncle were once in Bangladesh. Migration is in my blood, like that protagonist in Shyamal Ganguly's story, who drinks water from a tap at Champahati station, sleeps on the platform, and when asked, replies, 'I had so many things once upon a time, but now I have lost interest.' Now, in order to see the moonlight, he steps down to the road, accompanied by Shyamal 'Bangal'. But, in reality, the consumerist world has taken a toll on us. Sentiments are on the rise. Jobs are now graded, but then they always were.

In the early days of our arrival in Kolkata, I would often visit a friend's house (which actually was a building under construction), hoping to get something to eat if my visit coincided with breakfast. But such hopes were very often frustrated. My friend Yakub, having starved a whole night, went to that friend's house, only to be treated to tea and biscuits. I asked him what he did then. He said, 'I drank water from the corporation tap.' He owned so many plots of land at Pathankhali, and later joined a teaching service at Basanti and started various other businesses. This fellow could choose to go back to his village, but we could not. Death of a son or a daughter is too painful, for those of us who have lost our parents, entombed our glorious childhood, for those who have been deserted by their lovers and wives, the void is too deep, the grief too heart-rending.

Jobs are unavailable now, and this is a global phenomenon—none can deny this unpleasant truth. Maybe there will be no war, and there will be no requited love, but those girlfriends and lovers, who are now rearing their own sons and saying, 'We are bringing up someone else's son-in-law, my wife and my friend's wife who do not live with their parents-in-law, and those old men and women who are not served tea by their daughters-in-law, are nursing a deep sorrow.' No point talking like the poet Shakti Chattopadhyay, 'Give me sorrow, I love it.'

The Left built no industries in the last three decades because of the fear of labour problems and lack of profit. People are losing jobs every day because it is difficult to keep pace with technology, and it is equally difficult to renounce desire like Ramakrishna Paramahansa. So the gap keeps widening between the two ways of life. And in this cleft, the human race must thrive. A few days later, antibiotics won't work, and it is doubtful whether the Sundarbans will be in the Sundarbans at all. Where, then, will we find our land? Had there been general awareness, this country would not have to see the scams of Sarada and Narada. Dreaming is good, but one must remember that dreams need to be proportionate to one's situation. One relative of mine used to take his son to school every day burning petrol worth ₹700, but I could not afford that. That son has now become a computer engineer, and, in contrast, my daughter has ranked very low in the merit list, and is not eligible even to be a seamstress. Our next generation will not get jobs the way I managed to, and this is the fact that Chondro possibly could not explain to his son, and I too have failed to explain to my daughter. I am an ineffectual father afraid of some fancied death, and sleeping pills give me serenity at night. Sleep is the only peaceful bliss; it really is.

Bhushon Pal shook his son vigorously, and said, 'What is there to stare at? What is there in this damned swampy land? The real land is on the other side.' My daughter and my friend's son, too, believe that my land is just a quagmire. In my office, in restaurants, and even in pubs, people ask me, 'Can you bring me a maid from your land?' I shoot back a sharp no. This has strained my friendships with many, but what else am I supposed to do? Before and after the Aila,[1] many Sundarbans dwellers migrated to south India—even those like me who failed to procure jobs. Some have found employment in undergarment manufacturing companies, some in bag manufacturing units, and some are engaged in manufacturing toxic products. Overtime jobs bring more money. When they come back to the village, they buy lands. Not a bad policy at all. Some, of course, are bringing back AIDS,

---

[1] A devastating cyclonic storm that lay waste the South Bengal, especially the Sundarbans and adjacent deltaic areas in 2009.

some new brides (some other's wives), and some are getting murdered. The old order no longer exists. Those who migrated to the south have subscribed fully to consumerism; when they come back, I am aghast at the amount of alcohol they consume. Poets have said that you cannot expect the apocalypse to stop just because you are blind. But why should catastrophe get stalled in this floating, borrowed life? If movement is life, and expansion is youth, then this onrush of youth is unstoppable. I may cry as long as I wish in the crowded chamber of my office, but that will not bring back Chondro's son to him. And I will never get back my pocketful of childhood, my hidden tears, and the lands that my father and uncle cultivated. This is life—if you can accept it, is alright, or else, be prepared to waste away on irretrievable memories. For a modicum of success in life, you will have to run hard—you may gain something in the bargain, and lose some. My unlettered mother used to say, it's good to lose your way and find it. I now stand at the crossroads of that lost road. There is no coming and no going—I see Bhushon and his family in front, in this incorporeal darkness.

Translated from Bangla by Arnab Bhattacharya
Originally published as "Bhushon o tar poribar" in *Aabad Sahitya* journal, Volume 3, Issue 1 & 2, August–October, January 2018

17

Tulsi's Chronicle

Utpalendu Mondal

Tulsi hurled the first stone but alas—it missed its mark and the rooster dashed off. But he returned, resuming his efforts to make out with their hen. Stick-thin as a grasshopper, the hen made vain attempts to escape. The rooster still managed to make its way through the brinjal bush and pinned her down. Tulsi then hurled another stone—this one sailed over the red tip of its comb. Unhurt, he resumed his pursuit. Tulsi was unable to control her rage any more. Blinded by the pain of humiliation, she picked up the thick stem of *goran* that stood nearby and threw it straight at the rooster and scored a direct hit. Crowing in pain, he ran amok, finally splashing into the pond. His red comb was ravaged and his neck covered with bloodstains. He shivered as Tulsi picked him up from the pond and sprinkled water on his head. He lay motionless for a while and then rose again, clucking his way back to the neighbouring house. What a life force it had, Tulsi wondered.

What was the point of a life like this? It would have been much better if she had died in her childhood. In fact, she had almost died of typhoid once. She felt angry with baba—if only he had not carried her all the way to see the doctor at Gosaba…

She could still remember the thrill of sitting upon his shoulder, clutching his hair, gazing at the things below from her high pedestal. She had wanted to pluck a *ban* leaf—was it for the savoury salty taste it yielded? Was that why she sought salty flavour in everything even now? She would never know…

It was a young, robust hen. Maybe, they could lock it…

Aha, how she missed her mother's cooking! They had hardly had any delicacies since baba passed away. It was only for the sake of her young brothers and sisters that she had left home for the first time. She struggled to remember the exact year—yes, she was yet to have her first period. From Delhi, she went to Purulia and then Dhakuria in Kolkata. The days in

Dhakuria were not that bad; her employers were all right. But it was her mother who wanted her to quit and return home after her second sister's marriage. And so she did. It was not that she had not been home before; it was just that she no longer felt at home here. Work was scarce in these parts—so was money. She could not even do the typical village chores these days. Moreover, collecting money from the people her mother had worked for was not easy...the villagers were mean! 'Not today, we shall pay you tomorrow', they would say one day. 'The sale of paddy has been poor', they would say the day after. But no one would employ them if they dared to protest against this. How could one survive here with dignity? No, the townsmen were not as mean. She fumed within. 'Please keep your cool', ma had pleaded with her—'We have to live here after all. You have to return here again and again. It is here that your baba breathed his last. We had come here as refugees from East Pakistan. The party workers have given us a place to stay and we could lose it if we create trouble. As the saying goes, one who can tolerate, sustains; the one who cannot, perishes.' Tulsi looked at her mother. A tapestry of wrinkles lined the contours of her face. The winds of Pakistan still ruffled her untamed hair. Her uncles lived there even now, they still had some land there. It was a pity that they had never been to that place. A sigh escaped into the salty air within the room.

'What's this that I have been hearing, *khuku*?'

'What have you heard, ma?'

'You hit Ramakanta's rooster with the garan stem this afternoon and tore its plume into two, did you?'

'It was ravishing our hen to pieces; I was just trying to chase it away...'

'Just that made you hurt it so severely? But those people are the only hope we have. Who else is there to look after us? It's only because of them that I have kept you back. Who else would help us find a suitable match for you?'

'But they did fix a match for your second eldest! Her life is now ruined!'

'But that is how a woman's life is, *khuku*.'

'I don't agree, ma.'

'Ah, so this is what you have learnt in Kolkata!'

'Why just Kolkata, have I not stayed in Delhi too? At least I haven't turned to prostitution in the name of going to Delhi, like some of your neighbours.'

'Shut up, you silly girl! Let nobody hear you saying all this. Words like these travel far!'

'How does it matter to me?'

'It doesn't matter to you, right? It doesn't matter to you that your little sister has left home, does it?'

'No, it doesn't. It's because of your callousness that she has left.'

'She's your sister, *khuku*!'

'She might be. But didn't she leave because she wanted money? She had understood the power of wealth very early, and to think that I have spent all my life supporting you...if only I had all that money with me today...'

The mother and her daughter ruminated in silence. Clouds gathered in the sky. *Morani* was approaching fast. There would be a thunderstorm. Rain would drench the soil and the roots of the chilli plant would be soaked in water. The eldest daughter of the village headman's mistress would be getting married into a wealthy family in the month of Jaishtha. The would-be groom was a schoolteacher. Tulsi wondered about herself. Where would she end up? Where? Where? And then she saw all the darkness hovering over the meadows moving towards her—it is this darkness that would finally...

The mother and the daughter sat amidst the glow of the lantern. They had no idea where her brother was. It had already rained once in the evening and now there was a chill in the wind. How long would winter last this year? The villagers refused to look for a suitable match when requested. She is dark, she is too old, they would say—ma declared as she chewed on the *sajne data*, the long, slender, triangular seed-pods of the moringa or drumstick tree.

Tulsi listened to her quietly. Ma continued, 'I wish I could ask them why they had not made proper inquiries before suggesting the match for your sister. But I cannot. The boy is not right in the head. It is impossible to understand even half of what he says. That's why they wouldn't let him speak the day we finalised the wedding.'

'You couldn't even wait for me to be there. Everything was finalised before I arrived.'

'What else could we have done? Waiting might have ...'

'Very well, now suffer the consequences! My sister has to spend her entire life with that half-wit now!'

The mother and daughter went to bed. The son had still not returned. He must be chatting somewhere. He too was somewhat dim-witted like her son-in-law—how on earth would he manage to make ends meet, the mother wondered. She was no longer as strong as before, so the neighbours hardly gave her work these days. Even if they gave her work, they refused to pay for it. Was it possible to make ends meet all the year round with the fruits growing in and around their home or by cultivating chillies in the little land they possessed? Even the boy was of no help. He could not work, so no one gave him any.

There was hardly any kerosene left. The mother and daughter continued to sit in the dark. 'I do not want to stay here anymore', Tulsi said, 'there is no one to look for a match for me.' 'Would you have had to wait for this long if your father was alive? He would have got you married long back', ma replied. 'Why do you lament for that which can never be! Who can escape one's fate!' Could she have changed anything even if she had money?

At her employer's place, Tulsi had seen in a TV programme how a man had taken advantage of a girl and tried to run away after promising marriage. The court had ensured their marriage. But who would appeal to the court on her behalf? That man at her employer's place...

Hadn't masterbabu from Purulia or even the B.D.O. sahib from Dhakuria come to her for a change of taste? What had she been able to do about it? Yes, today she had been able to make some amends. She had been able to beat and ward off her neighbour's rooster. It had almost died; it would have served him right. It was pecking their hen to death! She herself had been battered, did that mean their hen had to suffer the same fate?

One day mastermoshai too had...but there was no goran stem at her disposal then...or else... But then what could she have done even if there was? It was a foreign land after all. But wasn't this a foreign land too? Who was here to call her own? No one but her mother and brother. Bhai was a half-wit, hardly able to do a thing. Ma kept worrying about him. If only her father was alive...

There was a *gher* outside the house. They had mortgaged it to deaf Haran at a time of crisis. They wanted to pay him back later, but he did not return the gher to them. Now he could catch fish from the pond and earned money by selling them. A few days ago, she had crossed the gher to catch fish near the riverbed. She had just immersed the bulky net in the water when he charged upon her in full regalia.

'Stop fishing right now!'

'Why should I? You don't own it, the government does.'

'You've learnt to mince words in Kolkata, haven't you?'

'What's wrong with that?'

But Tulsi did not argue any further. He was a 'leader' after all. These so-called 'leaders' of the poor were nothing but touts of the wealthy. Because of them, those who owned lands here were forced to sell them off and leave the village for good. I will give them a piece of my mind before the elections, fumed Tulsi. How they would try buttering her, how they would ask about her well-being, how their eyes would seek her...as if they would devour her whole with lustful intensity! And look at them now! How could people live here? What did she have to look forward to? Work was scarce, but not gossip...How much did you earn there? Where did your employers work? How much did they pay you? The endless questions drove her crazy.

'Didi, see what I have got!'

She stared in the dark at the pile of shrimps.

'Where did you get these from?'

'They have made huge water tanks in front of our gher. I put some bait and plunged the net in one, and up came the shrimps!'

'But dinner is already over...'

'What can I do about it? I've got these for you, now do whatever you want with them.'

As anticipated, Ramakanta came over the very next day hurling words of abuse at her for hurting his rooster. Ma scolded her and bhai said, 'We might have to leave the village because of you. You cannot carry on with such a temper. Who can find a suitable match for you after all this?'

'Do you think I am that desperate for you to find me one?'

'Ma says they'd never find a match, they have so many objections.'

'But they did find one for her younger daughter and now look at her plight!'

'At least I managed to get her married, what can I do for you? Tulsi is too dark; she is too thin, they keep saying...'

'Shut up! I'm sick and tired of hearing you brood over the same old things all day long.'

As soon as the rooster crowed early next morning, Tulsi woke up and began her household chores. She sprinkled cow dung all over the courtyard after a very long time. She stared at the reflection of the trees in the pond... Baba would stand and brush his teeth here, she remembered. If he had been alive, he would have got her married long back. Girls her age had already had a child or two...such sweet little creatures they were! They too would grow up one day.

Ramakanta's grandchildren often come over to play at their house. They frolic beneath the trees in the season of mangoes and jamuns...we never rebuke them for that, she reflected. She had brought with her a packet of candies when she returned home. She gave some to each of the children. They were thrilled! The girl named Tumpa was just like her employer's daughter. She spoke so sweetly! 'Won't you go home?', the girl had asked Tulsi.

'No. I won't. I shall stay here from now on.'

'Why? Won't you go back to Kolkata?'

'No.'

'Did the babus sack you?'

'Why would they sack me? I left of my own will.'

'I'm leaving now, do look after the house.' Her mother's words startled her. For how long had she been standing here? She was leaving for work. She knew they would not pay her but still, she would go. She and the rest of the family would be able to stay in this village, Tulsi would not. This was not the right place for her, and she knew it very well. Agriculture had taken over entire fields. Cows no longer grazed there and no longer pushed ploughs. Electric ploughs were used now. So many things were happening these days; only a suitable match could not be found for her. No one, no one could find a husband for her. Tulsi completed all her work in a trance. She took her lunch, fed the goats, ducks and hens. She hugged the frail hen for a long time, it felt as if she was hugging herself. Hadn't she too become terribly thin and pale? Her collar bone stuck out starkly against her neck, and there were crow's feet under her eyes.

That little girl came visiting again in the evening. Her hair was now tied with a red ribbon. She rushed in and climbed onto her lap. Her mouth still smelled of milk. 'Won't you go back home? You've killed our rooster, go away', she said with her infant stutter. Her words hurt Tulsi deep within. She did not belong here, and it was this child who had revealed this stark reality to her. She cuddled her and gave her a piece of candy. The child ran away.

The mother and daughter continued to discuss their future at night.

'There is no point in staying here.'

'I agree with you. The younger girls are much more efficient. No one is ready to give us work anymore.'

'This is why I feel we should all go to Kolkata. There's a lot of money in the city. We'd get some work or the other, and money would pour in.'

'But what will happen to the trees here? They had been planted by your father...if we leave, they'd be felled and sold off.'

'Do not worry, bhai would be there. Let him live life his way. He just has to fend for himself. No one would ever find a match for me. Don't you see how the same people who had advised you to bring me back turn away when they see you now?'

'That's true. But the bride's side cannot afford to have much ego, my dear. You have to accept that.'

'I am no longer interested in marriage. I shall work in the city, earn money and live well. I shall return only after I grow old.'

'Do whatever you think best—what more can I say?'

'Let me go and find some work, and then I shall come and take you with me. You pack your things in the meantime. Sell off the animals, or else someone will steal them and you'll be able to do nothing about it.'

'I have taken care of them for so long...'

'Such attachments yield nothing but starvation. Spare me the pain.'

The night grew old, so did the world. Sultry winds seeped through the cracks of the crumbling household. The resident snake gobbled up a rat. High tide followed the morani.

Tulsi deliberately missed the first steamer. The next one was due in two hours. She stood in the courtyard, facing the *Tulsi-manch*. Baishakh was on its way. Ma had hung a pot of water above the Tulsi plant, just as baba used to. She could still remember her father's voice. His face, however, was fast fading into oblivion.

The little girl came running. Her hair was not tied in a ponytail; the red ribbon, too, was missing.

'Are you going home?'

'I am.'

'When will you come again?'

'Let's see...'

'You'll bring candies for me, won't you?'

'Yes, I will.'

Perhaps Tulsi had been waiting for her. She caressed the girl's cheeks and ran her hands gently over the little head, and then she waved goodbye.

The child went on saying—'So you are going home...'

Tulsi began to walk towards the riverbank. Being late might cost her another steamer.

Translated from Bangla by Urmi Sengupta
Originally published as "Tulsi samachar" in *Golpo Pnachish*, 2008

18

Silt

Pranab Sarkar

One

The letter has been delivered just a while back. Basir miyaan is illiterate. As Mohor, his son, reads reads the letter, the contours of the father's face change.

As soon as the letter has been read, Basir distractedly goes back to scraping the *bakhari* and the monstrous weapon slashes through his flesh. In a split second, blood starts gushing from the wound.

This has been happening nowadays. Once a seasoned boatman known to dance on the serpentine waves of the Matla, Basir has now become absent-minded. His life's journey is nothing short of phenomenal. In one of his many adventurous strolls into the jungle, he had conquered the uncrowned king of the Sundarbans with one strike of his oar. He had fearlessly fought against the baton charge of the zamindars and the police during the Tebhaga movement, followed by imprisonment—it can be safely said that he has his own share of a glorious past.

Basir miyaan, the ex-Secretary of the boatmen's union, was feeling nostalgic that day. Memories of his youth kept flashing across his eyes. The complexion of Amina, Mohor's mother, was as fair as the sweet potato—it seemed as if nectar would ooze out of her fair skin at just a tender tickle. Her abundant black lustrous hair was like the demonic creek, reaching her hips. Was Amina solely to be accused of having an intoxicating aura? The electrifying youth of the Matla river equally maddened Basir. He could not survive even a moment without proximity to the creek; all of his love and affection was reserved for it. It is hard to pinpoint when and how Amina and the Matla became synonymous to him. Restless waves churned within his broad chest—the Matla flowed incessantly—Amina's gait—their motions merged somewhere. Which man can control his senses after witnessing such a splendid scene? No one. Is it easy to control oneself? Is it?

Two

Amina had been blessed with a beautiful baby boy. He was named Mohor. He grew up; he began attending high school after completing his primary education. When Mohor was in Class 7, Basir suddenly realised that he was ageing. His ebbing physical strength and poor eyesight served as constant reminders of his dwindling youth. He was no longer enchanted and exhilarated by either Amina or the Matla. The restless churning within his chest suddenly came to a halt.

Mohor followed Basir's footsteps. He took charge of the boat. His deep-seated desire to become a *bhadralok*, a gentleman, abruptly took a backseat. Can anyone name one man who has not spent at least one night of his life in Lane No. 7 of the red-light area of Canning? Liquid cash. Virile boatman. Sensing the precariousness of the situation, his parents consulted each other and fixed his wedding with Saima, the daughter of Janab Gazi of Sonakhali. Basir said, 'How long will Mohor flutter like a restless bird looking for a mate, if he has reason to come back home? Hahaha! Tie a rope around that bastard's neck tightly and bury the leash deep into the ground, so that he can only bleat meekly.'

Basir's intuition was right. After his marriage, Mohor would complete all his work as early as possible in the morning and return home. Once he returned, he did not even come out of his home to pee—the entire night was seemingly spent in hushed whispers and wild love-making.

This was a different game of the river. Mohor had learnt about the port from his father. The Sealdah-Canning railway lines were made to facilitate the establishment of Matla as the complementary port of Hooghly. Trains from Sealdah would directly stop at the bank of Matla. A municipality had also been built at one time. But the sudden alluvial deposits led to an unprecedented increase in the water level of the river. Thus, the port project had to be abandoned.

The boat service now no longer reached till Gauti Deuli, Harinda (Harindaha), Aamjhhara and Hede (Hridu). The lack of water created an insatiable thirst within Amina. On the one hand, countless people were jettisoned on the bank of Matla on a regular basis. And on the other hand, similar loaded buses used to come at the dockyard from places like Sharbere and Sonakhali. With neither ships nor port, the dockyard only resonated with old memories; the Matla flowed silently between her two banks, thronged by thousands of people. On nearly fifty boats, a host of boatmen, with their malnourished bodies and pale faces, waited with oars in their hands.

Taking a drag from their *beedi*s, a cluster of anxious faces sat on the doubly-thatched slanting roof of the union room of boatmen. The constant decrease in the number of passengers willing to cross the river in boats had resulted in a steady decline of their income and gave Mohor many sleepless nights. From his rich casket of proverbs, Goney chacha picks up one to soothe Mohor's anxious mind, '*Chinta korishne Mohor. Allah jokhon royechen du bela du mutho bhhater jogaar thik hoe jabaan*' (Don't worry, Mohor! Allah is there, and will provide you two fistfuls of rice twice a day.) Mohor heard him silently and remained very quiet. He had been this way the past few days.

Meanwhile, a new kind of imported machine was being fitted in the boats to stride across waters. A three-bladed fan was also attached below the boat; it cut across the flow with a strong deafening sound. The motor-driven boat was thus named '*bhatbhati*' on the basis of the unmissable sound that it produced while moving. On the south of the boat bank, a new union has been established for the motor-driven boats or steamers of the dockyard. The babus would try to scare Mohor with their incessant threats—'Don't create trouble or else you will have to be ready to face the consequences. If we fail to create a smooth system for the cross-over of passengers, our reputation will be at stake. Don't create a fuss over this just before the election. If you want to join us, let us know.'

Mohor retorted, 'No, there's no need for it. I can never join your party by cheating everyone else. If I have to embrace death, I would prefer to die out of hunger with those who have rested their faith on me. I cannot even think of deceiving them.'

In spite of their legacy, the boatmen's union continued to struggle to earn their livelihood, following the constant decrease in the number of commuters ferrying across the river. The number had almost reached zero. There was a logical reason for this decline. Who would have walked for ten minutes after getting down from the bus to reach the dockyard? The villagers were slowly becoming sophisticated and snobbish; they refused to waste their precious time walking to the bank. The number of people ultimately turning up was not enough to sustain the boating service. The families of the boatmen thriving on and around the dockyard area were hence undergoing the toughest times of their lives. Neither was there enough hay to cover the thatched roof of their ferry room nor did they have enough kerosene to light their stoves. On the other hand, the bank with the steamers was brightly lit by generators and passengers crowded the bank the entire day.

The net worth of the steamer bank had gone up to a lakh. The brother-in-law of some MLA had become the new *ijjatdaar*. How could Mohor fight with such powerful people? Menial labour had succumbed to the machines. There was nothing common between the brother-in-law of an MLA and old Basir's poor son, Mohor, the boatman. Feeling quite helpless, Basir miyaan had started working on daily wages in the nearby fields of chilli, watermelon and bitter gourd at Simultala. He had to opt for this alternative of earning a livelihood to help his family survive.

THREE

The panchayat elections arrived in due course and Mohor made his discontent clear vociferously. 'I cannot become a puppet in someone else's hands!', he said. But Basir seemed adamant; he was unwilling to allow him to contest the elections. Other leaders also pleaded with him, 'You're a dedicated old worker of the union. There's no other man as efficient as Mohor in this region. Only he has the ability to build this country and fight for the rights of the poor. Only he can become an able leader.'

Ultimately, the hard labour of the poor and hunger-stricken boatmen helped Mohor win the election and become a panchayat member. The public wanted him to either become the *pradhan* (panchayat head) or the *upa-pradhan* (deputy head) but the party never gave its nod in his favour.

Actually, Mohor wasn't one to unnecessarily flatter people. Those who did lived on the other side of the bank—instrumental in the appointment of the pradhan, upa-pradhan and *sabhapati* (president). Mohor did not quite measure up to the candidates presently serving in these positions. Still, it could happen. Nowadays anything is possible. That is why sons of ill-famed fathers are now at the helm of affairs and teach the mantra of revolution to the poor.

Mohor said, 'All of them are thieves, traitors, manipulators and liars.' What did Mohor get in return for joining a party that thrived only on the intent of satisfying the greed of the leaders and their kith and kin? He turned out to be of no use to his rebel friends and even thought of leaving the party. But he wished to unmask all the hypocrites before finally doing so.

But unfortunately, Mohor could not unmask the culprits. Instead, he had to bear the brunt of a show-cause for speaking against the party. Holding the show-cause letter in his hands, Mohor flashed a sarcastic smile and said, 'It's alright.'

'Go, Mohor!' Basir advised, 'Go to Canning. Talk to Panchu da and solve everything. Listen, your Swadesh chacha has become a minister now; he loves me. We have fought so many fights together. I shall talk to him. I shall go to Calcutta.'

Mohor replied, 'Don't you dare! We'll see what's in store for us! But you shall never go to them. All of them belong to the same group. You think Swadesh chacha is not aware? He's the one controlling the entire game. I would rather die of starvation than beg in front of these people. You don't need to worry about all these things.'

Four

Mohor is a completely jobless man now. In the winter, some Bagda spawns had drifted into the creek. Goney chacha said that 'the richness of the plough has come to the creek'. For the last few days, Mohor and Saima have been catching these prawns with their nylon nets as their sole source of income to make both ends meet. The whole creek now lies covered by these nets. There aren't many fish in there. Mohor mostly sits in the desolate and dilapidated union room for the boatmen, smoking a burnt *beedi*. A boatman or two often sits with him. Sometimes he lets out a sigh on seeing the empty boats huddled up against the swamped embankment. His inherited title of 'Secretary' sticks to his throat, much like the unwanted iron rod in the plough over the cow's shoulders. At times he is unable to breathe.

As the day proceeds, Goney chacha, Nojor Ali, Monto Koyal, Rafeek, Khalek and Haran Sheikh come down to the ferry hut located by the side of the river. One could almost count the bones in their emaciated tired bodies. Mohor could not meet their gaze these days; he rebuked himself every day.

They stared wide eyed at Canning town, its huge mansions buzzing with excitement across the creek. Just then, a steamer passes by making a faint sound. The young boatman is humming a line from a Hindi song. Mohor, suddenly sarcastic, says, 'What kind of a song is this, *Choli Ke Peeche Kya Hai? Sala*, sing a Bhatiali if you're a man!' Suddenly the steamer gets stuck in the sand. The boatman shouts, 'It won't go in any further. Everyone, get down!' The passengers start complaining, 'Take us to the side!' The boatman says that he can not as the boat would not go in any further. He almost forces the passengers down into the knee-deep water. The men and boys roll up their pants and get down while the women pull their saris over their knees, afraid of getting wet. The young boatman grins and whistles at them.

Mohor is incensed, 'Look at what these rascals are doing! As if they don't have women in their own houses. They're out to destroy the reputation of the fisherfolk!' Haran Sheikh agrees, 'They are first-grade bastards.'

FIVE

The election season is back. Political leaders from the other side of the river have started pouring in and delivering heavy speeches. Rafik and Khalek were sitting in the bus ghat when they apparently heard two of the weirdest rumours. These rumours had spread like wildfire. It has been five years since their marriage, but Mohor still has not been able to father a son. Was Mohor impotent or was it because his ill-fated wife was barren? This rumour has been doing the rounds. Mohor's mother had tried everything—doctors, quacks, trinkets, talismans, exorcisms and even the Pir's *dargah*. But she has not been able to change her son's luck. Nothing seems to work out. Rumour has it that Mohor did not sleep with his wife anymore. They kept bickering all the time, with or without any reason. Some of them advised—'Give *talaq* to your wife, she has dried up. She cannot bear you a son. If the breasts are dry, how will she feed her son?' Mohor laughed to himself, he never said anything. A bunch of fools, he thought. They say that Saima's breasts have dried up, divorce her. That woman is the Matla river, you idiots. How will you divorce her? Go divorce her if you can, if you have courage. Mohor knows that Saima is as intoxicating as the Matla, the drunken creek. The day the creek's breasts swell with waves, the boatmen would earn a paisa or two and that very day, saplings of *sundari* trees would blossom in Saima's heart. If your field does not yield crop, do you sell it off to some other farmer? Only if you till the ground, put manure and fertilisers will you reap a good harvest. One needs to water it with one's own blood, breath and tears. Similarly, Saima wants the same love and care—affection that would overwhelm her and leave her in raptures.

One remembers Bhagirath's tale in the Hindu Purana. Was there any agro scientist or river scientist better than him? But who would understand Mohor—his mind's expression, his heart's sorrows, his secret language? Nobody. Nobody.

Basir miyaan had gone to Kolkata yesterday to visit Swadesh chacha. Throughout the Tebhaga movement in Sandeshkhali, Deuli and Kalketla,

Basir miyaan had been Swadesh chacha's companion. He was more of a friend and a shield to chacha, always ready to protect him. Neither the zamindar's goons nor the police could touch a hair on his head. Khalek started saying, 'Don't know whether it's a rumour, but the minister has told chacha that Mohor bhaiya's job is confirmed. Next Friday he's coming over for a speech at the Canning Railway Ground and he will then hand over the appointment to Mohor bhaiya.' Montu remarked, 'Why are you silent, Mohor bhaiya? Please say something. Chacha must've told you everything. We won't usurp anything, please tell us what you're hiding.'

Mohor remained silent and unflinching. Nojor Ali and Goney chacha started saying, 'No, no, our Mohor isn't such a guy.'

Six

Today is that Friday evening. On that side of the river near the Canning Railway Ground, minister Swadesh chacha is arriving for his speech. There is a festive spirit all around. Thousands of people have arrived on this side, near the dockyard dam and bus-stand, bearing flags, shouting slogans and blood boiling with excitement. One more election. Uncountable steamers and boats are tired of ferrying innumerable passengers. Today, there is no dearth of passengers or money. But the passengers will not pay right away. Everything is saved for later. An informal agreement has been made, but to actually receive the money was another thing. Even a barren mother would experience childbirth before they got it. Rafiq said 'It's useless! Absolutely useless! Money, my foot! The leaders keep saying "All year round we let you use the embankment. We look after you. If you can't do that for one day for us, it won't be good for you", and get the work done by threatening us. Everybody knows that by now.'

Golam Sardar is a panchayat member. He came and said a bizarre thing to us and went away. 'Arey! Why are you all sitting so quietly? Ferry the passengers one after the other. We'll pay you in time. Why bargain so much when I am here? Seems like you guys aren't concerned at all. Haven't you heard what Swadesh Babu said in the meeting? In the coming month, work will start in the Matla. The banks will be cut. Big machines will dig up the sand and make it deeper. The flow will again be strong as before, boats will fly again and the ponds and lakes won't have any dearth of water. There will be as much rice as fish. There won't be poverty anymore. Ha ha! It's time, Fakir chacha and Amir bhai, it's our revolution!' All the Amirs and Fakirs started shouting—'The revolution is going on, it'll go on!', while filling their boats with the people and moving towards the gathering in the city on the other side.

On hearing Golam bhai, everyone was overwhelmed with joy. They could now dream of a full day meal and enough earnings.

Not only them, Mohor dreamt as well—once again the Matla will flow roaring in its strong currents. The waves will rise up. The mad waves of the furious monstrous Matla. Riding on those very waves with his small boat, Mohor will chide and tame them. Those waves will rise in Saima as well, and they will fall upon Mohor's small boat, furious and mad. He will keep dancing on the waves. Milky white foam covers his entire face and chest. Mohor wields the oars with his strong hands. Such happiness. Such joy! What contentment!

Suddenly, Mohor withdraws. His excitement subdues. He regains his consciousness, smiles wryly and says, 'Reformation? They're going to reform the Matla? Huh!' Now he starts counting on his fingers—'One, two, three, four, five, six, seven, eight, nine. This makes it the ninth time. Everything is tomfoolery. Only fooling people with lies. Do you understand, Khalek? When the voting season arrives, they also come. They make promises and then forget about them. They do not keep their word. Nobody will understand my mother's pain, my wife's pain, my pain or your pain. This river is my mother, this Matla is my…'

Khalek did not understand Mohor's words. Nobody did. Everyone thought that he had lost his mind.

Mohor laughed, cried, tore his hair apart, rubbed mud all over his body and sang…On the other side, the meeting had already started. One could hear Swadesh chacha's speech. Along with it, one could see thousands crowding over the meeting, swarming from nearby villages, crossing the river into the city as if on command. Everyone was supposed to go two or three times a year, and everyone was, except one. And that person was Mohor.

At one point, people saw a strange sight that left them astounded—the mad Mohor. A towel was tightly wrapped over his lungi. He held a shovel with both his hands and picking it up over his head hit the sand with it. He was removing the bed of sand with his shovel. One, two, three, four, five—hit after hit. All the slogans floating in the air resounded around him—'Zindabad!', 'Fight now and forever!'—creating a different atmosphere. Fire poured out of his eyes, and his face was filled with loathing and anger. Mohor hit the ground with his shovel at lightning speed, all the while laughing like a maniac.

He could see Saima standing in front of his eyes. Her heart gurgled with water and waves, one after the other. The mad Matla reinforced its strange game with Mohor. Again, his entire body was covered with milk-white foam. Mohor let out a terrible scream, which pierced the air and the sky.

Nobody knew whether that scream, after many a collision with those swamped embankments of the dry creek, reached the Railway Ground on the other side.

Translated from Bangla by Ananya Bhattacharyya and Manjari Thakur
Originally published as "Chora" in *Paharadar*, 2001

19

The Maneater, or Merely an Account of My Travel

BIKAS KANTI MIDDYA

∞

1

This perhaps is not exactly what you would call a story; it is more a recollection of an experience—a description of the journey to the attainment of that experience. It has neither a meaningful subject nor any object but is simply a narration of things seen as I travelled. This story contains all there is to say. Or perhaps it does not.

Anyway, by the time the steamer left Dhamakhali, the number of passengers was enough to unnerve any inexperienced person.

Every dog is a king in its own locality and not a single one lets go of the chance to show its power in its own area. When even dogs refuse to do so, what would stop a human?

That was why the ugly demon-like owner of the boat, following in the footsteps of the conductors of buses in Kolkata and refusing to take note of the objections raised by anyone, continued to load more and more people on the boat. In these places the measure of crowd or load in the boat is calculated not simply by the number of heads but by the gap between the edge of the vessel and the surface of the water. The edge of our boat was almost touching the water. Name one thing that had not been loaded! Humans, human babies, goats, goat-kids and their fathers, poultry, puppies, dried fish preserved in ice, *jhyatla*-mats, rice and coal, sacks of salt, tins of mustard oil, drums containing kerosene, and the wind carrying the whiff of country liquor stored under the wooden deck.

The myriad smells and sounds were thus overwhelming and it was impossible to discern one from the other. The crowd seemed to be a micro replica of India itself; people ranged from Hindus and Muslims to Christian tribals, travelling from one village to another, from a relative's house to one's own, or returning from Kolkata—from girl-students of colleges to net casters, to travellers from the market towns to the villages, from shopkeepers to suppliers. We were journeying from the city to the salt-land; city here meaning Kolkata and salt-land indicating Chhotomollakhali in particular and more generally the Sundarbans. The people referred to as 'we' consisted of only three characters—the narrator himself with his wife and their six-year-old daughter.

The *nouko*—no, here they don't use the term; it is either 'boat' or bhutbhuti. The bhutbhuti sputtered its way to the market of Mollakhali. It had started from Nyajat. It chose to travel upstream instead of taking the Raimangal which was the bigger river. The speed and the noise were equally powerful. The greed of the owner of the boat has already been referred to. Unsurprisingly, the boat was made to stop at every landing. Passengers waiting on the bank got in, and if not, then passengers got off the boat. In some places, embarking and disembarking took place simultaneously. Durga Puja was close and it was the Ramzan month as well; the period of fasting was about to end with the celebration of Eid. Migrant villagers were returning home. Shopkeepers were returning with newly bought stock for their shops as well. In addition to them there were the ordinary passengers. The boat was journeying from the north to the south—somewhere in the middle of the two 24-Parganas; it was high tide so it would take longer than usual to reach the destination. The question on everyone's mind was if it would be possible to reach before the evening set in—this by the way was not a question or a description. This was the gist of the conversation between two passengers. The enquirer was yours truly and the answer-giver was an outspoken local fellow, tall, shaven-headed and light-eyed. He had a supercilious attitude, perhaps because he had sensed I was new here. He talked a lot, but his verbosity only betrayed his ignorance. Nonetheless, he was reluctant to let go of the opportunity to establish his superiority. I realised that for someone as inexperienced as I was, in this voyage the talkativeness of the lanky fellow was an inevitable accompaniment to the sputter of the boat.

It was he who informed me—on the left was the North 24-Parganas, on the right the South. The Minister for Education was from the left, the Minister for Irrigation from the right. One belonged to the Namoh caste, the other one was a Pod.[1]

---

[1] Reference is to the castes of the ministers. Both belonged to the lower stratum of caste hierarchy.

I said, 'With two ministers in such close proximity, the prosperity of this area must be at its peak!'

The lanky one seemed to be a philosopher, a wise man and a farmer rolled into one. 'Prosperity only? Destiny too, the sister of prosperity. The political parties these two belong to are always locked in some conflict or the other: factional conflicts, CPM and RSP, etc. Not a single day passes without violence of some kind taking place.'

I was surprised at the level of indifference in someone born and brought up in this environment. What a saintly distance the gentleman maintained. I said, 'The physical appearances of the people here as well as the living conditions are proof of the poverty they suffer from. What motivates poor people like these to indulge in violence?'

Before I had even finished speaking, the gentleman burst out—'Poor people have less money but more obsessions. The scoundrels might not have enough food in their belly, but there is no dearth of intrigue in their hearts. Politics is at the very core of the rice they boil; it is the hooch in their very joints. They will die off due to this, one by one.'

It was evident that the gentleman was agitated for some reason. I preferred to move out of the shed on to the deck to avoid listening to the torrent of abuses the man was hurling toward some invisible mischief-makers.

The sun was beating down on the crowd with fiery intensity. People were as closely packed as chicken being transported in an Arambagh hatchery van or like caterpillars on branches of the *sajna* or *shiuli* trees. All of them were sitting on their haunches—their habitual posture. Whether it was the tribal couple or the dealer of dry fish, the owner of the ice factory, or even the faithful Muslims observing the *roja*—all sat on their haunches. The baby in arms of the tribal couple defecated like a duck, and a few moments later the duck in the packet defecated as well. Village women gossiped about domestic issues. Hawkers were plying their trade just as they do on urban vehicles—soft drinks, paans, *beedis*, lemon lozenges—four for one rupee each. Everyone was busy with their work and so no one objected to the misdeed of the tribal child, nobody got irritated because the duck had defecated. Only the faithful Muslims sat quietly. They were reluctant to talk and only responded to queries. It was difficult to believe in the truth of the words of the lanky one after seeing the mass of people on the deck. They all looked so harmless that even imagining them wielding guns was well-nigh impossible. How could they understand the language of the gun—they who lacked even the language to express their own feelings!

But my meditative state of mind did not last long. My daughter called out, 'Baba!' from under the shed and broke my reverie. It was absolutely no business of mine. I was out here on a trip with my wife and child. My destination was the residential quarters of the hospital my brother-in-law worked in—we would see the forest, the river, the high and low tides, fresh air, freshly caught fish, and if we were lucky enough to see the tiger in the wild, it would be a real story to tell the people of Kolkata. What need was there to gather such detailed information about the political scenario here?

Thinking thus, I quit the company of the people on the deck and went back under the shed.

2

Today was Saptami. I had planned to escape the urban excitement, the crowd, the blaring loudspeakers, and all of the Bengali hoopla by going away to the forest for a couple of days. But there was no respite here either. The sound of the loudspeakers coming from the villages by the riverside and the rush of children, women, men including the elderly was enough to establish the fact that Durga Puja is indeed the national festival of the Bengalis.

The urban mind is like a pigeon stuck in a coop; it gets deliriously happy with a little bit of open sky and fresh air. In addition, here was the golden sun of a late autumn afternoon stretching from the receding piece of land in the middle of the riverbed to the wide rice field fading into a distant village. Elsewhere one could find flocks of mynahs side by side, goat kids nestling against the mother goat and a calf running along the side of the river with its tail up. Our noisy boat passed by a rise on the riverbank where an old man was weaving a net on a bamboo frame under a peepul tree. There was no spark of interest in his eyes—yet life was like a poem here. There was an abundance of greenery, of detachment, of open sky, the freedom of the fresh air—it was so difficult to believe what the lanky man had said about this world. I had tried my hand at imaginative literature in my middle age, as a result of this the emotional quotient of my writing was very high. I chose not to remember the lanky one any longer in order to retain my mental peace.

During our journey, the moon which had been accompanying us from above had taken on a silver hue. Our boat touched the landing at Chhotomollakhali by the time it was evening. The market of Chhotomollakhali was just by the riverside, illuminated by rows of lights. On the opposite bank were Aamtali, Puinjali, Kumirmari—all were lit up by rows of tubelights (people here call them 'rods'). They burned perpetually, even when there were no festivals, as the electricity was produced by burning wood and the powerhouse was close by.

Meanwhile, the high tide was over and the ebb tide had started, so the boat ended up stopping at the broken landing instead of at the jetty. I disembarked with my daughter and my wife teetering on bricks stuck in the mud. Piles of garbage from the market covered the bank of the river beside the broken landing (where usually the water of the high tide did not reach). In the failing light of the evening some pigs were still grunting and frolicking in the garbage consisting of leftovers from the market.

After the arduous journey which had lasted five hours, I had not imagined that the hospital quarters would be this beautiful. In a locality like this, especially a village where communication and electricity supply were so poor, we had not expected to find running water and electric lights.

Next to the hospital was a pool (with fishes) bordered by rows of coconut trees. A bevy of white ducks roamed about fearlessly from the gate of the hospital to the side of the pool, making their presence known through constant trumpeting.

The double soling brick road was bordered by mango, *jamun*, jackfruit, *babla*, *lambu* and *jibon* trees; it was hard to imagine that the soil was saline. Equally difficult to comprehend was the fact that the Sundarbans were so close by and that in the not-so-distant past this area used to be a part of the jungle where tigers roamed, and that even now the big cat made sudden visits. What was even more surprising was the fact that despite being a government hospital, the walls were free of posters on family planning or prevention of AIDS. The yellow wall was only covered by a list of rules regarding the regimen of treatment of tuberculosis. Apparently, social health was top notch, the only worry was people's physical condition.

Our intention behind the visit to Chhotomollakhali was to see the forest, a tiger or two, spend time in a healthier environment, and to meet new people as well as to see new places, but my father-in-law had added a chore to the list saying, 'As you're travelling to rural areas, perhaps you can also enquire if there are any marriageable girls there. The nature and behaviour of young women from the city is suspect, as you know from experience. Girls from villages are still unspoilt. Please ask around when you're there.'

Carrying this load of expectations we entered the hospital complex, where the doctor was busy with his private practice. Seeing us, a middle-aged woman opened the gate of the hospital quarters and we realised that she was the domestic help. The responsibility of welcoming us had fallen on her shoulders and it was a task she carried out with unexpected professionalism, saying, 'Boudi, there is still some lunch from the afternoon. You may eat if you're hungry. I'll come again at seven in the evening.' It was evident that she worked in other residential quarters as well.

This was a bachelor's establishment. We had not been sure about the arrangements there, so it had seemed reasonable to carry our food with us. We had hardly served the *muri* and *shingara*s bought from Chhotomollakhali on to our plates, when someone who seemed to have come straight from a pyre, an interruption incarnate, opened the gate and entered the room without so much as a by your leave, 'Kakima, O kakima, where is our kaka?', and prostrated herself.

'Oh dear, what on earth are you doing? Does one touch the feet of someone younger in age?', my wife hopped back a few steps but there was no escape for her.

Pat came the response which seemed to have had been rehearsed, 'What if you're younger than me? By relation you are senior.'

I was a bit angry with my brother-in-law. Were these living quarters or was it a busy street crossing? I found myself deeply irritated by this 'interruption'—what did she mean by 'seniority in terms of relation'? My keen appetite was ruined.

But when she persisted and asked, 'Kaki, who is this fellow?', I lost my cool for a moment and it seemed to me even the father of Mini would have been less embarrassed when he faced questions by Mini.[2] But it did not take me long to figure out that she was 'not quite all there', so I replied tongue-in-cheek to this so-called niece of ours, that I was an attendant waiting upon her kakima, and was actually carrying her luggage.

But before she could sort out this puzzle her kakima herself answered, 'He is the brother-in-law of the doctor here.'

The 'interruption' seemed to have had both questions and answers recorded inside her. 'Oh, it's the brother-in-law of our kaka. Which means you are my pishemoshai. Where is pishima?' and she prostrated herself once more in front of me. I did not try to avoid it. It was evident she had a lot of respect for us, and in return we could give her nothing. Silently I blessed her, but she was not ready to forego the gift that usually accompanies such

---

[2] Reference to Tagore' short story *Kabuliwala*, where the narrator's young daughter used to embarrass him by asking uncomfortable questions

blessings. She immediately asked, 'I touched your feet, are you going to let me go empty-handed?'

Really, there was no end to my stupidity! We simply had to remedy that by giving her a fistful of muri and a couple of shingaras, but the questions continued unabated. She knotted the shingara and muri in the *anchal*, wrapped it around her waist and then resumed the interview. 'Pishemoshai, we'd have been happier if you brought pishima along.' Instead of complicating the situation further and with the intention of getting rid of her I pointed toward my wife and said, 'She is actually your pishima.'

The information seemed to shock her, 'O God, I really thought she was our kakima!' Since the kakima had now transformed into pishima there was another round of prostration for her, followed immediately by another query, 'Tell me pishima, are you really Bangals?'

I thought the next question would be about the Bangals' obsession with the High Court.[3] I muttered to myself what a strange creature this was, but asked loudly, 'What about you?'

I am not sure why but the question seemed to trigger a torrent in response—'My name is Binapani. We are Hindus. Baba gave me a sari this time, and kaka gave me some money. My husband was admitted in this hospital. Since then, I've started calling the senior doctor baba and the junior one kaka.'

Finally, the reason behind her obsession with the kaka-kakima and her garrulity were explained. Not only was her name Binapani, she seemed to be the goddess of words and knowledge herself. Only, instead of a veena she was carrying a broom. However, it still seemed impossible to dislodge her from where she was.

But we were spared the task as the next visitor did it for us. This was no ordinary visitor, suddenly I found a tall and bald figure standing just outside the verandah. He had sunken eyes and cheeks; his large teeth jutted out reminding one of a tiger. The teeth resembled spades so their exhibition was easy. When the stranger greeted us from outside with all his teeth exposed, for the initial few moments I mistook him for a tiger, but coming out on to the verandah I found it was indeed a human, not a big cat. He stood there with folded hands and said—'Namoskar, when did you all arrive?

---

[3] Refers to a Bengali popular saying about the gullibility of Bangals who were from the countryside and would be awestruck by the majestic buildings of Kolkata, especially the Calcutta High Court.

I am Nitai Tarafdar, the diet supplier to the hospital (representative of the hospital canteen). The doctor will arrive soon.'

Courtesy demanded that we offer him shingaras, and these he accepted gladly, rubbing his hands. The gesture was definitely fly-like but the attitude was canine. If he had a tail, it would have certainly wagged.

When Nitai was halfway through his own meal, my brother-in-law arrived. We breathed a bit easy as he finally left with his shopping list. We then learnt the details of Binapani and Nitai's lives. Binapani's son and husband used to smuggle wood out of the jungle. Her husband fell prey to a tiger and though he was rescued and admitted to this hospital, he finally succumbed to his wounds after seven days. Binapani lost her sanity after that. Her son continued to go to the forest. He was married but neglected his mother. She did not put down roots anywhere either, spending the major part of her day sweeping in the hospital, and working as a sweeper at other places as well. She muttered to herself all the time. The broom was her constant companion.

Nitai Tarafdar on the other hand was an interesting character, like a star that had deviated from its orbit. He had been a Naxalite once; now he was an agent for the Revolutionary Socialist Party. For some time he had worked as a middleman between the police station and the settlement office. But ever since he had bagged the contract of supplying special meals, not food, for 25 to 30 patients in the hospital, he was doing rather well with free government accommodation and a profit of 50% as perks. In addition, he had some 'side' businesses as well. He had settled his son in a windowless room in the Chhotomollakhali market as a video display operator. 'Select' movies for select viewers were shown there. The earning was not negligible. Moreover, once a month he brought a marriage registrar over from the town for registration of local marriages. Along with all this, he was currently following my brother-in-law around, doing everything from shopping to running errands of any kind. In exchange he received some pocket money and breakfast and dinner and if something good had been cooked, then lunch as well, all at the expense of the doctor.

The first night of the trip we dined on the country chicken brought by Nitai. The next day was a holiday. That was the reason why Nitai's shopping bag was overflowing with *parshe*, *bekti*, *koi*, catfish and crab. As the cook was late in preparing the dishes I went out on my own before I took a shower. On my right was the river, almost overflowing its banks with the high tide, and on my left lay mud huts with thatched roofs. Beyond them were the paddy fields half-submerged in rainwater; the green seemed to almost touch the blue sky. The trees close to the river bank were of the mangrove kind, with aerial roots—*bani* and *keora*. The trees on the left bank of the river grew in the clayey soil—rain tree, tamarind, neem, coconut, occasional mango, jamun and jackfruit trees. Like the trees, the human accommodations were also varied—some were huts built on pillars of the wood from the tress of the forest, some had walls of clay, and some were made of cement. My brother-in-law had informed me that there were three kinds of economic stratum here: the local rich, local poor and people who had amassed riches in towns. Most of the rich people were prosperous from selling paddy, to this category had been added businessmen and owners of fisheries. They were aided by political parties. The poor, on the other hand, are poor everywhere, they do not have any specific identities. But there was a difference between the urban poor and the island poor, as the latter were not crafty by nature. They gave straight answers to queries. The most complicated lot apparently were the middle classes—complicated bastards and devils of the first order. They were the first to raise protests if there were lapses, but were also most likely to choose a wrong way of life—the bourgeoisie in every country have the same nature.

There were a number of other places in the Mollakhali market apart from Nitai Tarafdar's son's place, where side-by-side with the bigger video parlours there showed films with pirated CDs. Micro CDs had flooded the market. The most delectable rumour was that Dr Pralay Das, who had obtained his MBBS degree backed by the money begotten of paddy sales and also owned a fishery, was watching blue films with his wife. The next-door neighbour, grocer Ananta Mondal discovered that the blue films that Dr Pralay were being transmitted on his TV set as well. Since then, there was an unending secret supply of BFs in that locality. I continued to think of this as I walked along. Paddy fields and long canals joined together to form fisheries and small ponds filled with *shapla*s and *shaluk*s. Kingfishers sat in wait for the fish on *babul* branches emerging out of water, and elsewhere dragonflies were mating. In this endless cycle of creation how could anyone blame Pralay for playing his part?

3

The next day we geared up to fulfil the real intention behind coming to Mollakhali. We wanted to see the forest and the tiger. I was the most excited of us three; in fact, I had not even slept properly the last night. I had never been to any forest, neither seen a tiger outside of a zoo. And here I was now, going to the tiger's own land. My fear and excitement were inevitable.

My brother-in-law had arranged for the boat. It belonged to Kamalbabu, the owner of the pharmacy where he had his private clinic. Kamalbabu was a good man; he actually was a politician and dealt with the general public and so had to either be good or present himself as 'good' to them. He was an elected member of the Zila Parishad and was the right-hand person for the Zila Sabhadhipati. Ministers or dignitaries chose Kamalbabu's residence as stopovers when they were in the area. We started our journey early in the day with a letter from him (addressed to the forest ranger).

But as soon as we got into the boat and noticed the number of passengers, I recalled my father-in-law and his instructions.

There were very few passengers. Apart from the boatman and his son there were four of us and three others including the sister-in-law of Kamalbabu, his daughter who was an HS student and his son who was in Class 7. Kamalbabu wielded enormous power in this area. I was already aware of the rumour that he had a dormant desire to marry off his sister-in-law. But Kamalbabu had to fulfil the demands of his brother-in-law and sister-in-law in order to reach his goal. As we had been issued an invitation for lunch at Kamalbabu's house before the boat had even left the bank, this was a possibility which could not be ignored so easily. His sister-in-law had seemed a nuisance at first, but was presentable and was a graduate from Pathankhali College. I had no objections, particularly as my brother-in-law was a divorcee following a very short marriage. All I wanted right now was to tour the Sundarbans; my principal objective was to see the tiger. I was suddenly reminded of the short story "Tope" (The Bait) by Narayan Gangopadhyay. The swift invitation for lunch led to the formation of a multidimensional image of the very story in my mind. In the soft light of the early morning the demonic sputtering of the mechanised boat on the quiet river made me uneasy, but the temptation of seeing the forest and the tiger was too strong.

Our boat moved forward passing on its way Kumirmari, Marichjhanpi, Baghna and further south to Burir Dabri. Water, water and more water. My mind did not get tired seeing water all around; on the other hand the wide expanse of forests triggered a complex feeling of fear and excitement. Eating and recreational activities were all taken care of within the boat. It was a large vessel and passengers were too few.

Our boat kept close to the riverbank as it journeyed on its course. Villagers on tiny boats were catching prawn seedlings. Fishermen had spread large nets in the middle of the river and sounds from tape-recorders and FM radio came floating out of the trawlers. The noise of the boats drowned the sound of the waves as well as human voices.

After we presented the letter from Kamalbabu to the assistant ranger (a very helpful gentleman) of the forest at Baghna and introduced ourselves—the brothers-in-law—we received permission to travel further south. The ranger was a very helpful gentleman. The boat—controlled by the machine, and the trees—nurtured by the forest, ran side by side. The boatman Kalipada—the father of Bhola—was my guide. Even he had sensed my obsession with forests and my lust for tiger-sighting. He introduced me to the trees of the forest, the water and the fish, crabs and other creatures inhabiting it—everything that was visible to us. Strange trees made their appearances in the forest, their names I had heard perhaps—*pondu, dhundul, goran, genoa, gol, garjan, bani, keora, hental, tawra, sundari*. It was Kalipada who informed me, 'The tiger hides itself in the hental bushes.' I asked him, 'How do you know that?'

'With my life, babu.'

'What do you mean by that?'

'I realised how dangerous the hental bushes were only after I lost my father to the tiger.'

'How long ago did this happen?'

'I was almost Bhola's age then.'

'What happened after that?'

'Since then I have been serving Kamalbabu. I drive his boat now. Sometimes I also catch fish.'

I asked exactly like an urban journalist-in-training, 'What varieties of fish does the river yield?'

'Different kinds, babu. Like *rekha, med, pankhaki, paira, danne, chhile, pellet, gurjaoli, tare, kaepet, banshpata, parshe, bekti, nihete, aar* and many more!'

'And how do you catch crabs?'

'For that, babu, you have to enter into deep and narrow creeks. It is very risky.'

My questions sounded pretentious even to my ears. I wanted to ask myself what value these hypocritical questions had for an urban writer who would write stories based on vicarious experiences of the Kalipadas of the world who actually bled.

But I had no courage. I was half-dead with fear as we walked along the protected lane to the watchtower after disembarking at Burir Dabri. The happiness of seeing nature was completely eclipsed by the anxiety for self-preservation. Bhola, the twelve-year-old son of Kalipada reprimanded me, 'How can you visit the forest if you're so afraid for your life? What will you do when you see a real tiger?'

Our visit finally came to an end with the sighting of a deer, a monkey and wild fowl. When we returned to our quarters that night somehow there was cooked deer meat for dinner. It still seemed to carry the flavor of the grass and the soil. Later we heard that that had also been managed by Kamalbabu.

We suspected that Kamalbabu was very well connected. But the next day when we visited his house on his invitation for lunch, we found that our assumptions had fallen far short of the reality. We were served sixteen courses of fish and meat with a chutney of wild *keora* as accompaniment. The garden was a riot of colours. There was no lack of trees in the Sundarbans, and no dearth of furniture in Kamalbabu's house. But the trees were brought to Kamalbabu's garden and domesticated according to someone's caprice, as none of them were indigenous to the forest; all were imported. They were not the common trees of Bengal like jamun, jamrul, mango or jackfruit. Most were imports from the south of India. There were grapes, apples, pears and pomegranates; white, red, blue hibiscuses; white roses, black *rangans*; gourds on the ground, pineapples in pots; perennial mangoes, jamuns and litchies; litchie-flavoured eggplants; coconut trees with the capacity of producing a thousand fruits, or producing green coconuts only annually, and much more. It was a forest inside another, almost a different kind of world. It was difficult to say which one was natural, and which one man-made.

After the meal we were taken for a visit to the fishery. It stretched over fifteen bighas of water. Parshe and prawns were farmed here. The owner informed us that officers from the Department of Fisheries in Andhra Pradesh had come for a survey and assured him a sum of five lakh rupees the next year.

We saw everything—the fish, the fruit, and the girl as well. On our journey back the pet ewe of our maid Dolly also gave birth to her lambs—everything was a good omen.

As it was Bijaya Dashami, we were offered another invitation even before the *bijaya* greetings were over—'Please be ready for an outing tomorrow afternoon. There will be a boat-race at Amtali bazaar, we'll go to watch it together.'

I objected, 'But the day after tomorrow I have some urgent business. We're leaving tomorrow.' I was tempted to stay back as I had never seen a boat-race, but there was a seminar. I had to write my paper, and I had to include my observations on the socio-economic conditions here.

Kamalbabu refused to take my objection into account. 'Of course, you'll go, but the day after. Come, watch the *baich*, you'll like it. This boat-race is a major event in this area.' The temptation was too powerful to be ignored. This seemed to be a good way of getting acquainted with the culture here as well. I said, 'We'll watch the boat-race, but we didn't get to see the tiger.'

'Come for a longer visit in the winter, will try to show you some. But you know what, the sighting of the tiger depends much on one's luck.'

I said, 'Luck betrayed us this time. Let us see if Lady Luck is kinder to us in the Christmas holidays. But I shall definitely come. I'm determined to see the tiger either in the open or inside the forest and to spend the night in a fishing boat.'

The fervour with which I spoke made Kamalbabu ask me, 'What seems to be the matter? I can understand your desperation to see the tiger, but what is this about spending nights in fishing boats?'

It is said that when the young deer starts growing its horns, it tests its strength by butting its head unnecessarily into different objects. I had started fancying myself as a writer. So I needed experiences, lots of them. Like a ragpicker I had started out on an errand to fill my empty sack with experiences. Before I could respond, the doctor interjected, 'Actually my brother-in-law has started writing a bit, that is why.'

It made Kamalbabu laugh. 'Yes, of course. Arrangements will be made for tomorrow, and also when you revisit with more time in hand.'

4

The next day, as planned, Kamalbabu's boat was ready for viewing the boat-race. Despite being in a hurry we went to watch it as it was to be a new experience.

There was a confluence of three rivers near the Amatali bazaar—it was a wide expanse. There were two hundred boats and ten thousand people at least with viewers on water as well as land. The sputter of the motor launches, the sound coming out of the loudspeakers, the drumbeats of the immersion, the raucous celebration of the public—there was a mad excitement centred around the boats competing in the race. The supporters of specific boats were shouting themselves hoarse—it was a normal enough atmosphere for the occasion. In the first race the leading boats came very close to one another and the competition was at its peak; but the accident happened during the second race.

If the boat which had come first in the first race also led the second one, the competition would have had come to a peaceful end. But a member of the team of the boat in the second position, presumably to keep the competition alive, struck the first one unethically, and the former turned around and fell back. This minor action on the water immediately had its reaction in the form of fights on land. The celebratory mood of the crowd turned sour in an instant. The violence was unimaginable. Though the boat we were in was on the water, the riot on land made us tremble; my wife was upset and my daughter started crying in fear.

In the evening there was a *jatra* performance in the Amtali bazaar—the title had been changed from *The Hanging of Dhananjay*[4] to *The Convict at the Gallows*. The earlier fight had been resolved for the time being with police interference and the help of local leaders.

With all the excitement over, we wanted to get back home without any more hassle. That night we returned to our quarters, but next day on our way back early in the morning we got stuck in Amtali bazaar. I got off the motorboat with luggage and my family with the intention of travelling on a motor van from Sandeshkhali which was on the opposite bank to Dhamakhali, but found that the jetty was full of people. I could hear crying—five women including two young women were lying prostrate on the ground and crying inconsolably. One of the young women seemed pregnant. A handful of dusty kids were also part of this mourning. The crowd was whispering and there were a feeling of suppressed tension all around. A few steps before the jetty started, there lay bodies of two dead young men with their throats cut.

I had seen dead bodies earlier—of natural deaths, deaths by disease or by accident. But that was the first time I saw murdered bodies—fresh blood, turned-away faces, open eyes. The sight made me close my eyes in horror.

I opened my eyes to find Binapani with her inseparable broom, and the outspoken lanky fellow, my acquaintance from the first boat, in the crowd.

---

[4] Dhananjay Chatterjee was given life-sentence on conviction of rape. His story has been the represented in popular media many times over.

In a moment I remembered his words, 'Poor people have less money but more obsessions. The scoundrels might not have enough food in their belly, but they have no lack of intrigue in their hearts. Politics is in the very heart of the rice they boil, hooch in their very joints. They will die due to this, one by one.'

In a minute there was an unannounced *bandh*—markets, motor vans, vans and motorboats, everything stopped functioning. But it was imperative that we returned that very day.

Sensing the atmosphere my not-quite-six-year-old daughter said, 'Baba, go and see the tiger now.'

In support, my wife, 'Now decide what you want to do. You and your obsession! Is it that easy to see tigers?'

I kept quiet for a few minutes before defending myself, 'You're quite right. The sighting of the tiger depends on one's luck, but you know what, that is true only for wild tigers. But we've experienced the violence unleashed by the maneater who has entered the human habitation, the land of the saline and soft soil, though we didn't see it with our own eyes. Don't you think witnessing that is also a matter of luck? Let my seminar go to hell. At least I got to experience something real and authentic here!'

Translated from Bangla by Sucheta Bhattacharya
Originally published as "Narokhadok athoba nichhawk ekti bhromon brittanto"
in Debprasad Jana ed., *Katha Sunderban*, 2008

20

The Will to Live

BISWAJIT HALDER

In the middle of autumn, the echoes of Chandi Path filled the sky. It was two days after Mahalaya. Durga Puja was only five days away. The frenzied phase of shopping was, more or less, over. Only the people of Saatjelia Colony *para* were left with their shopping. This para was situated on the banks of the Gomor river and primarily consisted of shanties. The people here were mostly fishermen living on half-empty stomachs and a diet of *shaak* and rice, and earned their livelihood by catching Bagda spawns in the river. However, the women of this para were more adept at this task.

The lives of the girls belonging to poverty-stricken patriarchal families in this land are similar to those of the girls in tea gardens—girls who pluck two tea leaves and a bud with their flower-like tender fingers and who are forced to grow up suddenly as their tender fingers become blunt over time due to sheer hard work and struggle, unbeknownst to them. Similarly, for the girls of this land, there is no question of attending schools—leave alone completing their education—owing to their poverty. The direction of their lives depends on the course the river takes. These are women who by having to migrate from the bend of one river to another, end up as wives even before their adolescence is over. Their lives hinge on fishing nets which they must throw and pull daily. No one knows when their hands become stronger than these nets—even more so, their minds.

The men in this para do not waste their time catching fish. They go to the forest on the other side of the river to gather wood.[1] At the end of the night, amidst the darkness, five to seven men leave in a boat with choppers

---

[1] The Bengali word for gathering or collecting wood or for cutting down trees in the Sundarbans is *khep*. There are other words for tasks such as fishing or gathering honey, etc.

and axes in tow. They return at the end of the day after sunset. What they are left with after giving the owner of the boat his share does not amount to more than eighty to hundred rupees per head. Their happiness knows no bounds on the days they return after cutting trees. On those days, they are the buyers of the most expensive items in the Tuesday market. Some of these men even end up going to the goldsmith with an advance to get nose rings for their wives.

Mahadeb had gone to gather big logs this time, which was an arduous task involving very hard work, but the money to be earned was also more. One could easily earn one thousand to one-and-a-half thousand rupees for eight to ten days of work at a stretch in this area. Pack your bags, stock up rations, keep the crocodiles in the water and the tigers in the forest and of course the forest guards at bay, and there would be no deficiency in their poverty-stricken household for about ten days. Even Panu Morol, the owner of twenty-five *bigha* land in the para could not challenge them when it came to food, behaviour and lifestyle.

Aghor, Shashi, Rabi and Mahadeb are companions in Sheetal da's boat. Sheetal not only owns the boat but also steers it, which is why he does not have to row against the tide for two or three days at a stretch while going to gather wood. He just sits next to the rudder at the rear of the boat. Sometimes, if he is in a good mood, he starts humming songs about the greatness of Bonbibi.

It was one of those days, and he was singing the tale of the tyrannical Dakshin Rai's defeat to his heart's content

> 'Barkha Gazi says, noble mother, listen to me,
> And take pity on me.
> Do away with your anger towards Dakshin Rai,
> For this reason, I have come to you.
> On hearing this, compassion arose in mother,
> And she lovingly began to speak.
> In these eighteen archipelagos, I am the mother of all.
> Sorrows of all those who call me *maa* will be washed away…'[2]

---

[2] The song which is dedicated to Bonbibi is originally in Bangla and is taken from a text called *Bonbibi Jahura Nama* (1881 CE) by Munshi Mohammad Khater. The Bengali lyrics are as follows:

> *Kohen borkha gaaji shuno nekmaai,*
> *Tomar hujure maago ei bhikkha chai.*

While listening to the sorrowful tale of deliverance, the companions fling their oars into the water, creating a splash. As they imagine the idol of Bonbibi, they stare at the forest and bow their heads in utmost reverence.

Shashi also bows his head in reverence once. Then, turning towards Mahadeb who is standing beside him, he says, 'Do you see Mahadeb-da? Do you see the way she has become one of our thirty-three crore gods! So what if she is a Muslim girl!'

Mahadeb does not think it necessary to reply to Shashi. He is lost in a world of his own while listening to Sheetal's tune. He thinks about the brother-sister duo and the cruel father who on the orders of his eldest wife gave away his younger wife Golal to the forest. Without any means, the helpless Golal gave birth to two children in the forest by herself. Those two orphans grew up to become the rulers of the forest—Bonbibi and Shah Jangali. Poor man-eater Dakshin Rai! The mother-son duo[3] had to be satisfied with their share of Kendokhali after losing the battle with Bonbibi and Shah Jangali. Mahadeb took an oath, 'We must observe ma's Hajjot with pomp this time. I will make Sheetal-da read the *puthi*. Sheetal-da has a melodious voice!' He couldn't help but praise Sheetal da's voice.

Puja is around the corner. This is why Mahadeb did not want to prolong his stay in the forest this time. Apart from that, he realises that the stock of rice at home would not last for more than a couple of days after his departure. During high tide, one cannot find many Bagda prawns either. His wife Haridasi who catches fish will have to make do somehow. Who knows whether Bidhu and Mangal are crying and making a scene at home by asking for new clothes for the Puja!

Dakshin Rai-r por kop koro dur,
E khatir aailam tomar hujur.
Etok shuniye maayer doya upojilo,
Sodoye hoiya maata bolite laagilo.
Aathero bhaatir modhya aami sobakaar maa,
Maa bole je daake taar dukkho thaake na...

[3] The mother-son duo here refers to Dakshin Rai and his mother Narayani who lost the battle against Bonbibi and her brother Shah Jangali. Kendokhali is a forest tract full of honey. Hence it was allotted to them.

Bidhu and Mangal are Mahadeb's sons. They have been desperately anticipating their father's return at Sheetal's house. Every morning, the moment the boys start to cry and hanker for new clothes for the Puja, Haridasi sends them over to Sheetal's house cleverly, saying, 'Go and see whether your father has returned yet. He said that he'll be bringing new clothes this time.'

The toddler Punti also cries, not for new clothes but milk. Rice has been scarce for the past two days at home. Around this time of the year, no one wants to lend any money either. Before Puja, nobody wants to end up empty-handed themselves. Due to the shortage of food, they have had to take out every single grain of rice from the pot[4] as well.

This is why Punti cries a lot these days; even more so when her biting does not yield even a single drop of milk from her mother's dry breasts. Haridasi, unable to bear the pain, cries out, 'Oh God, this girl will kill me!' Subsequently, she slaps her daughter, who starts to cry even more loudly.

On hearing her cries, the neighbour Rathin's wife brings over a bowl of rice starch. Haridasi tries to cool it down by blowing on the bowl and holds it near her daughter's mouth. On seeing this, Dinu's handicapped wife shivers and cries out, 'Dasi-di, what are you doing! How could you hold such a warm bowl of rice starch near the girl's mouth without cooling it down properly! She will have an upset stomach! Cool it down and add a pinch of salt in it at least.'

'Let her have an upset stomach. I'll be at peace only when all of you die.'

There is a lot of frustration in Haridasi's words, but Dinu's wife also observes that she has removed the bowl of rice starch from Punti's mouth. By then, Punti has also stopped crying and is giggling while staring at the cheap dangling nose ring on Dinu's wife's nose. On seeing this, Dinu's wife also starts to laugh, and with a sudden pull takes Punti on her lap with one

---

[4] The Bengali source text uses the words *ghoter aagchal* which is very specific to the Sundarbans. Every home in the region has a *ghot* or an *aghandi* (literally meaning a pot) where people pour in a handful of rice each time someone in the family brings rice from the market. This pot of rice is not touched unless an emergency arises, since this pot is supposed to be used as the last resort. Since the words are extremely culture-specific, an exact English equivalent is difficult to find.

hand and while caressing her head says, 'You unlucky woman, should you be saying such things on a Thursday!' On remembering what day it is, Haridasi quickly bites her tongue.

It is almost evening. Lamps have not yet been lit in all the houses. The small, shiny waves of the salty river water can still be clearly counted from atop the road. Anil, Kedar and Monotosh had returned in their boat after cutting trees yesterday. Subal and Aziz's boat had come back this morning. They knew that once Puja started and if they did not return early, the dealers would reduce the price of wood. As a result, they would have to sink piles of wood in the river in fear of the forest guards and spend the entire duration of the Puja empty-handed. Once the Puja ended, it would take about fifteen days to a month for the prices of wood to rise again. By then, the creditors would have also started to harass them. Therefore, the woodcutters try to come back from the forest while the prices of wood are still high; most of the people in this para have come back home accordingly. The only boat that is left belongs to Sheetal.

This was the first time that Mahadeb had gone out in Sheetal's boat. He used to go in Kedar's boat earlier. However, the last time, after coming back and taking his share of spices and supplies, he had had an argument with Kedar's widowed elder sister. The argument was regarding the fact that apparently, Kedar's widowed elder sister had kept more than their share of the turmeric powder. Mahadeb's fault was that after he came to know about this from his wife Haridasi, he had gossiped about this with the rest of the companions of the boat and had told everyone. And that was it! The moment this gossip reached Kedar, he had dropped the main conspirator Mahadeb from his crew; a boat owner like Kedar could not tolerate the audacity of an ordinary boatman like Mahadeb.

After trying here and there for almost fifteen days, Mahadeb found a place on Sheetal's boat. Usually, just before the Pujas, nobody wants to let go of their old companions. It was only because an old companion in Sheetal's boat, Pochen, had typhoid, did he take in Mahadeb. One could say that luck was on Mahadeb's side.

Soon, the darkness of the evening envelops everything. The shrill cry of crickets from the shrubs on the sandbank makes it seem like it is already midnight. The reflection of the pristine Sarat-Panchami moon on the ripples in the Gomor river resembles bolts of lightning. In that hazy darkness, the oarsman pulls in the oars noisily into the half-immersed boat. After this, the boatmen tow the boat onto the riverbank near Sheetal's home once and for all.

Jumping out of the boat, one of the boatmen runs along the sandbank and ties a rope to the gneyo tree on the bank. After a while, he returns to the boat and says something to his companions in a hushed tone. He then runs onto the road along the dam. The man is instantly recognised by the villagers as Rabi. These villagers are all family members of the companions of Sheetal's boat. For the past few days, they have all been waiting for Sheetal's boat to return.

Rabi reaches Haridasi's house and recognising her at once lowers his head. His behaviour makes Haridasi apprehensive and she asks, 'What is the matter, thakurpo? Has Bidhu's father quarrelled with you again? I know his ways. I've been tormented by him in the same way all my life. He just refuses to mend his ways! What can one do! He is like your own elder brother. Please do not mind.'

Rabi is embarrassed by Haridasi's words. He keeps his head lowered and mumbles, 'No, boudi, it's not that. But...but...' he hesitates to speak but then looks into her eyes, vehemently nods and says, 'We don't know how that creature managed to seize such a stout man with a single blow and dragged him off into the dense forest. We chased the animal with hatchets and spades, but couldn't find him. All five of us tried our best, sister, but we could not bring Mahadeb-da back despite our frantic efforts.'

Even before Rabi can finish, Haridasi, who had been starving for the last few days, collapses to the ground. A villager quickly grasps her and prevents her frail body from falling onto the riverbank. Punti begins to wail as she falls and is gently lifted by one of the villagers. Immediately the villagers attend to Haridasi: they lift her up and lay her down on the road. Someone runs off to fetch water.

Rabi quietly stands in a corner guiltily and observes everything. Finding him standing alone, Shibu's mother, an elderly woman of the neighbourhood, comes to him. The seventy-eight-year-old woman leans on a stick for support as she asks him, 'What Rabi, did you guys not perform the *maal*, the rituals?[5] Who was your *bable*, the one supposed to perform the rituals, eh?'

---

[5] The Bengali source text uses the word *maal* which can be loosely translated as 'rituals'. It is the responsibility of the *bable* or *baole/baoliya* of a boat to get

On hearing Shibu's mother speak, Rabi comes back to his senses. He sighs and replies, 'No, aunty, Aghor uncle did ask us to get back to the boat well in time. He said that once the evening set his spells wouldn't work anymore. However, it took us some time to cut down the sturdy branches of the pashur tree. On hearing his repeated warnings, the moment we were trying to get onto the boat...'

He could not speak any more as he was on the verge of tears.

'Right, so you'd done something wrong. Otherwise, a mishap like this couldn't have happened in the presence of a bable like Aghor. He is someone who can effortlessly make our *bondhu* dance to his tune and goes around collecting honey in the forest by tying a *gamchha* around its jaws. How can something go wrong with his spell!'

By then, some of the villagers had already left Haridasi and had thronged around Rabi to hear what he was saying. Everybody nodded their heads in agreement with Shibu's mother. They were familiar with the stories of the fakir who went around the forests collecting wood having put the tiger to sleep using the leaves of the golpata tree. Therefore, they were by no means skeptical about Aghor's abilities. Rather, they were proud of the fact that the person who could tie the jaws of ferocious animals with a gamchha was no pir or fakir but a man of flesh and blood, Aghor Mistri, an ordinary villager who led a life exactly like theirs.

Today is Aarang. The *dhaaks* at the Haatkhola puja pavilion are beating the rhythms of *bhashan*. People from the neighbouring villages have crowded in the pavilion. Preparations are being made to send goddess Durga, along with her children, back to Kailash. As part of the ritual, women are sprinkling vermillion on each other before the idol of the goddess.

The children are preoccupied as well. Some are having sweets from paper bags. Some others are holding packets of snacks. Some are playing with flutes, dolls or toy guns, while others are holding the balloons that they have brought. Everyone is enjoying with their family and friends, dressed in their colourful new clothes.

Bidhu and Mangal have also received new clothes for the Pujas. The village headmen have gifted each of them a cheap loincloth. Haridasi has received a white saree. She is walking from one end of the pavilion to another with

---

down before everyone else and perform the *maal*, which includes chanting mantras and performing a few rituals in order to ward off evil spirits, tigers and other wild animals.

Punti in her arms. In front of her, Bidhu and Mangal are walking up to the cheerful people in the crowd, extending their hands and saying,

'Babu, can you give us some money? We have to offer our baba's *pindo*.'

Translated from Bangla by Ishani Dutta
Originally published as "Jijibisha" in *Uttariyo: Samaj o Sanskriti Bishayak Patrika*,
Vol. II, January 2019

21

Kanu

Biswajit Halder

After a lot of deliberation, when Phanibhushan realised that there was no way out, he decided to sell off his cow and calf to pay back his debts. With whatever was left behind after repaying his debts, he would buy a fishing net. You could still manage to make a living by catching fish during high tide in the river, but it is impossible to run a household by selling only milk. So he and his wife decided that they would sell the cows at the village market next Tuesday.

But the couple's idea was met with opposition from their ten-year-old son, Kanu. When Kanu brought back the cow and the calf after the grazing session in the afternoon and heard that their Dhabala–Subala[1] would be sold off, he went to his father and broke down.

Phanibhushan was indeed remorseful seeing his son's sadness, but the moneylender's repeated threats overshadowed what would have otherwise been a warm moment between the father and the son, and Phanibhushan's remorse soon turned into rage. He shouted at Kanu, 'Shut up! You donkey!' Then imitating his son's voice, he said, 'Eeh!. . . Don't sell Dhabala–Subala! So what will you eat if I don't sell them? You'll be happy when people humiliate me, won't you?'

Kanu did not understand his father's reaction; he kept quiet on seeing him so livid. On finally realising that there was no hope, he ran to the cowshed and began caressing Dhabala. Imagining their fate and reminiscing about his lifelong relationship with the cows in the face of their separation, Kanu started sobbing.

---

[1] Names of the cow and its calf, meaning the fair one and the strong one respectively.

Dhabala did not understand this. She just felt proud of her little master's touch and to express that, she began to shake her body merrily. Seeing her mother's joy, Subala began to lick Kanu's feet out of affection.

Phani's wife Motimala went to the river early in the afternoon on Tuesday. She got a good catch of Bagda and came home early. Applying some vermillion on Dhabala–Subala's forehead, she touched their feet. Then she called Kanu, 'Kanu dear! Our Dhabala–Subala are going to be sold today, won't you offer prayers to them?'

Kanu was sleepy and still in bed. He had almost forgotten that today was market day and their Dhabala–Subala were to be sold off. After yesterday's incident, he was hoping that his father would reconsider and not sell the cows, at least for his sake. But after hearing what his mother just said, he leapt off the bed, came to the verandah and realised that his expectations were not realistic at all. His father was tying ropes around the cows' necks, and these poor cows, the means of a little income for the family, happily wore them. Kanu could not bear to see this. He ran to Phanibhusan and fell at his feet, crying profusely.

Sitting in the verandah in the evening, Phanibhushan was thinking of ways to collect ration for at least a week without being bothered by moneylenders. If he could somehow manage to work for a shift on Ishan's boat, he would not even have to worry about returning the money. Just then, Nabin Morol entered his house. As soon as he saw Phani, he shouted, 'Hey Phani, you said you'd meet me at the market and return my money! Where were you?'

Failing to find any excuse, Phani responded like an innocent child, 'Khuro, I can't pay you back this week. Please don't worry; I'll give you back the money on the next market day, some way or the other.'

Nabin Morol went into a flying rage as soon as he heard this, 'How long will this "next week" go on? Do you realise that your one hundred and fifty rupees has now amounted to five hundred rupees including interest?'

Phanibhushan kept his calm and said, 'I know that, khuro. I had thought of selling the cows today to pay you back, but just as I was going to leave for the haat, Kanu started crying so much....' His voice choked at this point. After a while, he coughed a little and started again, 'How do I make this child understand that if I fail to pay my debts, the moneylenders will take away our shelter too?' Phani stared at his broken, dilapidated roof.

Morol softened a bit on hearing this. He echoed Phanibhushan's refrain, 'Of course; why would the moneylenders let you go if you don't pay back the money! Just as you understand this well, you must make your son understand it too. Who will allow you to keep a debt for so long, like I have? Forget the money; your wife borrowed a *pati* of rice from my home last month, have I asked you to return that? Go to Jiban Ghoshal, you won't even get a morsel !' Morol then lowered his voice and continued, 'Okay Phani, do something, give your cows to me, I will consider your debt cleared and will also give you another four hundred rupees. That will be a bit of a loss for me, but what else can I do? I cannot cheat you! I have seen you since you were a child. I don't think your son will have any problem with this arrangement. Whenever he misses them, he can come to my cowshed to see them, right?' Morol broke into a burst of amicable laughter to convince Phanibhushan.

Phanibhushan did not utter a word but nodded in agreement. Realising that he had struck when the iron was hot, Morol put on a smile, raised his voice and said, 'Bouma, are you there? Can you give me a glass of water? It has been so hectic today! So, how is my grandson? What is he doing? What is his name—Kanu, right?'

Hearing Nabin khuro call her, Motimala hastened to cover her head and stood near the door, 'Kanu has not been feeling well since afternoon. He's resting.'

Morol was surprised, 'What?' He changed his tone and said, 'Of course. It's been so hot since the last few days, I was not feeling well in the afternoons either. So, are you done with cooking? Or will you do it later? What will you cook, tell me? Vegetables, fish, meat—everything is so costly that it seems better to give up eating altogether!'

Motimala's sari slipped off her head when she heard about cooking. She raised her head to say something but looking at her husband's eyes, she stopped. Phanibhushan too glanced at his wife once and then looked away. Morol well understood this little act between the husband-wife and changed the topic. He went back to what he was saying earlier, ' So I was saying that please don't allow the child to go out in the afternoons. If he gets a fever, it'll only get worse in such heat.' He stood up to leave and said, 'I will leave now. Phani, please come to my place tomorrow or the day after and take your money. Let the cows stay here for a couple of more days. Your khurima will come every day to take the milk. When your son agrees, send the cows to me. I'll take your leave now, bouma.'

It was the beginning of June. There were clouds all over the sky, but not a drop of rain. The weather was extremely sultry. Phanibhushan had gone to cut some *dum* five days ago and would return tonight. Kanu went fishing with his mother every day. On days when they got a sufficient catch of Bagdas, Kanu would get a rupee or two; and on days they did not, he did not get anything either.

Motimala was a little unwell today. She was dehydrated from an upset stomach after having a curry of *jadu palang*. The thought of having palang curry again for dinner if she failed to get Bagdas in the afternoon made her go fishing with Kanu. But as soon as she realised that they would not have much luck that day, she decided not to waste her time trying and pulling up her fishing net said, 'Let's go home, Kanu, there aren't too many of them around today.'

'There is chance yet, ma. You go home; I'll try for a while and then come back.'

'Come back soon, my dear. I'm not feeling well. Then we have to go to the shop as well. There is no rice in the house, remember?'

After his mother had left, Kanu tried pulling the fishing net through the western side. But he was only a little boy. With his little strength, he could barely pull the net against the flow of water. But was there any other way than to keep trying? His mother had just said that there was not even a handful of rice in the house.

Motimala went home, put aside the fishing net and went straight to the Ghoshals' pond in her wet saree. She sat near the pond to gather *matipora shak*.

While pulling his net through the water, Kanu slipped into a reverie and suddenly started to remember many things. He remembered their dear Dhabala–Subala and how he took them to the field every day. That day, when Nabin dadu was taking them away, they were crying a lot, but dadu pulled them away anyway! Kanu's cries had not been able to stop it from happening.

Kanu was so engrossed in his thoughts that he did not notice the daylight had faded. When he realised that it was quite late, he pulled up his net, kept his things on the bank and went into the river again to clean the mud that was stuck in the net. The movement of the fishing net made the salt water of the river shimmer in the golden light of dusk. Just as Kanu had folded his net to get back to the riverbank, an invisible force pulled him deeper into the water. Kanu tried his best to return to the shore. Frightened, he started to shout and struggled in vain. After a while, he couldn't even shout. In the blink of an eye, he disappeared.

A lot of people had gathered on the bank by now. Someone spoke of taking a boat into the river, someone said that they could have tried to find him had it not been dark already. Someone ran to Motimala to give her the news. Motimala dropped whatever she had gathered and ran to the riverbank. Just then, Kanu's body floated up and disappeared again, as if the little boy had come to say goodbye to his mother for a moment.

Like a mad woman, Motimala ran to take her son in her arms. But the people around her held her back as she sat down and started wailing.

Slowly, the fading light of dusk transformed into thick darkness that enveloped the villages on both sides of the river. The river was no longer visible from the embankment, but Motimala's teary eyes looked unblinkingly at the dark water, trying to find her son.

Translated from Bangla by Tias Basu
Originally published as "Kanu" in *Uttariya*, Volume II, January 2019, Kolkata

22

The Immersion March

Pabitra Mandal

They had all given up. It was no use anymore. Together they had kept the embankment in place for too long by shoving chunks of clay or lumps of straw and hay from both sides. But it was beyond repair now. At the moment, they were all heading towards their homes in haste to take care of their personal belongings. The base of the embankment was muddy and slippery because of the rain and the overflowing salt water.

Udayan too made his way through the water as fast as he could. He was soaked thoroughly in salt water from the river; his half-sleeve shirt and lungi were drenched as well. The water rolled down his bald head along his moustache and entered his mouth but there was no time to even spit it out. At fifty or fifty-five, Udayan had a well-formed body and grey hair. His round face sported a silver and black unshaved beard and his eyes were bloodshot.

There was commotion nearby. People were abandoning their houses and running frantically into the open fields. Further along that direction lay the metalled road, a few pucca two-storeyed buildings on the roadside, the high-school and a primary school with a terrace.

Seeing her father in this state and observing the condition of her neighbourhood, ten- or eleven-year-old Anu had gone stiff with fear. Dazed, she had failed to understand what her father said while running. Her mother Anita said, 'There's no more time. Let them do what they can, we've got to survive.'

'Yes, let the cattle and the goats die', Udayan snapped. 'The two cows are secured with long ropes. I've let the goats loose, let them do what they can. You hold Anu's hand, I'm taking the bag!'

But he stopped dead in his tracks as soon as the words were out of his mouth. With eyes focused straight at the fields he lowered his voice, 'No going out anymore.'

It had followed Udayan almost at the heels. Catching bits of straw in its mouth, the snake-like hoods of salt water were advancing at a frenzied pace across the fields. Crossing mid-field in no time, the water was now pushing the boundary of an adjacent locality. In the field, some obstructions had made the water surge.

Anita said, 'What now?'

Anu said, 'Ma, aren't we going to the school building?'

Udayan's voice was soft, 'It's not possible to step onto the fields anymore, child. No one knows where the rushing waters will fling us.'

Their eyes met and chill ran down their spines. Tears started flowing from Anu's eyes but not a sound escaped her lips.

By now the water was lapping the edge of their house. But it was no longer possible to go anywhere.

Fortunately, they had kept the trunk containing useful papers and other important things at Milan's house yesterday. Milan was like a brother to Udayan and lived just a few houses away. He had built that house only last year entirely with installments of money from the Indira Abas Yojana. As such they did not have any money to spare and were probably in debt. It was a scrappily erected structure of five-inch walls with an asbestos shade supported by bamboo beams on a thirteen-by-ten area. In any case it was better than a straw-thatched roof on mud-baked walls or a fence. Milan did not stay in this house. He lived near Champahati or Piyali and gave tuitions to a few students there to feed himself and his aged mother. It wasn't possible for him to acquire more degrees after his B.A. because of acute poverty. He was applying for jobs now, taking examinations, sometimes qualifying and sometimes not. When he did qualify, he failed to cough up the money required before joining service and his prospects grew dim. It was an impossible situation indeed.

Udayan had stored Milan's Ujjwala Yojana gas cylinder, the oven, the two trunks along with several bags and bundles one by one into the space above the shade. In return for this help, Milan's mother had allowed him to keep his little trunk there. This little gesture had left Udayan grateful.

If only they could stay there. Anita had even hinted at it. But Udayan dismissed the idea and she was visibly disappointed. He was suddenly reminded of his dead father's words, 'One shouldn't leave one's homestead and family deity alone at the time of disaster.' When cyclone Aila had hit, they had left home but when they returned there were many things missing. Were the swirling waters alone responsible?

His plan was to send Anu and Anita to the school building but that clearly was not possible any more. The water had already submerged their feet and was now swiftly rising. The courtyard was completely swamped, and the gusting winds were blowing the straw-bits, torn leaves and broken twigs. There was no way to access the rooms or verandah even. The supporting poles of this straw house had been hollowed out by termites already. Only a few of the bases were still holding up and at any moment the house might collapse. This morning's exercise in tightening the roof with ropes and cords hadn't made it any more dependable. The storm was too violent for that.

Had it been just the two of them, they wouldn't have worried so much. But they had Anu with them and she was just a child, facing such a calamity for the first time. She had not been born when Aila had hit.

They were standing under the ancient mango and palm trees and the water was rapidly rising; it had reached up to Anu's waist.

If only her grandmother had taken Anu along with her this morning! The old woman had comfortably marched to the high-school building with Udayan's eldest brother's youngest son. None of them saw her going; such was the opportune time she chose. She did not even inform them! But then again, why would she? Their current relationship did not permit that anymore. There was trouble in the family and partnership quarrels. The mother was now divided between the younger and elder siblings. She stayed with each of them for six months every year. It caused trouble during her illness, and the wives grumbled—'Is she only your mother?' Anita's comments caused even more trouble. So the old woman was now stubbornly settled in the older brother's house.

Anu received neither her grandmother's affection nor the pleasures of a joint family. Her father had to wander about in other people's farms in search of a few paisas while her mother was perpetually irritable, tending to the home front, the cattle, the goats and the land. Even a kind word elicited an aggressive response from her. When this was pointed out to her, she would say, 'It happens. Stay at home for a day and see, your daughter is such a bother!'

By now the waves were going over their heads too.

The hut was being battered and ripped apart by the wind. The shed threatened to crush them as it fell; Udayan and Anita shoved it away. It was difficult to say which way the shed floated on the brimming waters in the drowning field; it was impossible to see beyond the waves. A *poshu* beam, made by his father—old and worn out but sturdy—served as a pillar in their house but the sheer force of the waves wouldn't let the house or the beam stand. His father's handiwork floated away and disappeared in the dancing waters.

Anu had been made to sit on a thick side-branch of the mango tree. Her soaked dress was making her shiver. Seeing this, Udayan brought her down from the branch. The salt water felt warm now and he urged her, 'Grab my neck!'

Anu held her father tightly, coiling her arms round his neck. The coconut tree was just ahead of them. Embracing the tree, he bobbed up and down with the dancing waves. Anita was close, holding on to the mango tree. Anu said, 'Oh mother, my legs feel numb!'

Just that morning they had all had a bit of *panta*. Anita had cooked something, her eyes smarting in the smoke. But they hadn't had the chance to eat properly. It was all still neatly stored in the room under their humble bed. Who knew where the pots and pans, plates and bowls, jars and glasses were now! Udayan said, 'Wait a little, child, the low tide is setting in.'

It was eleven o'clock now. Anita looked fraught with anxiety.

Coiling his left arm around Anu, Udayan pressed her more firmly to him. With his right hand he held the coconut tree. Under this cover the battery of the waves disintegrated into mere thuds and so this position was somewhat more comfortable. Not having noticed this advantage earlier, Udayan had had a tough time battling the waves for so long. With his left hand he grasped Anu's legs and tried to keep her warm by kissing her face. Their condition was truly unimaginable.

The wind continued to change direction and the floating debris was now heading straight towards the river. Udayan could no longer see the embankment; it had probably collapsed by now. The river was now at ebb tide. Anita said, 'Look! The kindling is floating away.'

'Oh, forget your kindling! Look at the logs, planks, pillars and posts!', Udayan snapped. Waves tossed them about as Anu heaved herself up on the tree even more.

Suddenly, Anita-shrieked, 'Isn't that our trunk?'

Udayan took a quick look. Yes, the shape looked very familiar. The colour was tar black, painted by his own hands. Bobbing up and down on the dancing waves and weighed down by a heavy padlock, the trunk was half-submerged. Still, it could be recognised alright. This meant that even Milan's brick house was ruined and inundated now. Where would Milan's aged mother be in this disaster? Udayan tried to hand over Anu to Anita. She exclaimed, 'There's no need to go!'

'Will not going help? Everything is inside it.'

This was true. Ration cards for the three of them, food security card, Aadhar card; voter cards for the two of them, bank book for Jandhan Yojana, record of property and homestead, documents for wood, the receipts for panchayat's tax, and some gold and silver jewellery—everything was inside it. Anita knew this. She did not stop her husband from going but hugged Anu even more tightly. Anu was growing up. She needed to be married off. Her wish was to send her off in new ornaments refashioned from the old ones. Would it be possible to get new ones again?

'Anu shrieked, 'Oh, baba, don't you go!'

'But without it we'll cease to exist, child. I'll be right back.'

Letting go of the coconut tree, Udayan proceeded, braving the waves. His target was the box. Carrying the child on her hip, Anita sat on the thick branch of the mango tree, steadily gazing at the man she had just embraced. Unable to move through all the debris, he now dived underwater. If he didn't swim fast, the box would float away and be lost forever. His head bobbed on the surface through the leaf litter. The trunk was still far. He dived again. Now he was at the right spot but the current had moved the trunk farther away. He dived and pierced the water surface again; he was no longer visible. The rain had subsided for a while but the steady downpour had begun again. Anita couldn't see anything clearly.

Failing to grab the trunk would indeed be an irreparable loss. Even a lifetime of pursuit would not help them to get the papers back. Approaching the babus for special favours was sheer waste of money. Where would they get all that money? Even the knick-knacks were....

For quite some time now she hadn't heard from him. Anita screamed in panic, 'C-a-n y-o-u h-e-a-r m-e !

No reply. Or had she not heard anything due to the turbulent wind and waves? She screamed again.

Anita continued to hold Anu in a tight embrace, crying silently lest the little girl feel scared. Her eyes desperately searched for signs of Udayan. The deluge of rain had made her vision hazy and heart restless.

Fixing her gaze on Anita's face Anu asked anxiously, 'Ma, why hasn't baba returned?'

Raindrops and tears—could the girl tell the difference? Unlikely! Widening her lips in a dry smile Anita replied, 'Well, it's about time now for him to return.'

'How far did he go? He wasn't lost in the river, was he?'

Anita rebuked her, 'You shouldn't utter such thoughts, my dear! He'll come back any moment.'

But by now Anu was bawling. Holding each other tightly, they wept copiously.

Some more time passed. The rain continued to fall with the same intensity as before. Waves crashed and broke at Anita's feet. By now she had misgivings as well but was scared to express them to Anu.

'Where are you two?'—It was Udayan's voice, stifled by the rain, wind and salt waves.

Anu yelled, 'B-a-b-a !'

'Y-e-s-s-s, c-o-m-i-n-g!'

Anu's face glowed. Anita hugged her daughter tightly in joy. She cried out, 'G-o-t t-h-e b-o-x ?'

'N-o-o!'

Surely the man was not joking amidst all this calamity! Anita's gaiety dwindled somewhat. That trunk held their future in it. A part of the resources was for Anu's wedding, and it also carried the proof of their citizenship. If Udayan hadn't found it, they would probably become refugees in the coming days. Who knew where they would drift away next in the mess of space and time! Who knew for how many years the homestead, the crops and the farmlands would lie without harvest owing to the assault of the salt water! They would have to migrate as labourers to Bengaluru, or to Tamil Nadu or the Andamans. No, even that journey wouldn't be possible. These days, Aadhaar and voter cards were required for travelling to prove one's identity and citizenship. Raids were carried out on the way.

Abruptly, Anita seized Anu's lean neck with strong hands. She would finish her off. Along with the box they would give away this one too. There's no future left for her, is there?

Anita's pressure on Anu's neck tilted the branch where they were sitting to one side. Anu slid along the slope of the branch straight under water. She could swim though.

Her thoughts confounded; Anita too plunged into the water. She groped around but could not find Anu.

Suddenly from behind her Anu floated up onto the surface and grasped her mother.

Anita yanked her close in an embrace.

Having swallowed a lot of water by now, Anu was gasping and could not breathe. With full force Anita pressed the girl against her bosom. If only she could spew some of the vile salt water from her mouth.

Was it tears of joy in Anita's eyes? It was impossible to tell as her head, hair, eyes and face were drenched in the rain and salt water. The relentless drumming of raindrops continued to work up a flourish of melodious symphony.

Translated from Bangla by Pritam Bandyopadhyay
Originally published as "Bhashan jatra", 2021

23

Nostalgia or Stories of Roots and Soil

APARESH MONDAL

TALES OF MANEY-THAKURDA AND SHONAPISHI

The Biswas family of East Bengal was rich. They owned about fifty acres of land. Their well spread-out family home, alive with the chirping of birds, stood under the peaceful shadows of mango, jamun and jackfruit tress. Buzzing with daily wagers, paid cattle grazers, maids, cooks and members of the family, it was an elaborate household. The eldest son of the family, Mahesh was set to marry Jogin thakurda's[1] only daughter Shona pishi. It was an ideal match. Jogin thakurda was the beloved eldest son of the Mondal family of Dayoruli. They had about twenty *bigha*s of yielding paddy fields. On one side of it, the canal Thakurun khal met the Kalindi river. The bloom of crops in the fertile alluvial soil would make the neighbours jealous. So, when Shona pishi's marriage was fixed, Jogin thakurda had said, 'My dear daughter is divine, just like the idol of a goddess made of pure gold. She will fill the Biswas household with golden light.' Shona pishi's fair face would turn red with embarrassment, 'Baba, you are too much...' Her smile would fill everyone's hearts with joy.

After Po thakurda's first wife died in that country, he married again. It was not an extravagant event. He married only so that his two sons, Jogindra and Mukunda would not be deprived of mother's love. He had two more sons from the second marriage, Shailendra and Haran. Po thakurda also had a daughter from his first marriage. She had been married to a man from a respectable family of East Bengal (later East Pakistan) in a grand ceremony.

---

[1] Thakurda means grandfather. Names or address also of endearment like Jogin, Po and Maney have been affixed to thakurda to refer to different grandfathers.

East Pakistan was then ruled by the Urdu-speaking government of West Pakistan. Around 1951, the Bhasha Andolan created great turmoil in East Pakistan. Jogin thakurda sensed danger—no, one couldn't stay in this country anymore. The oppression by the Pakistani Army had become unbearable. In the meantime, Shona pishi's in-laws had shifted to the Thirteenth *laat* in Hingalganj on the other side of Bengal after selling their land at a very cheap price. Before shifting, Shona pishi came to bid farewell to Jogin thakurda and the other uncles. With tears in his eyes, he said, 'My heart breaks; may you all stay blessed.'

Bishu was the eldest son of the younger brother Mukunda. He was five or six years old at the time. Although he had been to Shonadi's in-laws' place once, he did not know her properly. He did not even remember the visit clearly. In 1957, they too had come to this side with whatever they could escape with. The BSF guarded the border—Shuklal Majhi cunningly got them to the other side, escaping an otherwise sure death.

The Sarkars had been planning things for quite some time by then. They had managed to strike a deal with some well-to-do Muslim landowners from West Bengal who exchanged their land with the Sarkars. That was how they got close to the Raychaudhri zamindars of Taki. The Sarkars used to oppress their employees just like zamindars did and did not care about their wellbeing at all.

After coming to West Bengal, Jogin thakurda, Mukunda thakurda and everyone else took turns working for the Sarkar family. My father, Bishu, started working as a cowherd from the young age of seven or eight. He used to work just for a meal and a mere five *sikis*. At the end of the season, if the employer was happy enough, the employees got a new *gamcha*. Thakurda used to work for the entire rainy season in exchange for one *mon* of paddy. The month of Bhadra would pass in ploughing, making the land fertile and sowing paddy in nearly 50–60 bighas of land. On the other hand, not even half of that paddy remained after paying off the debts that were taken for the family. That was the reason why my father and uncles would work in exchange for daily meals.

Jogin thamma used to cry, 'Please go and see how my dear daughter is doing!' as Jogin thakurda comforted her, 'Our dear daughter is living a good life. Mahesh is not a bad man. He belongs to a good family.' But thamma would be adamant, 'They have such a big house, who knows how she's managing? You better take Bishu with you and see for yourself.'

In the afternoons, the women of the Bachhar household would gather around the water tap in the south and chat with the East Pakistani women of Muslim households, discussing the kind of country East Pakistan was and how the Muslims mingled with the Hindus. Jogin thamma used to say, 'The Muslims of our neighbourhoods were very nice.' Before coming to this country, Abul chacha cried a lot. He had said, 'You've been our neighbour for so long, may you be safe in the new country. In our golden country Hindus and Muslims are brothers, but the dogs of West Pakistan provoke us to partition…Who knows if the country will be free or not…There is so much blood all around… The women of the Bachhar family—they are so nice…' Batashi thamma used to say, 'Can you really separate relations of blood by dividing a country?'

…

Father shivered at Shonadi's words, 'What did you say, Shonadi? With another wife…?'

'Yes, he can't tolerate me. I didn't know that he had another wife. He even has two sons with that wife. I came to know this only after coming here. The other woman is very bad. Influenced by her, Mahesh beats me up!'

It took about an hour to reach Shitoliya by boat from the Thirteenth. Mud whirled beneath the turbid waves of Kalindi-Kalagachi. Shonadi's heart ached again in pain. She cried, 'Bishu, my dear, there is so much pain in my heart. It often aches.' Frightened, Bishu asked, 'Shonadi, haven't you been to a doctor?'

Shonadi sadly replied, 'Who would take me to a doctor? I don't even have a home.' Bishu screamed in anger, 'Grant me permission, I will go and break that idiot Mahesh's nose. Animal! This country is very heartless, let's go back to East Bengal!'

Shonapishi's Death

Mahesh Biswas left the Thirteenth, the area of Sandler sahib, and went to Hiranmaypur after mortgaging (or selling) his lands to his brothers. He shifted with his second family along with Shonapishi. Bishubaba respected Shonapishi a lot despite the age difference. There was no one more beautiful than her in the family. The women of the Bachhar family would often say, 'The girl is so beautiful, how can Mahesh not like her?'

Batashi thamma would say angrily, 'You asked why I was always worried? The beautiful girl would manage her household well? Now see how irresponsible her husband is!'

Bishubaba had rightly wanted to break Mahesh's nose. But Shonapishi had said, 'Don't do anything like that. They might be inhuman; but we are better than them.'

This country heaved a much-needed sigh of relief after all those years of anxiety, bloodshed and deaths. Would rootless refugees ever find the fertile soil of East Bengal here? The four grandfathers got four plots of land from the Sarkars and were finally ready to put down roots. The family slowly settled down. The Congress party was in power at the time. Partition had created an economic crisis in India and imported provisions had to be distributed among the large population. To add to that, there was the Kashmir issue. The rate of production had also fallen sharply. Flour, corn and Milo were the only rations available. There was no proper distribution of ration—hoarders stocked crops to sell in the black market. People were begging for leftovers in the streets. During the Khadya Andolan, the police killings in the tarred roads of the city caused a bloodbath.

That monsoon, Bishubaba had just started work at Tarapada Gharami's property; he was the only person to ox-plough Tarapada's 60 bighas of land. Tarapada Gharami was fond of Bishubaba. One day, while baba was tilling the southern lowlands of Gharami, Jogin thakurda came to him crying, 'Bishu, your Shonadi is no more. Come quick! She fell on her face in front of the Harimandir in Gharamipara...' A shocked Bishu left his plough and ran.

'Let's walk fast. Have you informed the uncles?'

'Yes, they didn't come, saying that they could not leave their fields.'

'Huh, pretending to be a laat sahib with two bighas of land! Let them be, they do not need to come. You go and call a couple of people from Mistripara!'

Baba buried his beloved Shonadi on the salty banks of Kalagachi in Gharamipara. It was later heard that Mahesh had been taking care of Shonadidi. She had a tumour on her outer chest and had been taking homeopathy medicines. She was pregnant too! Alas, she could not see her father's home one last time. Bishu would often sob in sadness and his stomach would cry in hunger.

Jogin thakurda would cry frantically too. 'Shona...my dear Shona... Shona, my bird of the forest!' He had a habit of saying the word 'maney' while talking. Since then, he had come to be known as 'Old man Maney'. The boys of the neighbourhood would tease him—'Old man Maney. Maney... where are you going, Maney? Look, there is your daughter!' Bishubaba would scold the young boys, 'Why do you guys tease him? The poor man has lost his senses in grief of his daughter. Go…go off to your work!'

BISHUBABA'S STORY

Shejka's financial condition had improved by now. He worked extremely hard all day long. His fortunes had continued to rise ever since he joined Shibpada's house for a paid job. He bought agricultural lands one after another along with ponds and houses. His courtyard would be filled with crops at the end of the year. He employed labourers as well. His nephews however, worked as daily labourers to earn livelihoods. A dispute has started regarding the *khoi* tree beside the pond in front of Bishu's house. They were hell bent on depriving him of his rights. 'You people bought the pond in front of my house from the government. You wouldn't even let me use the water. But some twenty bighas of land are lying just like that in East Bengal. The green field around Thakurun khal. Alas, I am landless, friendless here in this country, and there…!'

Bishubaba's cousin had visited from the other side once. He told Maney thakurda, 'Let's go to that country, mama. You have so much land there… some of it got submerged in the river, and a Kalibari, a Bonbibitola and a Pir Baba's shrine now occupies some bighas. But there would still be about ten bighas left. All of you should visit; I shall help you all cross the border myself. A little bit of land might still be recovered if you come.'

While having lunch, Bishubaba said, 'After Shonadi's death, jyatha did want to go back to that country. He might have thought, "I have no sons, let my nephews divide my land among themselves." I told him, "I will go with you, jyatha. Let's go to that country; we'll have a lot of money if you sell your land…we will no longer be poor. There is so much fight over this little piece of land…this is unbearable!" But that old man did not go back. Otherwise, would we be living in such difficulty today? We were not supposed to live in this condition!'

I sat there, helpless, not feeling like eating. Ma said, 'Now eat. There's no point thinking about that. What was supposed to happen, did not happen. And what should happen, will also not happen. Our shejo brother will continue to live like a king and we'll always be poor. We don't have the right to wish for things.'

I protested. 'No ma, we can't accept this injustice. They've secretly bought the pond, almost like cowards. I am quite doubtful about the legalities of buying a pond given by the government though. But while measuring the house, a corner of the pond and the leaning khoi tree have been found to be within the boundaries of the home. Legally, that too should have three equal shares—for baba, kaka and shejo thakurda.'

After lunch, I took a siesta as I had not been feeling well. There was a friendly match in the colony in the afternoon. But my father's sad and hopeless face continued to occupy my thoughts. The afternoon sun turned into embers. The shadows of the khoi trees moved in the courtyard like evening insects; the solitude was overwhelming. Mother had gone to the river to fetch water. A sweet southern breeze was flowing. I was washing up when I heard Nutu shouting, 'Come Pocha, let's go! Everybody has gone out.' I replied at once, 'Yes, let's go!'

THE STORY OF BISHUBABA AND TARAPADA GHARAMI

Mukunda thakurda was depressed after Maney thakurda's death. Thamma, Maney thakurda's wife, had to beg for her meals after her husband's death. Every household was poor back then. On some days, she managed some rice, and on other days, she had to make do with water. Sometimes she would get some flour, corn or Milo as ration. All of these would last for merely five or six meals. Mukunda thakurda craved some rice. He would tell Bishubaba, 'Go Bishu, see if someone will give us a little rice! I can't tolerate it any longer. God, this country is so cruel!' Bishu would run towards Tarapada Gharami's house. Tarapada was a kind soul who never turned away anybody in need. 'Kaka, it seems like I cannot save baba this time. Feeding him only corn and Milo...' Tarapada said, 'He is a man from East Pakistan; he cannot live on these kinds of food. Go check the barn to see if there is anything!' 'Kaka, there is no paddy up here. You sold it to Jiten Dash that day.' He replied, 'Look around, and take anything that you find. Save the man. Swelling of the limbs is not a good sign.'

Maney thakurda had died some ten or twelve days back. Nobody in the household was talking about it. Maney thamma and Mukunda thakurda called shejo thakurda and told him, 'Look Haran, borda has just passed away, we're still in mourning. You've been doing good for yourself; can a *shraddha* ceremony not be arranged?' But Haran thakurda had been so arrogant! 'If you so want to do it, do it yourself...why ask people to do it for you?' Mukunda thakurda had almost fallen to his feet—'I wouldn't ask if I could do it. I can't do all this. He's your brother, you should do whatever needs to be done.' Haran thakurda responded, 'He might be your half-brother, but you have his father's blood. You should do whatever needs to be done. Have you forgotten all this?'

Tarapada Gharami gave his wise opinion: 'You can't say this. Haran, stop this argument. At least do the *ghat-pindo* ritual with ten people in attendance. I will try and help you with whatever I can! Or else, the village heads will ostracise you!'

FATHER, MOTHER AND OUR BROTHERS AND SISTERS

The thin darkness of the evening had spread a net over our courtyard as small gusts of wind blew. The sky was dotted with stars that shone brightly. It seemed like someone had covered the whole courtyard with milky light from the sky. Dulduli had returned from her hostel last week. She got a long holiday after her Higher Secondary examination. At first, I thought of going on a vacation but later I dismissed the idea. It seemed selfish to search for happiness by escaping from my parents, sister and the poverty that engulfed us.

I had returned from the colony quite some time back. Ma was cooking under the *puimacha* in the courtyard. Sitting beside her, baba was venting his grief. Flames fumed in the oven. Ma consoled him, 'Let it go. Don't involve others.' I came forward and asked, 'Ma, what happened?' She shot back, 'What happened? Will you ever understand our pain? You heard everything in the afternoon; still you were not there for the judgement today. Go...go and play. That will fill our stomachs.' I teared up, 'I don't know anything! Baba, what happened?'

Baba was an emotional person. He broke down, 'I failed; I failed to stand up against my enemies. It was my dream to build a desk and a chair for you from my share of wood. My dear son has studied on the floor all his life. No ancestral home, no land—I haven't been able to keep anything for you.'

I was dumbfounded; a heavy weight settled on my chest. It was almost as if on one side were our co-owners, the Kauravas, and on the other side were us, the exiled Pandavas.

I later got to know that baba had planned to take me to the judgement. The neighbours, even the panchayat had almost agreed. Baba had tried to gather people from the neighbourhood that afternoon. He had anyway never received any fair judgement till now. Everybody apparently thought of me and suggested to him, 'Bishubaba, your son is young and good at his studies.

It's better not to involve him in problems regarding property. He'll anyway go off to college in Kolkata in a couple of months.' Baba sighed, 'Of course, what everyone says must be right. By God's grace, the kid has been doing well. He'll not be able to concentrate on his studies if he is saddened by these affairs. You gave a fair judgement—trying to restrict my son's progress. Even my own Kaka has said that we do not need the share.' Everyone unanimously gave the judgement in favour of the shejo one.

Time went by with bouts of happiness and sorrow. Baba worked at other's households. Ma and my little sister went fishing. Inflation in the prices of daily consumables had left the lower middle class exasperated. My sister had to give up her studies after Class 6 as we could no longer afford it. Ma had made a call to my mess about two months back. She said, 'Sushama says that she will not continue with her studies anymore. The price of rice and oil is exorbitant and it is tough to make both ends meet. She accompanies me to the river when I go fishing. I've decided to make a pair of earrings for her by saving up some of the money I earn by selling prawns. Others in the locality wear jewellery too...besides, she is growing up...'

I told ma, 'There is no need to send me money any more. I've started giving a few tuitions.'

She asked, 'When will you read if you give tuitions?' I said, 'Don't worry, I'll manage.'

I went home towards the end of Bhadra. Didi was not in the house. I got to know that mashi came just after I left for Kolkata and had taken didi with her. Didi now worked at some elite household in Baranagar and earned a salary of five hundred rupees; food and stay were free.

Pujo was near. The newly sown paddy in the watery fields had ripened. Swarms of fishes played under the hyacinth-covered water. Those times reminded me of didi. I could clearly see her in the shadows of the dry paddy of Bhadra; I could visualise her dark, short figure and curly hair and see her picking earthworms by digging the mud with the end of a fishing rod. I could hear her whisper, 'Shh, don't make a noise! See, I'll surely catch a fish with the hook.' I was transported to my childhood in an instant. My cousins went to school every day after having fish curry. If anyone asked me, I would proudly say that I had also had fish...

Ma went by herself to the swamp of the north with the fishing rod that day. My sister followed her with a lamp. Ma suddenly scolded her, 'Put out the light! Rival fishermen are watching us. If they spot us, will we have this fishing rod?' Would we ever see the day when we eat fish?

Sushama fell asleep every evening. The poor girl had to stay in the water all day long. In the afternoon, she had been showing her toenail to me and saying, 'See dada, this toenail hit a brick and has broken; it's paining a lot.' It was indeed a painful sight—blood and pus were seeping through. My heart skipped a couple of beats.

A light wind was blowing from the south. Near the palm tree in Bachharpara I saw the old lady Gayen sitting with her fishing rod. I asked her, 'Grandma, aren't you afraid?' Indifferently, the old lady said, 'What fear! Pujo is almost here. My grandchildren have been after me. Pagol Mal buys those fishes. At least some money comes in' … Every morning, Pagol Mal came to her house and shouted—'Got any fish?' Making everyone jealous, old lady Gayen sold a lot of *koi* fishes. Was the old lady for real or a ghost?

We had never owned a pond. We still did not. On days old lady Gayen felt well, she went to the stream and cast her fishing net. On some days, she got a catch and on some days she returned empty-handed. It seemed like the fishes too behaved in an unpredicatble manner; they were also making fun of us. Ma became desperate to do away with poverty from the family. She would cry relentlessly whenever we did not manage to make meals for all five of us—sometimes silently, sometimes aloud. My little sister often lamented, 'I'm inauspicious. Had I not been here, didi and you would have had a happy life. The expenses would also have been lesser.' I used to scold her, 'Shut up! Always speaking rubbish!'

Mashi always said that Kolkata offers better prospects. Didi had gone there to earn some of that money. But the poor condition of our household still did not improve. She ate in the kitchen, even if it was leftovers of her elite employees—but she could at least eat two meals.

Baba had returned from his work and ma was about to serve lunch. He gave her a white envelope and said, 'Take this. You have a good husband. I've bought this medicine for your dysentery from Binoy's shop while coming from Rati Baul's place. Have it on time. Is it bleeding?' Without turning back, ma replied yes. Baba said, 'You all eat so much and…Couldn't you have bought it in the morning from Binoy? You'd have got better by now!' Ma said, 'I feel shy. How can I speak about such things?'

Baba gazed outside as he ate and said in a low voice, 'Shejka's antics never end. The brawl regarding the pond and the khoi tree has ended long ago! But he has told Pochen of Malpara—I will call the police if Bishu crosses his limits. Just listen to his words! Granted, he is tricking us, but why is he interfering with the part-owners?'

Pujo was near. The air and sky were filled with the fragrance of autumn. It was quite late into the night and the whole locality was silent. Baba, ma and my sister were fast asleep, but I could not sleep. My childhood and youth were flashing in front of my eyes. Baba was growing old, my little sister was growing up. Didi needed to be married off too. I continued to think how I could handle these responsibilities. If we had at least some land, somehow, we could have managed. But there were troubles all around and no redemption was in sight.

In my childhood, baba had once said, 'Once you grow up, you should take revenge of our deprivation from our assets. I'll not say another word until you grow up.' I could not sleep remembering his helpless and miserable face. My heart ached. I kneeled like a lost man and thought about the revenge I was supposed to take on behalf of my hardworking father. Have I grown up enough or should I wait some more? When can I point my finger at shejthakurda and ask him why he crucified us with lies and deprivation all these years? Why are we, the helpless, always punished like the crucified Jesus by your conspiracies? But remember, you devil, I am coming…and I will have my revenge.

My eyes were burning and my heart had turned to stone. As soon as I put my head on the pillow to sleep, an owl screeched harshly in the date tree outside.

Translated from Bangla by Tias Basu
Originally published as "Pichhutan othoba shikor matir golpo"
in *Nonadangar Manush*, 2016

24

My Childhood: An Oral Narrative

Archana Mandal

I was born in the village of Chhoto Rakshaskhali, an area surrounded by rivers and streams. The village was so named because it was beside a *khal* of the same name. One village away, where my cousin Anjana lived, one could see the tip of the Bay of Bengal. There was another village called Boro Rakshaskhali just across the river.

There was a high school in the middle of the village which had ten teachers. There were four primary schools in four directions if one went out of the village, also with four teachers each. Now, I hear they only have two teachers. There are some contractual teachers as well—paid from contributions raised from the parents of the students. Five rupees are collected from the parents of each student every month, and that sum is used to pay the contractual teachers.

I was the youngest of five siblings; we were four sisters and one brother. I was a month old when my parents decided to move to the Sundarbans. My grandfather had bought twenty *bighas* of land in Chhoto Rakshaskhali and it was divided among my father and his four brothers. Everyone else sold off their portions; only my mother remained, still holding on to our land. It was a mud hut then with a straw roof, which needed to be thatched every season. That is where I grew up.

Times were difficult when I was growing up. There was no proper road in the village; I had to wade through calf-high mud to reach school. I would take off the white dress on the way and carry it with me and put it on only on reaching the school. I studied till Class 8. I was the only one from our family who went to school; none of my siblings could do so. My elder brother moved to Kolkata to work in someone's house; he must have been around fourteen or fifteen then. His bond with us gradually became tenuous after that. The school I went to was called Kajallata Shishu Shiksha Niketan. We had to pay two rupees as fees every month and had to buy our own books.

But my mother could never afford the fees leave aside the other contributions that students were expected to make now and then for various celebrations and occasions. Nor could she buy our books—we hardly had enough to eat, how could we think of buying books? The teachers at my school were very considerate. They were the ones who gave me books. One teacher would get me a book, and the next day, another teacher would do the same—in this way, I managed to somehow continue my studies.

My mother could not afford to buy me exercise books either. Initially, I just used a broken slate that had been discarded by one of my distant relatives—they were somewhat better off. Later, I used discarded paper—people often write on one side of the sheet and discard them; also, exercise books which still have blank pages. I managed to scavenge paper from such sources and used them to write my lessons. But I could continue my studies only till Class 8. The education came in useful. After that, I gave tuitions to children of the area; I used to teach up to Class 5 but could never muster the courage to go beyond that. At night, I used to go fishing for shrimp to add to the family income.

School was a mixed experience for me. Most of the teachers were very helpful and took special care of me because they knew of my circumstances. I remember, once, I was very tense about my exams. All my classmates had received admit cards to sit for their exams. I had not paid my fees, so I did not get mine. One of the teachers realised my predicament and told me not to worry about it, assuring me that the school would let me take the exam in any case. And that was indeed how it went!

But not everybody was so kind. I remember one of my classmates who was fair and belonged to a well-off family. She used to call me names. One day, she told the others in my presence that I had come to school looking like a monkey. There was also a teacher who used to call me Ma Kali as I was very dark. Not once during my entire schooldays did he ever call me by my name!

One day, I had coaxed and cajoled my mother into lending me a pair of glass bangles. When this teacher saw me wearing the bangles, he gripped my arm till the bangles broke. Ma Kali has no use for these things, he said. I was distraught! It had taken so much effort to get ma to lend me those and to allow me to wear them to school! What would happen now? I went to the headmaster, disconsolate, and recounted the episode. The headmaster took me to a shop just outside the school, which sold glass bangles. He got me new ones from there, and instructed the shopkeeper to give me new bangles every time they were broken. This continued for a week or so. I would go back to class with new bangles, which would then dutifully and unfailingly be smashed by the teacher. After a week or so, the shopkeeper told the teacher that he owed him a substantial sum. Astonished, he said he had never bought anything from the shop in the last few weeks. The shopkeeper then told him that the headmaster had instructed him to replace my bangles every time I reported them broken, and to charge the amount to the teacher concerned. This immediately rid him of his habit!

My school had both boy and girl students. We were given khichuri for lunch most days. Sometimes, we even got bread and bananas in the mornings. Our school and many other schools were managed by a man called Sukumar Singh. He sometimes brought guests to the school, including foreigners, Christian missionaries and nuns. They would donate money which helped to run the school. We would often put up performances for the guests; there were so many things we did—*sari nritya*, where the girls danced in two rows with the sari in the centre, and the *ghoti nritya*, where we would dance, balancing earthen pots and bowls on our head. And of course, there was the *bratachari* dance, where we used to move around performing with sticks in our hands. One day, during a bratachari performance, somebody's stick landed heavily on my left thumb; I still have trouble flexing my left thumb after all these years.

There were around fifty houses in our area. The residents cultivated their land and harvested some rice. What they produced lasted them a fair part of the year, but not the whole of it. We used to grow vegetables on a little patch right next to our house and also used to fish a lot.

Rathayatra was the primary festival in our village. Kali Puja was also celebrated. There was no Durga Puja; I did not see a Durga idol until I was in Class 7, when I visited Midnapore. Gajan is an important tradition in the Sundarbans; I grew up watching Gajan performances. I still remember the performance of Naren Shikari. He was amazing! When he acted dead, his limbs would go absolutely stiff—no amount of pushing or pulling from anyone could make him break out of it!

There were no shops or market in our village. There was a bazaar in Patharpratima; that was also where we would have to go to sell the produce of our fields. One needed to take the boat across the Ganga and buy provisions from the Patharpratima market every Monday. The boatman would charge us one rupee for each journey.

We were very poor and sometimes did not have enough to fill our bellies. On some days, ma would pluck the *girey* saag that grew near the river. Girey is a kind of leafy vegetable that has a lot of water; we would boil it and survive on that. Also, *shapla* is very common in the area; we often used to depend only on shapla to fill our bellies.

I remember something that happened to me one day when I was ten or twelve. The fishermen had spread out their nets to trap shrimp spawn. I was holding on to the bamboo poles and the net and swimming across when I suddenly saw the fisherfolk gesticulating wildly from a distance. I could not understand what the matter was but I tried to come back, sensing there was some sort of danger. But it was slow going, and I suddenly saw a crocodile hurtling into the net. Had the net not been there, it would have certainly got me. In the meantime, the fishermen had also advanced in order to save me, and a boat that had been hovering around also reached me. They caught the crocodile in their fishing net. As they rescued me, they gradually unfurled the net and let the crocodile free. I saw then that the crocodile had an iron mesh fixed to its mouth. Actually, the crocodile reserve was only about an hour from our village; sometimes, when there was an increase in their numbers, they would release some of them into the river, putting iron meshes on their jaws. This was done so that they could not attack humans. They would however be able to eat the fish that would slip through into their mouth through the gaps in the mesh. Thus, they would not starve to death. After a while, the mesh would drop off and the crocodiles would be free to take on anyone again. There were also deer and tigers in the reserve though I have never seen a tiger myself. It is not as if everyone from the Sundarbans meets tigers every day.

I was married off when I was fourteen or fifteen. A 'good' match had been found and my parents were afraid that good prospects would be lost if I did not get married right away. They were also very happy as I would be going away to Kolkata, where people could earn much more than they would in the village. Everyone knew that Kolkata was a land of opportunity.

But the marriage did not work out at all. After it broke down, I went and took a room near Vidyadharpur. It cost me fifty rupees a month then, which was difficult for me to pay as I hardly earned anything. Then, a mashi who lived nearby told me she could get me work with a centre. She introduced me to the owners of the centre, and they gave me work. I would initially get twenty-five rupees a day, of which the centre would deduct five rupees. Sometimes they assigned me to Gariahat, sometimes to Tollygunge. I also worked for six months in Good Hope Nursing Home near Baghajatin. I was so poor I would sometimes buy a hundred grams of muri in the morning, and would survive on it. When the other didis asked me to join them at lunch time, I would make excuses and say I was not hungry. Then, I would mix the muri in water and have it. Whatever was left over would sometimes take care of dinner as well.

I would travel from Vidyadharpur to Jadavpur by train on my way to work. In Vidyadharpur, I lived in a Muslim neighbourhood. It had around fifty houses, and I was the only Bengali[1] in that all-Muslim neighbourhood. One day, I had finished my duty and returned home and gone to bed. There was a knock on my door late at night. I opened the door and saw some of the boys of the neighbourhood—they asked me to get them a vessel as they had some prasad for me. It was the time of Eid after all, so they were going from house to house, sharing the prasad. They saw me when I came out with the vessel and realised I was a Bengali, immediately apologised and ran away. They had got me some beef from the Eid celebrations! I heard Billa-da from the neighbourhood shouting at them and abusing them soundly. He had realised what the matter was. After a few months, I realised it was not possible for me to stay on in that neighbourhood as the only Bengali woman there, that too, a single woman. Still, it was a good place and I got a lot of help from my neighbours. Water was not available round the clock, and I would often be at work when water ran in the taps. Billa-da would often get his daughter to draw a couple of buckets of water and keep them on my front door so that I would not be without water. He was a sort of caretaker for the bustee. The owner had deputed him to keep things in control. He was originally from Bangladesh who had married a widow and moved into her house in Park Circus.

Collected and translated by Sayantan Dasgupta

---

[1] Mondal makes a distinction between Muslim and Bengali, equating 'Bengali' with 'Hindu'. This is a common usage in popular discourse.

Glossary

aalbheri	elevated mud dividers that separate long stretches of fields
Aarang	also referred to as Vijayadashami, is the tenth and the final day of the Durga Puja. On this day, the idol of goddess Durga is immersed in water.
Agrahayan	the first month of the Bengali calendar
atol	indigenous traps to catch small fishes
bable	Every boat which goes into the forest in order to gather wood or honey consists of boatmen and a *bable* who is also referred to as a *bauliya* or *gunim*.
Bagda	tiger prawn hatchlings
bakhari	a long bamboo section used to hang load on both ends and carried on the shoulder
Bangals	Bengalis who had migrated to West Bengal from erstwhile East Pakistan during or after partition of India
banigachh	a special mangrove tree in the Sundarban region
baroyaritala	*baroyari* refers to the public. *Baroyaritala* is a designated public place, generally a marketplace or a shrine, where people gather.
beedi	a type of cheap cigarette made of unprocessed tobacco wrapped in leaves
beguni	Bengali batter-fried brinjals
Bhadra	the Bengali calendar month from mid-August to mid-September
Bhasha Andolan	a political movement demanding the recognition of Bangla as an official language in the then Pakistan; the movement eventually led to the Bangladesh Liberation War and emergence of Bangladesh as an independent state.
bhashan	the act of immersing goddess Durga on the tenth and the final day of the Durga Puja, which is also referred to as Aarang or Dashami

Bhatiali	a genre of folk songs specific to the boatmen of certain parts of Bengal
bheri	a watery space chiefly used for aquaculture
bhutbhuti	steamboats popularly used in the rivers of Sundarbans
bigha	a traditional Indian measure of area of flat land
Binapani	refers to Goddess Saraswati who is the reigning deity of speech, music and the arts, usually represented as carrying a *veena* in her hand
bondhu	There is a prevalent superstition in rural India that one should not take the name of an evil spirit or else the evil spirit would appear in front of them. In the Sundarbans, a tiger is considered a big danger when one is in the forest cutting wood or gathering honey. Therefore, the people in the region do not refer to a tiger by its name but instead refer to it as *bondhu* which literally translates to 'friend'.
bordi	term used for an elder sister; in schools of Bengal, the headmistress is often called bordi by her students and colleagues.
boudi	sister-in-law; can also refer to one's brother's wife or a married woman
bouma	daughter-in-law
brahmadatti	ghost of a male brahmin; these ghosts are seen to wear a sacred thread and sport a shaved head with a strand of hair in the back of the head.
Chandi Path	tells of the greatness of Goddess Chandi or Chandika (the most powerful and terrifying form of Goddess Parvati in the Hindu pantheon) from the *Markandeya Purana*; the Chandi Path is recited in honour of goddess Durga every year during Durga Puja on Mahalaya.
Charak	a folk festival celebrated in parts of southern Bangladesh and West Bengal in honour of Shiva
chhanchi	wild green vegetables widely consumed in the Sundarbans
Choitro	the Bengali calendar month from mid-March to mid-April; refers to the spring season in this case
dadu	Dadu is a form of addressing one's grandpa. Here, the word is used endearingly as a mark of affection.

Dakshin Rai	He is believed to be the demon king or ruler of the beasts in the Sundarbans and Bangladesh. According to the mythology of the region, he is the arch-enemy of Bonbibi who is also considered by many as the ruler or the protector of the forests and the people of the region. Dakshin Rai is also revered by many and is called upon by the people before they enter the forests to gather wood or honey for protection against tigers—a disguise that Dakshin Rai is believed to take in order to attack the people.
daowa	a balcony-like open stretch in front of a mud house right before it opens into a courtyard
dhaak	a percussion instrument essential to the rituals of a number of pujas, including Durga Puja
dhaaks	folk drums of various shapes and sizes
doira	a variety of wild seedy banana
done	traps with baits attached to hooks to catch big cat fishes
dum	logs of *dhundhul*, *posur* (Cedar mangrove), etc.
duni	a river
fakir	A 'pir' is generally a title given to an elderly Sufi master or spiritual guide. Similarly, a 'fakir' is a Muslim ascetic who has renounced all worldly possessions and has taken the vows to solely survive on alms and worship.
Falgun	the Bengali calendar month from mid-February to mid-March
Fotikir Shib	an anthropomorphic representation of the tiger; here it is compared to a folk version of Lord Shiva.
gamchha	a towel made of coarse cotton
gangbheri	an embankment which protect islands from the saline tidal rivers by holding back their twice-daily high tides; long stretches of field converted to pisciculture farm
ganja	marijuana
garan	a tree found in the Sundarbans; the timber of this tree is valuable
gete	a kind of bamboo that is particularly strong and durable—it has more bulk and the circumference of its hollow shaft is minimum

gher	a small section of the backwaters enclosed by bamboo poles for private use
ghol	a whirlpool in the middle of high tide
ghoni	a kind of net with closely-woven holes
gneyo	*gneyo, paashur* and *golpata* are names of mangrove trees found in the Sundarbans and surrounding areas
gomosta	government appointed revenue collectors in the rural area
gonmukh	first to fifth days of the lunar cycle, when the tide is strong
gopa	a bigger variety of net made of twine to catch bigger fishes
goran	a plant typically found in the marshy wetlands of the Sundarbans
gunin	a traditional healer; such healers are still popular in rural areas as they are believed to have the ability to combat various ailments including snakebite
gurudeb	a traditional way of referring to a teacher
haat	an open village market which is held either daily or weekly
haatbar	the specific days on which the haat is organised
haat-besti	a local term for a handbag for carrying items to and from market place
hajjot	It is a day of worship for Muslims in the Sundarbans. Woodcutters, fishermen and honey gathers celebrate *hajjot* on three different days in a year. Woodcutters celebrate on the first day of Magh which is the eleventh month of the Hindu calendar. Fishermen and boatmen have their *hajjot* on the day they refer to as Maaghi Purnima, which takes place in Poush, the tenth month of the Hindu calendar. Honey gatherers celebrate *hajjot* in Chaitra, the first month of the Hindu calendar.
hatishur	Heliotropium indicum—an annual, hirsute plant that is a common weed
kash leaves	leaves of Kash flower (Saccharum spontaneum) which flourishes during autumn and signifies the advent of festive season in Bengal

hetal	another native tree found in the forests of Sundarbans
hinchey	also known as *helencha*—buffalo spinach
ijjatdaar	provider of a decent living
jadu palang	a kind of small shrub growing on the banks of the river in the Sundarbans. It has no taste. However, people pick up this vegetable and cook it due to lack of other costly food.
Jaishtha	the Bengali calendar month from mid-May to mid-June
jatra	a popular folk-theatre form of Bengali theatre, spread throughout most of Bengali-speaking areas of the Indian subcontinent
jhati	Miniket rice, a long-grain single boiled rice of West Bengal region
jhellas	a type of long and stout grass used for weaving mats
jhentla	a kind of mat for daily use in the Sundarbans
jotedar	this title is used to refer to a person who owned extensive amount of land in Bengal
kaka	father's younger brother
kakababu	An elderly person is often addressed as kakababu. The word comprises two common words, 'kaka' meaning uncle and 'babu' meaning gentleman.
kakima	wife of father's younger brother
Kalyug	Kalyug refers to the last phase of the cycle of time in the Puranas. Colloquially, it is used to talk about dark times or poor state of affairs in a certain time.
kantha	a blanket made by sewing layers of clothes
Kartik	the Bengali calendar month from mid-October to mid-November; in Hindu mythology, one of the sons of Shiva and Parvati
kayasthas	a caste of people who historically were record keepers of the state; the kayasthas come right after the brahmins in terms of hierarchy in the caste system.
Khadya Andolan	In 1958, the Communist Party of India and other left organisations created the Price Increase and Famine

	Resistance Committee also known as Khadya Andolan, a mass movement in response to the food crisis.
khalbalanga	wide-mouthed, earthen cooking pot
khebla	a kind of net with big holes in it
khoi	a variety of puffed rice
kholla	another variety of trap to catch fish
khoka	a term of endearment used for young boys in Bengali households
khuku	term of endearment often used for young girls in Bengali households
khuro	an informal way of referring to an uncle
King Yama	god of death in Hindu mythology
konchor	the end of a cloth that one is wearing, especially the end of a saree or a dhoti
kotkoti	crackers made from gram flour
krosh	a unit of distance; one krosh equals 2.25 miles
kupi	water tanks made of mud and clay, used to store water and breed fish
laat	the area under the jurisdiction of a laat sahib
lafa	a bamboo platform covered with mud placed across moving water where fishes jump up while trying to escape
lungi	a long piece of brightly colored cloth (cotton or silk) used as clothing (a skirt or loincloth or sash, etc.)
maal	country liquor
Magh	the Bengali calendar month from mid-January to mid-February
mahajan	moneylender
mandash	a raft made with stems of the banana tree
matipora shak	a leafy vegetable which generally grows on its own in the muddy soil after the paddy has risen
mejo jyatha	jyatha refers to father's elder brother while mejo refers to the position of succession.
mon	a unit of mass that roughly equals to 38 kilograms
morani	state in between extreme high tide and low tide, commonly observed in the backwaters of Sundarbans

nayeb	a managerial position in a zamindari
North 24-Parganas	an administrative district of West Bengal
notey	green amaranth—Bengali leafy green food item
ol	arum
Panchami-Sarat	Panchami refers to the fifth day of the lunar fortnight in the Hindu calendar. In this case, it is Panchami in Sarat which refers to the autumn season.
panta	steamed rice that soaked in water and had the next day when it begins to ferment; *panta bhat* is generally had in summers and is believed to cool down the body.
para	neighbourhood
papad	deep fried delicacy popularly served in village fair
pashu	a kind of wood available in Bengal
pati	a small pot made of wicker or cane used to measure rice
patna	a kind of fishing net made of string used to catch small fish
payelling	local term for a bamboo-made structure made along the course of the river in between the river water and the dam so that flood water does not directly impinge on the dam; a device to preserve longevity of the earthen dams
phoot	a variety of net with medium holes
pindo	also known as *pindodaan*, this is a ritual that is performed by one's family members after one dies, especially by the male members of a household in which an offering is made to the dead.
pishemoshai	husband of a paternal aunt
pishi/pishima	pishi refers to aunt, specifically father's sister
Poush	Bengali calendar month from mid-December to mid-January
pradhan	village head
pronam	refers to the act of praying with folded hands to an idol or touching the feet of idols or elders

pui	a creeper plant used as a vegetable
puimacha	a shed created for the vines of *pui* plant
puthi	an ancient manuscript generally containing religious tales, mostly read on a religious occasion
saba	obeisance
sabhapati	president
Saptami	seventh day of the lunar month when Durga Puja takes place
Sarada, Narada	two financial scams of West Bengal of the last decade
sarbaharas	in the Communist Party parlance the have-nots; the proletariat class
shaak	loosely refers to greens or green leafy vegetables such as spinach
shapla	a variety of water lily
shejka	shejka or shejo kaka refers to uncle; the uncle younger to one's father is boro kaku and the one younger to boro kaka is shejo
shnajal	refers to a fire lit from cow dung cakes to keep mosquitoes away from cows or horses
shraddha	the last rites performed by the family members of the deceased person
siki	an old form of currency; one *siki* equals to a quarter of a rupee
South 24-Parganas	an administrative district of West Bengal
tana-jal	fishing-net; a specific kind of net tied with a rectangular frame, in front of which a long rope is attached to pull it. The people of the Sundarbans make money by fishing with this net in the rivers.
thakurpo	literally translates to brother-in-law. It is a very commonly used word in Bengali and is mostly used by women to refer to their husbands' brothers and friends.
thamma	a term of endearment for a grandmother
thopa	a rudimentary trap for catching crabs

Tulsi-manch	The Tulsi plant is considered to be holy in Hindu religion. Many households in rural India spot a Tulsi plant mounted upon an earthen platform in the courtyard, where it is watered and worshipped daily by the women of the family.
Zila Sabhadhipati	president of the district council

Notes on Contributors

Panchanan Das has been writing poetry, lyric poetry, limericks and rhymes for the last four decades. His songs have been recorded by eminent singers like Dhananjay Bhattacharya, Dipankar Chattopadhyay and Suprakash Chaki. He also writes novels, belles lettres, one-act plays, and more recently, short stories. His writings are characterised by the struggles of the working class.

Bimalendu Halder was born into a peasant family in Maheshpur village in South 24-Parganas. He holds an MA in Bengali from Calcutta University and has worked for a bank. He is the author of two collections of short stories—*Labanakto* and *Aksah-Mati-Mon*. He has also written plays, and his poems and short stories have been published in a number of periodicals. He has researched and written extensively on the languages, history and folk cultures of the South 24-Parganas.

Biswajit Halder was born and raised in South 24-Parganas. He has been a Jadavpur University RUSA 2.0 Post-Doctoral Fellow and holds a PhD. He is author of several research articles, short stories, poems and books such as *Lok-Oitihyer Dharay Dui Chabbish Parganar Shiva Sanskriti: Chadak, Dharmodel, Gajan o Balagaan, Ramayan Gaan: Chabbish Parganar Ramkathar Moukhik Oitihya* and *Panchanan Daser Panchapadee*. He has also created several documentaries on oral narratives and performances of West Bengal.

Jaykrishna Kayal was born and raised in Khejurtala village of the South 24-Parganas. He has published a number of short stories in various magazines like *Kathasahitya, Desh, Chaturanga* and *Nabakallol*. Some of his books include *Nabhimul, Jowar, Baronabot* and *Rangamatir Pothey Pothey*.

Pabitra Mandal was born in the remote Kumirmari village in South 24-Parganas. He has a BA and a BEd and teaches in a Higher Secondary school. His first published story was "Dukhejatra". His collection of short stories, *Nishi Jyotsnar Chhaya* was published in 2011.

Prasad Kumar Mandal was born in Putia village in North 24-Parganas district. A retired administrative officer of the National Insurance Company, he has successfully documented the life-narratives of the hapless marginalised communities residing in the perilous waters of the Sundarbans delta. His major anthologies of short stories include *Mancher Baire*, *Manav Sarovar* and *Pindodaan*.

Bikas Kanti Middya is Professor of Bengali, Rabindra Bharati University. Middya is a known face in the little magazine circuits of both West Bengal and Bangladesh. His novels include *Parashmani*, *Mahaprayan*, *Ubhachar* and *Ananta Jagey*.

Aparesh Mondal was born in Sitalia, Sandeshkhali in the Sundarbans area. He has an MA in English Language and Literature and a BEd as well. He was awarded the Mahendranath Karan Smriti Puraskar in 2016 for his collection of short stories called *Nonadangar Manush*. He has also authored another collection of short stories, *Horang O Anyanya Galpo*.

Archana Mondal hails from Chhoto Rakshaskhali and has studied till Class 8. She works in Kolkata as a domestic help.

Niranjan Mondal was born in Kachukhali village, South 24-Parganas district in 1955. A superannuated bank officer, he has evinced keen interest in the life-stories of the Dalit communities of the Sundarbans—fishermen, wood-cutters, witch-doctors, shrimp-catchers and other fringe-dwellers. He has also researched extensively on the folklore, local history and archaeological remains of the mangrove region. Some of his remarkable anthologies of poetry are *Afuran Aranyaneel* and *Bisanno Canvas*. His recently published novel, *Ujanbhatir Kathokata* and anthology of short stories *Badabaner Padabali* have earned great critical acclaim.

Utpalendu Mondal hails from Gosaba, South 24-Parganas. A chronicler of the tales of Sundarbans, Mondal has published collections of short stories like *Abad Maler Itihas*, *Sumaner Bharatbarsha*, *Galpa Panchish*, novels like *Gourdaha*, *Namsankirtan*, *Fera*, *Setu*, and stories like "Akashlinar Baba", "Jaljangaler Baromasya" and "Aila".

Shyamal Kumar Pramanik was born in Nila village of South 24-Parganas. He has published collections of poems, novels, short stories as well as research articles in history. He was awarded the Ananya Nandanik Sahitya Puroshkar in 2000 and the Shaktikumar Sarkar Smriti Puroshkar in 2006.

Pranab Sarkar was born in Sandeshkhali in the North 24-Parganas. Some of his noteworthy stories are *Knakra, Jomir Alir Maa, Boothnath–Cinema o Ekti Meye, Bhabnagarer Manush* and *Purono Kolom Othoba Scenter Shishi.*

About the Translators

Pritam Bandyopadhyay is Associate Professor, English at Haldia Government College, affiliated to Vidyasagar University. He is former sub-editor, *Ananda Bazar Patrika.* His translations from Bangla into English have appeared in various anthologies.

Tias Basu is a PhD Research Fellow in the Department of Comparative Literature, Jadavpur University. She has co-translated *I, Anupam (Ami, Anupam)*, a novel by Nabaneeta Dev Sen, published in 2019.

Ananya Bhattacharyya received her MPhil degree from the Department of Comparative Literature, Jadavpur University. She currently works as State-Aided college teacher, Department of English, Seth Anandram Jaipuria College.

Arnab Bhattacharya is a critic, author, editor and translator. He has translated a collection of short stories by Troilokyanath Mukhopadhyay titled *Of Ghosts and Other Perils* (2013). Another important work is his English translation of Troilokyonath Mukhopadhyay's work *Konkaboti* (2018).

Sucheta Bhattacharya teaches Comparative Literature at Jadavpur University. She has myriad and eclectic academic interests which include literature of nineteenth-century Bengal, Latin American literature, the culture of the borders, to name a few. Her passion however remains nineteenth-century English Literature, especially the minor Victorian writers. Her other passion is translation.

Swagata Bhattacharya is a Guest Lecturer in the Department of Comparative Literature, Jadavpur University. She has a PhD from Jadavpur University and is a former post-doctoral fellow in the same department. She teaches French at the Ramakrishna Mission Institute of Culture, Kolkata.

Arpita Chatterjee is a musician, researcher and translator. She has co-authored the Bangla translations of Amish Tripathi's three-volume bestselling Shiva trilogy. She runs Sangeetika Seva Trust, an organisation dedicated to music appreciation and headed the Academic Research Department of the ITC Sangeet Research Academy from 2004 to 2009.

Suchorita Chattopadhyay is Professor, Comparative Literature and Coordinator, Centre for Canadian Studies, Jadavpur University. She is also Principal Investigator for the project 'Locating Indigeneity in the Global South: Revival, Conservation, Sustainability' at Jadavpur University under the RUSA 2.0 scheme. Apart from her other academic publications, she has published *Amader Bhagini, Anandaghatini*, a Bangla translation of the African novel *Our Sister Killjoy* by Ama Ata Aidoo in 2007.

Srishti Dutta Chowdhury is a PhD student enrolled at Purdue University. She has been a Project Assistant in the Department of Comparative Literature, Jadavpur University under the RUSA 2.0 scheme.

Banya Datta is a graduate from Osmania University. She is a freelance translator and has completed a certificate course on translation from the Centre for Translation of Indian Literatures, Jadavpur University.

Ketaki Datta is Associate Professor, English, Bidhannagar College, Kolkata. She is a novelist, short story writer, critic and translator. She has published *The Voyage* and *The Last Salute*, English translations of novels by Jarasandha and Santosh Kumar Ghosh respectively. Many of her translations of Bangla short stories have been published in *Indian Literature* (Sahitya Akademi).

Sanghamitra Deb earned her MPhil degree from the Department of Comparative Literature, Jadavpur University.

Naina Dey teaches English at Maharaja Manindra Chandra College. She is particularly interested in the area of Gender Studies.

Ishani Dutta is currently pursuing a PhD from the Centre for Comparative Literature, Bhasha Bhavana, Visva Bharati. She has worked as translator for the project *Tagore in English: Essays of Decolonisation* under RUSA 2.0, Jadavpur University, and is a project fellow for Project Anuvad under UGC-UPE Phase 2: Cultural Resources and Social Sciences, Jadavpur University.

Koushik Goswami has a PhD from the Department of Comparative Literature, Jadavpur Universitya. He did his MPhil in English from the University of Burdwan. He received a JU-RUSA doctoral fellowship and was a Humanities Visiting Scholar at Exeter University, United Kingdom.

Keshab Hira completed his MA in English from Rabindra Bharati University and has taught English in many international schools both in India and abroad.

Baisali Hui is Professor of English, University of Kalyani. She did her doctoral research on Indian Partition writing, and trained in the study of Linguistics and English Language Teaching at CIEFL (EFLU), Hyderabad. She has presented papers and chaired sessions at many conferences including those at RELC Singapore, Bangladesh and the University of Vienna, Austria and has published articles in national and international journals on literature and language.

Saikat Maitra is Assistant Professor, Indian Institute of Management, Kolkata. He was awarded his PhD from the Department of Anthropology, University of Texas.

Nirnoy Roy is a PhD scholar in the Department of Comparative Literature, Jadavpur University.

Oly Saha is Assistant Professor, English, MUC Women's College, Burdwan. She is also pursuing her PhD in Comparative Literature from Jadavpur University.

Urmi Sengupta has a PhD from the Department of Comparative Literature, Jadavpur University. She is currently a faculty member, Communicative English, British Institutes.

Soham Sinha is a PhD student in English at Syracuse University. He earned his MPhil degree from the Department of Comparative Literature, Jadavpur University.

Manjari Thakur earned her MPhil degree from the Department of Comparative Literature, Jadavpur University. She is currently a PhD student at Queens' College, Cambridge University.

About the Editors

Dr Indranil Acharya is Professor and Head of the Department of English, Vidyasagar University, West Bengal. He was the Deputy Coordinator of the UGC-SAP (2009–2014) and State Coordinator of the People's Linguistic Survey of India. His authored/edited/translated books include *Beyond the Sense of Belonging: Race, Class and Gender in the Poetry of Yeats and Eliot* (2011), *Survival and Other Stories: Anthology of Bangla Dalit Stories* (2012), *Many Coloured Glass* (2013), *Towards Social Change: Essays on Dalit Literature* (2014), *Listen to the Flames: Texts and Readings from the Margins* (2016), *Paschimbanger Bhasha* (2017), *Smritibiloper Pore* (Translation of G.N. Devy's *After Amnesia*, 2017), *The Languages of West Bengal* (2019), *Mahatma Gandhi in Bangla* (2022), *Geographical Imaginations: Literature and the "Spatial Turn"* (2022) and *The Almond Flowers and Other Stories* (2022). Dr Acharya is the Chief Editor of *Janajati Darpan*, the only international multilingual publication series from Bengal on indigenous studies. He has also been a UGC Visiting Professor to the Department of English, University of Delhi in 2019–2020.

Sayantan Dasgupta teaches in the Department of Comparative Literature, Jadavpur University. He is also Coordinator of the Centre for Translation of Indian Literatures and Joint Director, School of Media, Communication and Culture there. He is secretary of the Comparative Literature Association of India. He has edited several anthologies of translation, the most recent one being *Dalit Lekhika: Women's Writing from Bengal* (with Kalyani Thakur Charal). He has also edited books like *A South Asian Nationalism Reader*, and his translation of Girishchandra Ghosh's *Jyaisa ka Tyaisa* was published as *Tit-for-Tat* by the Sahitya Akademi. His English translation of Bimalendu Haldar's short story "Labanakto" was on the English PEN shortlist for the PEN Presents Award 2022. He has edited *Celebrating the City: Kolkata in Indian Literature*, an anthology of essays on literary representations of Calcutta-Kolkata in Indian languages. He currently edits the *Jadavpur Journal of Comparative Literature*.